USA Wrestling

Coach's Guide

to Excellence

USAwrestling
T.M.

Library of Congress Cataloging in Publication Data:

Penager, Brett, 1965-

USA WRESTLING COACH'S GUIDE TO EXCELLENCE

Publisher: I. L. Cooper
President: Joanne Cooper

Library of Congress Catalog Card Number: 95-67292
ISBN: 1-884125-27-1

Developed and published with Cooper Publishing Group LLC. For more information about this and other publications, contact the Publisher: Cooper Publishing Group LLC, P.O. Box 562, Carmel, IN 46032.

10 9 8 7 6 5 4

Contents

SECTION II: PROGRAM DEVELOPMENT

SECTION III: PSYCHOLOGY OF COACHING

SECTION IV: DEVELOPING WRESTLING SKILLS

SECTION V: TRAINING AND NUTRITION

SECTION VI: SPORTS MEDICINE

Acknowledgements

The scope and content of this book would not have been possible were it not for the help and assistance of many persons which contributed to its completion. USA Wrestling would like to say "Thank You" and acknowledge all of the professionals and organizations that gave of themselves, and their time, for the benefit of this great sport of wrestling.

Included in this list are: Dr. Larry Johnson, Delnor Community Hospital, for his contributions in the infectious disease chapter; Dr. Thomas Justice, Lock Haven University, for the chapter on weight training; Dr. Dan Gould, Kansas State University, for his contributions in sport psychology; Craig Horswill, Gatorade Sports Institute, for the chapter on weight control; Jim Scott, Grand Valley State University, for his leadership and work on injury prevention; Marty Loy, University of Wisconsin-Stevens Point, for his wisdom and contributions on fundraising and promotion; and all of the wrestling leaders of the past and present who have built the foundation on which we stand today.

A special thanks also goes out to the entire staff of USA Wrestling under the direction and leadership of James Scherr, Executive Director; Mitch Hull, National Teams Director; and the National Coaching staff which provided much of the tenets and material of what is needed to be the best. These coaches include Bruce Burnett, National Freestyle Coach; Mike Houck, National Greco-Roman Coach; and Roye Oliver, National Development Coach.

Finally, this book truly would not have been possible without the patience, understanding, and excellent professionalism of Cooper Publishing Group and its fantastic staff.

Foreword

The goals of USA Wrestling as the National Governing Body of amateur wrestling in the United States has been, and will continue to be, to possess the most powerful and comprehensive wrestling program in the world. In order for this to be attained, we must have the world's best coaches to develop our athletes. This can only be achieved by one method . . . The continued improvement and development of our coaches at every level, through the implementation of an educational program that is second to none.

The content of our National Coaches Education Program (NCEP), though very beneficial to us in the past, had many areas in which we felt needed improvement for its future success. This text is part of that commitment to excellence. It has been compiled with the assistance of the premier wrestling professionals in the country and is also one of the only books of its kind that is primarily written for the betterment of the *coaching* of wrestling.

Within the four levels of the NCEP, the Bronze level is the one that will have the most dramatic impact on the future success of wrestling in the USA. This is due to the sheer numbers of wrestlers that will be affected by the largest segment of coaches in the country. Though available for purchase by anyone, this book is designed to be used and implemented at this level.

Our goal, and that of this book, is to provide for these coaches the knowledge and expertise needed to properly affect these athletes in a positive and beneficial way. In doing so, the future of this sport and the success and enjoyment of its participants will be ensured for generations to come. We hope, also, that the joy of coaching will be derived from those who benefit from the knowledge presented in this text.

Preface

Impact of Coaches

I have come to a frightening conclusion
I am the decisive element in the gym, on the field, or in the pool.
It is my personal approach that creates the climate.
It is my daily mood that makes the weather.
As a coach, I possess tremendous power to make an athlete's life miserable
or joyous.
I can be the tool of torture or an instrument of inspiration.
I can humiliate or humor, hurt or heal.
In all situations it is my response that decides whether a crisis will be
escalated or de-escalated and an athlete humanized or dehumanized.

An Adaptation of Haim Ginott

Within this country, the profession of coaching is one of the only careers in which there are basically no formal education requirements, no special training schools, and no professional certification needed to get started. Though many states and scholastic institutions are now requiring some of these qualifications, for the most part anybody can help their child or a team and be called a coach.

For those who understand the benefits of participating in athletics, this fact has proven to be a major factor in the shortened and sometimes terrible athletic experiences of the youth in this country. When a child or person is not coached properly, the benefits of sport are not worth the physical and mental abuse often demonstrated by unknowledgeable coaches. It is for this reason that, as the National Governing Body for the sport of amateur wrestling in the United States, USA Wrestling has taken a leadership role in the education of wrestling coaches—so that the benefits and enjoyment of this sport may be passed on to the world's most precious commodity, its youth.

USA Wrestling's National Coaches Education Program (NCEP) has been an integral part of the success of our nation's wrestlers at every level. From the volunteer to the professional coaching ranks, this program has helped to educate and train coaches on the specific skills necessary for the vocation of coaching wrestling. Though our country is blessed with many of the world's greatest athletes, were it not for their tutelage and development by our great coaches, their's and our country's success would be greatly diminished. Great coaching at every level is the backbone of every great athlete.

This text is part of USAW's restructured NCEP Bronze level. It is a book that targets the knowledge and skills that wrestling coaches need to be successful in their chosen profession. Unlike many wrestling texts, this book specifically focuses on the needs and desires of the *Wrestling Coach*. We sincerely hope, that in some small way, it may help to assist you in becoming the best coach that you wish to be.

Section I
Philosophy of Coaching, Risk Management, and Effective Teaching

Code of Conduct for Coaches

As the subsequent chapters will attest, the coach has a number of responsibilities to a variety of groups. The following *Code of Conduct* reflects a summary of these responsibilities.

1. The coach shall strive to acquire and implement the most current knowledge of the rules, strategies, and teaching methods of the sport.
2. The coach shall strive to structure a safe environment for the athlete during practices, matches, travel, and other team functions.
3. The coach shall strive to work closely with parents and community members to promote an understanding of the role of athletics in the total educational experience.
4. The coach shall strive to have the welfare of the athlete as the primary concern when making decisions that relate to the care of injuries, rehabilitation, and return to activity.
5. The coach shall strive to promote effective communication with wrestlers, officials, fellow coaches, parents, school administrators, and community members.
6. The coach shall strive to serve as a leader and model in the development of appropriate conduct for the athlete both within and beyond the sport setting.
7. The coach shall strive to use strategies in practice and competition that reflect a standard of fairness to all competitors and that are designed to encourage play within the letter and spirit of the rules.
8. The coach shall strive to keep the concepts of winning and losing in proper perspective.
9. The coach shall strive to enforce team policies with fairness, consistency, and an appreciation for individual differences.
10. The coach shall strive to be knowledgeable of the state association's policies pertaining to the sport and shall ensure that the regulations governing eligibility are upheld.

The joy of coaching is epitomized as a coach congratulates his athlete.

1
Role of the Coach

QUESTIONS TO CONSIDER

- What is the primary role that a coach should seek to fulfill?
- What are the potential benefits of participation in athletics?
- What are the potentially detrimental effects of participation in athletics?
- What are the principal goals a coach should seek to achieve?

INTRODUCTION

Participation in athletics can exert an important positive influence on young people. The high rate of participation in athletics and the broad community support these programs receive suggest that this belief is shared by many individuals. However, mere participation does not ensure that athletes will obtain all of the potentially beneficial effects. In fact, without proper coaching, positive parental support and guidance, there is a risk that the detrimental effects of participation may outweigh the beneficial effects. Therefore, the quality of adult leadership provided by coaches as they direct their practices, contests, and special events is the primary factor in determining the degree to which beneficial or detrimental effects occur.

The following paragraphs review the primary roles a coach must fulfill to assure that the young athletes' participation result in positive outcomes.

EFFECTS OF PARTICIPATION IN ATHLETICS

Participation in sport can result in positive and/or negative effects. It is important, there-fore, to identify the potential outcomes of participation so you can plan to maximize the beneficial effects and minimize potentially detrimental effects.

Beneficial Effects of Participation in Athletics

The benefits of participation are numerous and many occur within the context of a good program. Benefits include:

- developing appropriate skills;
- developing physical fitness;
- learning appropriate conditioning techniques that affect health and performance;
- developing a realistic and positive self-image;
- enhancing the likelihood of participation in physical activity throughout life;
- learning the rules and strategies of sport;
- developing a respect for rules as facilitators of safe and fair competition;
- obtaining enjoyment and recreation;
- developing positive personal, social, and psychological skills (e.g., self-worth, self-discipline, team work, effective communication, goal-setting, self-control); and

- denouncing drug use as the way to recreate, escape from reality, or enhance performance.

Many players achieve significant benefits in at least some of the components listed above. The extent to which the benefits are obtained depends upon the quality of coaching leadership and the frequency, duration, and intensity of participation.

Beneficial effects of sport participation must far outweigh any potentially detrimental effects if athletics are to retain their status in the extracurricular program.

Detrimental Effects of Participation in Athletics

When coaches identify appropriate skill, knowledge, fitness, and personal and social objectives for their athletes and employ suitable teaching methods, their athletes are likely to obtain the benefits previously listed. If, however, the coach selects inappropriate objectives or uses ineffective teaching methods, no benefits (or even detrimental effects) may result

When incorrect techniques and/or negative behaviors are learned by young athletes, it is difficult and time-consuming for the next coach to extinguish these inappropriate actions and attitudes and then to teach for appropriate outcomes. Therefore, ineffective coaching, whether intended or not, can result in detrimental outcomes for the participants. The value of a good coach can be placed in perspective by contrasting the beneficial effects of participation with the following detrimental effects:

- developing inappropriate physical skills;
- sustaining injury, illness, or loss of physical fitness;
- learning incorrect conditioning techniques;
- developing a negative or unrealistic self-image;
- avoiding future participation in sport and physical activity for self and others;
- learning incorrect rules and strategies of sport;
- learning to misuse rules to gain unfair or unsafe advantages;
- replacing the enjoyment of participation with a fear of failure; developing negative or antisocial behaviors;
- taking drugs in an attempt to enhance performance; and

- wasting time that could be devoted to other activities.

The benefits of athletic participation are directly related to the quality of the leadership provided by the coach.

Athletes and parents desire good coaching. Although many guidelines for effective coaching exist, they are commonly violated. It is important to remember, therefore, that beneficial and/or detrimental effects of participation in athletics can occur. The degree to which beneficial rather than detrimental effects occur is related to the quality of your coaching leadership. Accordingly, it is important for you to clearly understand your role as a coach, make correct choices, and take appropriate actions to maximize the beneficial effects and minimize detrimental effects of participation. This chapter, as well as other chapters in this USAW manual, will provide guidance in assisting you to make these choices.

GOALS FOR THE COACH

If your primary purpose is to maximize the benefits of participation while minimizing the detrimental effects, then important goals include:

- effectively teaching the physical skills, rules, and strategies of the sport in an orderly and enjoyable environment;
- appropriately challenging the cardiovascular and muscular systems of your athletes through active practice sessions and competitions; and
- teaching and modeling desirable personal, social, and psychological skills.

The contribution you make to your athletes is directly related to the degree to which you are effective in these three areas.

Winning is also an important goal for coaches and participants on athletic teams. Winning depends in part, however, on the quality of the opposition, calls made by officials, or extenuating circumstances. These are all factors over which you, as a coach, can exert little or no control. It is important, therefore, to concentrate on factors over which you have control (e.g., teaching physical skills, rules and strategies; developing physical fitness; cultivating personal, social and psychological skills; and creating team cohesiveness). As you become effective at these components of coaching, the elements that contribute to losing or winning a contest will occur naturally.

A large amount of time is invested by athletes and coaches irrespective of whether the benefits to the athletes are small, moderate, or great. Parents and administrators should demand that coaches continually focus on improving the ratio of beneficial to detrimental effects for their team by learning and applying principles of effective coaching such as those described in the various chapters of this USAW manual. The following paragraphs summarize the content of this USAW manual.

Philosophy

The attitude you and other members of the athletic staff have toward sports programs will have a significant impact on the way you coach. The mere fact that you are enrolled in the National Coaches Education Program (NCEP) reflects a commitment by you to enhance your coaching competence. Your role as a coach is to maximize the beneficial effects of participation, while minimizing potentially detrimental effects. Your athletic philosophy should be based upon the premise that athletic programs exist for the welfare of the athletes.

Positive interactions with the people you come in contact with are extremely important components of coaching. Good working relationships with the parents, athletes, fans, faculty, custodians, officials, and other coaches are important not only in establishing a successful season but also in modeling proper personal and social skills for your athletes.

Growth and Development

Effective coaching implies that coaches know how growing, maturing athletes are affected by the stresses of competition. Coaches must understand and deal with physical changes, maturing cognitive capacities, and gender differences. Basic knowledge of physical conditioning principles will help you design effective practices and training sessions.

Weight training has been used by athletes in an effort to improve performance. A coach must know how to administer and supervise an effective weight training program while being cognizant of the potential risks involved. Proper nutrition is another important factor that affects a player's performance. Caloric requirements along with specific nutrient needs should be conveyed to the athletes, not only in an attempt to improve their diets, but also to improve performance. The components of vision and their relevance in athletic performance are also important.

Sports Medicine

One of the potentially detrimental effects of athletic participation is risk of injury. As a coach, it is important for you to take steps to prevent injuries by providing a healthy and safe environment. However, injuries will occur even if every precaution has been taken. Sport injuries require immediate attention to help prevent further injury; reduce the risk of excessive blood loss or swelling; promote quicker recovery; and, in extreme cases, prevent permanent damage or even death. Rehabilitation may be necessary before an injured athlete can reenter practice and competition. General guidelines exist that describe who is responsible for the rehabilitation, what are the criteria for reentry, and who decides when the athlete returns to competition.

Many calisthenics and stretching exercises have been found to be detrimental to the anatomical structure and function of the athlete. A coach must use only safe physical activities. Finally, pre-participation athletic examinations and proper medical records are necessary components in a comprehensive and cohesive program for taking care of your athletes' health.

Psychology

The extent to which benefits are gained from sports participation depends largely on your ability to effectively plan and evaluate instruction. Your ability to communicate, both as a speaker and listener, will aid you in maintaining discipline and motivating your athletes.

During instruction, a coach should concentrate on desired objectives and reward and reinforce efforts to achieve these outcomes.

Your athletes are likely to model many of your traits and actions. Therefore, it is critical that you act as an appropriate role model and create an atmosphere in which you can positively shape the personal and social skills of your athletes. You should never lose your temper, yell at officials, or break rules to gain an unfair advantage. In essence, "actions speak louder than words" and you must "practice what you preach" if you hope to positively influence your athletes' behavior.

Substance abuse is an increasing problem in athletics to about the same degree as it is in current society. The accessibility and popularity of alcohol and other drugs highlight the need for preventive action by parents, teachers, administrators, and coaches. Sharing accurate information about drugs, increasing awareness of the pressures experienced by athletes, and teaching students to properly deal with situations where drugs are used are critical actions that a coach should perform.

Litigation/Liability

The potentially detrimental effects of athletics can extend from athletes to coaches as well. Knowledge of your legal responsibilities and rights as a coach will help you avoid lawsuits and, if practiced, protect you if litigation does occur. Appropriate insurance (medical and liability) is needed to provide for expenses and/or judgments if injury or litigation occur.

Sports Management

One of the first steps a coach should take is to identify goals and objectives for the season. Earlier in this chapter, broad goals were mentioned such as teaching physical skills, rules and strategies; challenging the cardiovascular and muscular system; and molding desirable personal, social, and psychological skills. The content of much of this USAW manual should help you in identifying objectives to meet the needs of your athletes. Next, these objectives should be organized into a plan from which practices, contests and other events can be managed efficiently.

Scheduling of facilities and transportation for practices and contests should be based on sound principles and procedures that are fair to all parties concerned. While the budget is usually allocated through negotiations with the coach, the ultimate responsibility to allocate resources within the budget falls to the coach. Therefore, it is necessary for the coach to learn as much as possible regarding budget management.

SUMMARY

Your role as a coach is to maximize the beneficial effects of athletic participation while minimizing potentially detrimental effects. Proper planning for the season by defining specific goals and objectives to accomplish this end is a necessary first step in your coaching duties. Much of the content of this USAW manual will help you in narrowing your objectives to meet the needs of your athletes. However, the function of teacher is not sufficient in fulfilling your role as a coach. You must also know how to organize, motivate, communicate, counsel, protect, model and manage. The NCEP program addresses each of these responsibilities.

2
Philosophy of Coaching

QUESTIONS TO CONSIDER
- What is the one common aspect of successful coaching philosophy?
- How is a philosophy of coaching developed?
- What is in a philosophy?
- What are the three areas of goal setting?

Your philosophy of coaching will determine your response in critical situations.

DEVELOPING A COACHING PHILOSOPHY

As a coach begins his/her career, one of the very first questions that must be answered is "What is my philosophy of coaching?" The development of a coaching philosophy will lay the foundation for everything you do as a coach both within and outside of your program. It must be thoroughly understood that regardless of the sport, there are numerous coaches that achieve success with entirely different methods and philosophies. However, the one similarity that all of these great coaches have, is an unshakeable belief that what *they* do to achieve their success is the best possible way to build their athletes, coaches, and program.

The development of a coaching philosophy entails many different components. Many coaches, especially in the beginning, coach in the same manner in which they were coached as competitive athletes. Many coaches model their style and philosophy after coaches they admire and respect. Still other coaches follow the steps and ideals of a mentor or head coach they worked under. All of these examples are commonplace and accepted methods of coaching. However, it is the superior coach who learns to combine many aspects of the aforementioned methods and then use and adjust them according to *his* strengths and weaknesses. In so doing, the formation of an individual philosophy is formed.

The fact that there are some basic principles that the best coaches center their methods around does not diminish the point that there is no "right" or "wrong" philosophy of coaching. The development of your own individual coaching philosophy will be the result of time, trial and error, mistakes, education, experience, and upbringing. The most important factor to remember and apply is to use and believe in a philosophy that works for *you* and fosters the success of your athletes and wrestling program.

WHAT IS IN A PHILOSOPHY?

The best coaches model their coaching philosophy to compliment their personalities, strengths, and overcome their weaknesses. This includes everything from the disciplinary measures they enforce to the style of wrestling their team will exhibit. A few examples of some questions you may want to ask are, "What style (takedowns, mat wrestling, counter attack) of wrestling do I feel is most successful for my athletes to perform?"; "What are my policies regarding weight loss?"; "What is my philosophy regarding athletics (winning) vs personal growth?"; "What is my position on academics as it relates to athletics?"; "What is my opinion on training wrestlers for competition?"; "What are my thoughts on winning?" These are just a few areas that would be considered a part of a coaches philosophy.

There are many different successful styles, personalities, and philosophies in coaching. The most important aspect to remember, is to develop a style and philosophy that works for you, your athletes, and the program. You must believe in what you are doing with unwavering commitment.

GOAL SETTING

Success in any endeavor is really the cumulation of many failures. This statement can only be understood when the "failures" are put in the perspective of "failing" to reach all of your goals. Without a goal to reach there can be no failure and without failure, there can be no success. As a coach, it is imperative to have goals in which to direct your actions and program objectives. If you don't shoot for or at a target, where do you aim? The establishment of your goals as a coach can be broken down into three main areas. These being goals that are set for your athletes (athletically, academically, etc.), team, and yourself.

1. Athlete Goals

As a coach, you are responsible for the development of your athletes in many areas. Regardless of whether it is athletically, academically, or socially, you must set the goals for your wrestlers to work towards and standards by which they must adhere. Though wrestling is an individual sport, it is your leadership that will determine the goals and success that your wrestlers will set for themselves. The best way in which to have both you and your athlete understand each other and have some agreement in objectives, is to discuss this with them one-

Figure 2-1. "To achieve victory, your goals must be set for victory."

on-one in private. It is important that as the head of your team you know the goals of your athletes, and in turn they know your expectations of them. This process will enable both of you to work together, not in conflict, towards the accomplishment of the understood goals.

2. Team Goals

The dynamics of a group working together towards a unified goal creates a powerful effect. With a team of athletes it is important to share your goals with each and every member. The effort and focus of your third and fourth string wrestlers is just as important as that of your starters to create unity of vision and purpose. Without this combined effort of all in-

volved, you will greatly diminish the possibility of achieving your goals.

3. Coaching Goals

Just as your athletes and team must set goals, you must also hold yourself accountable for the achievement of your goals. Coaches, at times, can get an athlete to do things that even parents can't. You are in a position to have tremendous influence, both positive and negative. Don't miss this opportunity by holding yourself to a standard lower than that of what you are asking of your team. As a coach, your athletes will emulate and copy what they see you do more than any other single person in their athletic sphere of influence. It is for that reason that you must set the example for what you expect them to do. When they see you *doing* what you have told them to do, your guidance and knowledge will carry much more authority, and in return your athletes will follow your instructions and the desired effect will be accomplished.

SUMMARY

The development of a solid coaching philosophy is a task that takes years, experience, modeling, education, and trial and error. There is no right or wrong way in which to coach. However, there are some basic principles of coaching that, when applied correctly, will greatly enhance your chances for success and the realization of your goals. The aforementioned principles will help to provide a foundation for you to begin your career as a successful wrestling coach.

3
Effective Teaching and Risk Management

QUESTIONS TO CONSIDER

- What should the coach know in order to be an effective teacher?
- What guidelines should the coach follow when teaching young athletes?
- What are the characteristics of a good practice?
- Identify qualities of a "good" drill.
- What should the coach know in order to conduct safe practices and matches?
- Identify the seven components of risk management that are required of all wrestling coaches.

Properly training and teaching athletes is a learned process of coaching.

INTRODUCTION

The modern day wrestling coach is called on to fill many roles, but none is more important than that of being a good teacher. In fact, if the coach is not a good teacher, all of the other roles will be diminished, too. The coach's effectiveness as a counselor, substitute parent, role model, friend, and mentor is increased if the coach is a good teacher.

Good teaching is the foundation for successful coaching.

EFFECTIVE TEACHING GUIDELINES

There are many ways in which you, as a coach, can impart information to young athletes. There are also many styles or methods that have been shown to be effective. Despite the variety of styles that coaches use, certain rules or guidelines are common to all good instruction.

To be an effective teacher a coach must:

- Clearly communicate what is to be learned
- Be able to evaluate the athletes' abilities
- Use a coaching style that fits the needs of young athletes
- Be consistent and systematic in teaching young athletes
- Be able to alter practice plans and match strategies on the basis of how effectively objectives are being met.

In the following section each of these guidelines will be discussed in more detail.

Communicate Clearly

The results that a coach expects young wrestlers to obtain can be placed into three categories:

Physical: pertaining to the development of the seven basic skills, as well as the physical conditioning that permits wrestlers to do these tasks without undue fatigue.

Mental: relating to the strategies, rules and responsibilities of the young athlete as a competitor and team member.

Social: referring to the personal characteristics of wrestlers, such as loyalty to a common cause, supporting team members, respecting opponents, official and spectators, listening to the coach's instructions, and conducting oneself as a responsible citizen.

You, as a coach, are responsible for identifying precisely what is to be learned by the athletes within each of the previously identified categories. **Athletes will not learn desirable skills, values, and attitudes simply by exposure** or by having adults wish that certain fundamental laws of good citizenship will be acquired. Learning requires instruction, practice under realistic situations, corrective action and then more practice. This cycle should be repeated until the desired outcome is attained.

Coaches should be certain that their definitions of what is to be learned are pertinent to the developmental levels of their athletes. Hence, some young wrestlers may be advanced with regard to social skills and be delayed regarding their physical skills. Others may be advanced or delayed in all aspects of the agenda that a coach wishes to teach during the season. For this reason, clearly stated objectives by you as the coach are essential prior to the time when you initiate any instruction. Failure to define your objectives will lead to chaos in your instruction.

Evaluation of Athletes' Abilities

The coaches should be able to assess the abilities of **all** wrestlers **prior to** determining the instructional objectives for the year. The accurate assessment of wrestler's abilities determines a coach's instructional strategies, as well as the expectations and goals that can be set for the season.

Assessment should include each athlete's status in the areas of physical, mental, and social skills. For example, a wrestler with excellent physical skills, but who has a bad attitude, could cause major disruptions on the team if the coach does not address the deficiencies in the wrestler's social skills. Conversely, wrestlers who have excellent social and mental skills will not be able to realize their potential as competitors if they are unable to translate these abilities because of underdeveloped physical skills.

The assessment of athletes' abilities is essential to a good beginning in the wrestling season, but assessment by the coach must also occur practice-by-practice, throughout the season. In fact, accurate assessment of wrestler's needs is one of the most essential components of good teaching. All good coaches have the ability to assess a situation and then take corrective action during the teachable moment when instruction has the greatest chance of being effective.

Assessing Needs and Taking Corrective Action

Physical Skills

Coaches can learn much about their wrestlers' physical skills by observing them in drills and matches. The assessment of physical skills depends on:

- knowing the correct way to perform a skill
- knowing the sequence of actions that result in the correct performance of the skill
- being able to detect your wrestlers' correct and incorrect actions
- being able to tell your wrestlers how to correct their faulty performance

Once again, the judgment of the coach is the key to improving your athlete's performance. If you are inexperienced in the analysis of skills you should obtain the outstanding videotapes on skill development that are available through USA Wrestling. Demonstration of the essential physical skills in slow-motion will assist you in observing the essential ingredients when the skill is performed at its normal speed. The explanations provided by the videotape's commentator can also be used as you instruct your wrestlers.

There is no substitute for experience when you attempt to identify errors and correct the physical techniques of your wrestlers. However, inexperienced coaches have learned that the process of observing and correcting mistakes can be enhanced by the following guidelines:

- choose a vantage point so that you can see the entire skill being performed.
- observe the entire skill before dissecting it into its parts; then have the wrestler attempt to correct only the one part or segment that

is most important to success. When this segment has been corrected, then proceed to the next most important segment.
- have the wrestler practice the essential component until the correct motor pattern has been achieved.
- be ready to encourage the wrestler while the new pattern is being learned; remember that the speed and total coordination with which the old pattern was performed will be reduced while the wrestler is learning the adjustments.

Assessing the physical conditioning of athletes in wrestling does not require sophisticated laboratory equipment. As a coach you will be able to determine which wrestlers have the stamina to consistently perform throughout an entire match or those who cannot finish moves due to lack of strength and power. Although improved techniques will assist wrestlers who are in position to perform their skills, success in the sport of wrestling depends on an athlete's ability to maintain good position and execute correct technique throughout the duration of a match, even when fatigued. Remember that skillful techniques are not a substitute for physical conditioning. However, in wrestling, physical conditioning is most effectively achieved by having the athletes practice the real-match situations and carefully selecting drills in your practices.

Assessing Mental Needs

Young wrestlers will learn the rules and strategies of wrestling most effectively by having you, the coach, anticipate what is to occur during matches and then ensuring that you construct similar situations in your practices. The "sixth sense" that some young wrestlers possess comes from having been in similar situations before, then recognizing the options available to them and choosing the correct course of action under the circumstances. Only if young wrestlers have experienced an identical situation in previous matches and practices can you expect them to make the correct decision. Therefore, your teaching in practices must be based on the situations that you expect them to encounter in matches. How they resolve these dilemmas will be directly related to their understanding of similar situations in practice and matches.

Figure 3-1. Teaching wrestling skills is a major part of coaching wrestling.

Assessing Social Needs

The interaction among your wrestlers will provide you with an indication of their social needs. Often, the most skillful wrestlers are also the most popular. Their social needs are likely to be met by the recognition that they receive from teammates, parents, and fans because of their wrestling abilities. The coach should ensure that the recognition for skill and ability should not overshadow the need to acquire the social skills of good citizenship. Too often skillful wrestlers are treated as though the rules of the team and society do not apply to them, only to find that they are societal misfits when their sports skills no longer shield them from the application of equal treatment.

Coaches should be particularly alert to the special problems of social development that are often present in immature wrestlers whose skill level is consistently below the average of his/her team and age level group. These underdeveloped wrestlers face the constant challenge of being unable to compete on an equal basis in the drills, and perhaps equally as important, they are frequently excluded from the comradeship that develops within a team.

The coach is the essential promoter of so-cial development within a team** and is the one who must recognize the contributions of the immature, underdeveloped wrestlers by praising their successes and placing them in situations where they are likely to succeed. When wrestlers recognize that the coach values the contributions of all team members, then the leaders of the team are also more likely to accept those whose contributions to team goals are not consistently evident.

GUIDELINES TO GOOD TEACHING

Although there are many ways to instruct young wrestlers, the inexperienced coach will find the following sequence easy to use and effective in teaching and refining skills. As you begin your instruction, it is best to remember that young wrestlers learn best by participating. They do not learn well by sitting and listening to coaches lecture about topics that too often seem abstract, but which adults think are concrete. **A good rule is, "When I speak, I want you to stop what you're doing and listen."** Do not violate your own rule by continuing to talk when wrestlers are not paying attention.

Prior to your instruction:

- be sure you have the attention of all wrestlers
- tell them precisely what you want them to learn; do this in one-minute or less, preferably with a physical demonstration of the skill
- have wrestlers practice the skill while you observe them and provide feedback
- have wrestlers come back to a group setting and discuss the adjustments that are needed for improvement
- place the wrestlers into groups by size and ability; continue to practice and provide feedback
- repeat the last two steps as frequently as needed until the desired level of competence is achieved.

The following ten steps to good teaching have been shown to be effective in a variety of settings, including the teaching of young athletes.

1. Be Realistic About Your Wrestlers' Abilities

Wrestlers will respond to realistic and challenging expectations. Conversely, expectations that are beyond their achievement will decrease the motivation of even the most skillful wrestlers. Set short term goals on an individual basis and adjust them when they are achieved. Wrestlers tend to achieve according to their coaches' expectations if the expectations are realistic.

As a coach you should expect to significantly improve the skills, knowledge of rules and strategies and attitudes of each of your wrestlers during the course of the season. Make a commitment to help each of the wrestlers realize these goals.

2. Structure Your Instruction

Your wrestlers' progress will be directly linked to how clearly you communicate and teach toward your intended outcomes. This means that every practice must have well-defined objectives and a systematic plan of instruction. The critical steps to a structured lesson are:

- select the essential skills, rules, and strategies from the many options available
- clearly identify elements of acceptable performance for each skill you include in practice
- organize and conduct your practices to maximize the opportunity your wrestlers have to acquire the skill(s) by using the effective teaching techniques contained in this chapter.

3. Establish an Orderly Environment

The achievement of objectives by coaches is directly related to the learning that takes place in a safe, orderly, and business-like environment, with clear expectations of what is to be accomplished at each practice. Wrestlers must be held accountable for being on time and coming to the practice ready to learn. Young wrestlers do not learn effectively in long, boring practices that involve drills that do not relate to their understanding of the sport of wrestling. Keep your practices organized, personalized, and pertinent to the needs of your team.

4. Maintain Consistent Discipline

You will find that keeping control of your team is much easier than regaining control once problems with misbehavior have disrupted your authority. Thus, your role is much easier if you can prevent the types of misbehavior that arise when coaches do not anticipate and avoid problems with discipline.

Preventing Misbehavior

Although threats and lectures may prevent misbehavior in the short-term, they create a hostile and negative atmosphere and, typically, their effectiveness is short-lived. Moreover, this type of relationship between a coach and team members does not promote learning the sport of wrestling nor does it motivate the wrestlers to accept the coach's instructions.

Sound discipline involves two steps that must be in place before misbehavior occurs. They are:

A. Defining how wrestlers are to behave and identifying misbehavior that will not be tolerated.
B. Identifying the consequences for individuals who do not behave according to the rules.

Preteen and teenage athletes want clearly defined limits and structure for how they should behave. This can be accomplished without showing anger, lecturing the wrestlers, or threatening them. As the coach, it is your responsibility to have a systematic plan for maintaining discipline before your season gets underway. Coaches who have taken the time to establish rules of conduct will be in a position to react in a reasonable and fair manner when team members misbehave.

Defining Team Rules

The first step in developing a plan to maintain discipline is to identify what you consider to be desirable and undesirable conduct by your wrestlers. This list can then be used to establish relevant team rules. A list of potential items to consider when identifying team rules is included in Table 3-1.

Enforcement of Rules

Not only are rules needed to maintain discipline, but enforcement of those rules must be carried out so that reoccurrences are prevented. Rules are enforced through rewards and penalties. Wrestlers are rewarded when they abide by the rules and penalized when they break the

Table 3-1. Items to consider when defining rules for your team.

Examples of Desirable and Undesirable Conduct in Wrestling	
Desirable Conduct	**Undesirable Conduct**
Attending to your instructions	Talking while you are trying to give instructions
Full concentration on drills	Inattentive behavior during drills
Treating opponents with respect	Fighting with opponents or using abusive language
Giving positive encouragement to teammates	Making negative comments about teammates
Avoiding illegal moves	Intentionally trying to hurt someone with use of illegal move
Being prompt to practices and matches	Being late or absent from practices and matches
Helping to pick up equipment after practices	Leaving equipment out for others to pick up
Bringing all your equipment to practices	Forgetting to bring a part of your equipment or uniform to matches and practices

rules. The next step, therefore, in developing a plan to maintain discipline is to determine the rewards and penalties for each rule. Your wrestlers can be asked for suggestions at this point because they will receive the benefits or consequences of the decisions. **When determining rewards and penalties for rules, the most effective approach is to use rewards that are meaningful to your wrestlers and appropriate to the situation.** Withdrawal of rewards should be used for misconduct. A list of potential rewards and penalties that can be used in wrestling is cited in Table 3-2.

The best way to motivate wrestlers to behave in an acceptable manner is to reward them for good behavior.

Table 3-2. Example of rewards and penalties.

Examples of Rewards and Penalties That Can Be Used in Wrestling	
Rewards	**Penalties**
Selected for varsity	Being taken out of the lineup
Elected Team Captain	
Leading an exercise or activity	Not being allowed to compete
Praise from you	Assessing janitorial duties: cleaning mats, cleaning locker room, etc.
Decals	
Medals	Dismissed for
	1. next practice
	2. next week
	3. rest of season

Remember that penalties are only effective when they are meaningful to the wrestlers. Typically, the types of penalties that are used for rule violations are ineffective because they are not important to the players. Generally, they do not leave room for positive interactions between you and your wrestlers. Examples of ineffective penalties include showing anger, embarrassing wrestlers by lecturing them in the presence of team members or adults, shouting at wrestlers, or assigning a physical activity (extra sit-ups, extra pushups). Assigning a physical activity for certain misbehavior may develop a negative attitude toward that activity. Avoid using physical activity as a form of punishment; the benefits of wrestling, such as learning skills and gaining cardiovascular fitness, are gained through activity.

Adolescents should not associate activity with punishment.

Although threats, lectures and/or yelling may deter misbehavior in the short term, the negative atmosphere that results reduces long term coaching effectiveness. A more positive approach to handling misbehavior is to prevent it by establishing, with wrestler input, clear team rules. Use fair and consistent enforcement of the rules, primarily through rewarding correct behavior, rather than penalizing unacceptable behavior.

5. Group Your Wrestlers According to Ability

Your wrestling team will most likely have wrestlers at various levels of ability. For effective learning the wrestlers at times need to be divided into smaller groups. The critical consideration for grouping wrestlers effectively is to have them practicing at a level that is needed to advance their wrestling ability.

The general guidelines to effectively group wrestlers are:

- when a new skill, rule, or strategy is being taught that all your athletes need to know, use a single group instructional setting
- as you identify differences in ability, place wrestlers of similar ability and size in smaller groups
- when a skill, rule, or strategy is being practiced where individual athletes are at several levels of ability (initial, intermediate, or later learning levels), establish learning stations that focus on specific outcomes to meet these needs.

Organize the groups so that there is a systematic order in which wrestlers take turns. Each group must know precisely what is to be learned. Supervise each group by rotating and spending short periods of time with each. Avoid the temptation of spending all of the instructional time with one group. If any group is favored during small group instruction, it should be those wrestlers who are the least skillful because they are also the ones who are least able to diagnose and correct their own errors.

6. Maximize Your Wrestlers' On-Task Time

Progress in skill development is directly related to the amount of time that wrestlers spend practicing these skills in match-like situations. Practices provide the opportunity to attempt a specific skill repeatedly under guided instruction. Coaches should anticipate match situations and then conduct their practices to simulate match situations, while still being able to adjust the environment to meet the developmental levels of the various athletes. **Practices are the most effective learning environment for perfecting physical and mental skills.** In order to ensure that practices are conducted wisely you should consider the following time-saving techniques.

- Reduce the number of athletes who are waiting by using smaller groups in drills.
- Provide sufficient equipment so that wrestlers do not have to wait for their turn to use it.
- Schedule your drills so that one leads into the next without major set-up time.
- Clearly outline and/or diagram each portion of practice and communicate as much of that information as possible before implementing it on the mat.
- Delegate assistants (coaching staff and volunteers) to help you with instructional stations under your supervision.

7. Maximize the Wrestlers' Success Rate

Successfully achieving a desired outcome and the motivation to continue to refine the desired outcome are highly related. Therefore, coaches must structure their practices so that wrestlers are successful in lessons to be learned. This relationship between attempts and successes mandates that coaches structure their practices so that wrestlers will succeed on a high proportion of their early attempts. The following hints have been used by successful wrestling coaches:

- reduce each skill, rule, or strategy into achievable sub-skills and focus instruction on those sub-skills
- provide feedback to the athlete so that, on most occasions, something that they did is rewarded, followed by specific instructions about what needs more work, ending with an encouraging, "Try again."

8. Monitor the Wrestlers' Progress

Wrestlers learn most effectively during practices that are accompanied by meaningful feedback. In wrestling, the meaningful feedback is most frequently provided by the coach or assistant coaches. The old cliché "Practice makes perfect" is only true if athletes are practicing appropriate skills in the correct manner. If left to their own agendas, young wrestlers may practice inappropriate skills or they may practice pertinent skills inappropriately. As their coach, you must be sure that the practices are conducted with the correct balance between feedback and independent learning.

9. Ask Questions of the Wrestlers

Young wrestlers generally enjoy their relationships with their coaches. Asking them questions is an ideal way to build the coach/athlete relationship. Questions should be designed to provide insight into: Why the player is involved in wrestling? Who are the significant persons in his/her life? What are his/her goals for the season? What parts of the match are personally satisfying or depressing? Coaches who know their wrestlers are most likely to be able to meet their needs by placing the wrestlers into situations that will enhance their self-esteem.

10. Promote a Sense of Control

Coaches must be in control of their teams, but control is not a one-way street. Wrestlers, too, must feel that they have some control over their own destiny when they attend practices and matches. They must feel that they will be rewarded for hard work, that their goals will be considered, and that their role on the wrestling team is valued and essential to the welfare of the team. As a coach you can promote a sense of control by:

- organizing your instruction to result in many successful experiences (i.e., opportunities to provide positive feedback).
- teaching your wrestlers that everyone learns various wrestling skills at different rates. Many of our World and Olympic wrestling team members started their careers on J.V. and lost more matches than they won. Teach young wrestlers to use effort and their own continuous progress as their primary guide. They should avoid comparing their skill level with that of other wrestlers.
- encouraging individual wrestlers to put forth their best effort. Reward such effort with a comment, pat on the back, thumbs up sign, or other means which will communicate your approval.

EFFECTIVE PRACTICES

Effective practices are those sessions that meet the needs of the wrestlers to carry out the objectives that are listed in the plan for the season. The keys to effective practices are **careful planning** and **sound instruction**. Both ingredients are under the control of the coach. Therefore, each of your practices should:

- be based upon previous planning, seasonal organization, needs of the team, and needs of the individuals
- list the objectives and key points that will be the focus of instruction for that practice
- show the amount of time allotted to each objective during the practice
- identify the activities (instructional, drill, or scrimmage) that will be used to teach or practice the objectives
- apply the guidelines for effective instruction included in this chapter
- include an evaluation of the strengths and weaknesses of the practice.

PRACTICE TIME NEEDED

The amount of time that wrestlers can attend to your instruction depends on their ages and developmental levels. Generally, wrestlers aged ten and under cannot effectively tolerate more than one hour of concentrated practice. As age advances and the abilities of wrestlers improve the practices, too, can be slightly longer. **A primary problem in youth wrestling is to use effectively the time that is available.**

Another common problem in youth wrestling is to define far too many objectives and then teach for exposure rather than mastery. The most important part of wrestling is understanding the basic skills. Make sure your athletes understand these skills first. When insufficient time is devoted to basic skills, the result is incompetence and frustration. A good rule is to distribute your practice time across several objectives. Then devote sufficient time to each objective so that a meaningful change in the performance of 80 percent of the wrestlers has occurred. Devote time in additional practices to the objective until the wrestlers are able to transfer the skill into match-like drills. At that point, they can be expected to transfer the skills of practice into their matches.

CHARACTERISTICS OF A GOOD DRILL

The two most important components of your practices are the **development of individ-**

ual skills and the translation of these **skills into match-like situations through drills.** Therefore, the drills that you select must be related to your objectives. Too often coaches use drills that are traditional or favorites of the wrestlers but that have no relevance to the skills to be learned. Such drills waste valuable time. Drills should be selected or developed according to the following features. Drills should:

- have a meaningful objective
- require a relatively short explanation
- provide an excellent opportunity for wrestlers to master the skill or concept
- keep wrestlers "on task" during the drill
- be easily modified to accommodate skilled and unskilled wrestlers
- provide opportunity for skill analysis and feedback to wrestlers
- the drill should be challenging and fun

Write your drills on single sheets or cards. After the practice, write your comments about the drill's usefulness directly on the card and file the card for future use. Good drills can be used many times during a season. Share your drills with fellow coaches. Such activities promote fellowship among coaches and provide the beginning coach with a repertoire of useful teaching tools and techniques.

PROTECTING THE SAFETY OF WRESTLERS

In addition to providing effective instruction, the coach has the responsibility of ensuring that all practices and matches are conducted in a safe environment. Therefore, the coach's primary responsibility can be summed up in this statement: **Teach for improved competence and safety every day.**

For over a decade courts, lawyers, and professional associations have been establishing the legal responsibilities of the youth sports coach. These responsibilities include providing adequate supervision, a safe environment, proper instruction, adequate and proper planning, adequate evaluation for injury or incapacity, appropriate emergency procedures and first aid training, adequate and proper equipment, appropriate warnings, and adequate matching of wrestlers and competitors. These duties are to be met by the coach while he/she is involved in any supervisory situation related to his/her coaching responsibilities.

RISK MANAGEMENT QUESTIONS TO CONSIDER

- What is risk management and why is it relevant to coaches?
- What are the three parts of developing a risk management program for coaches?
- What are the legal qualifications or competencies that coaches should have?
- How are the "reasonable expectations of wrestlers' parents" related to risk management?
- What are the management practices that will help coaches achieve their risk management objectives?
- What are the three steps coaches should take to implement their risk management program?

INTRODUCTION

Coaching to the Reasonable Expectations of Your Wrestlers' Parents

Assume that a prospective volunteer coach is interviewing for a position with a wrestling organization. The candidate is asked to, "identify the one quality you have which distinguishes you as the best candidate for this coaching po-

sition." If you were the prospective coach, what would your answer be?

For the inexperienced candidate, the likely answer is going to focus on past wrestling experience. After all, isn't that the primary qualification of many volunteer coaches? It is not uncommon for youth coaches to assume that past wrestling experience is a sufficient qualification. Probably many youth sports organizations have agreed.

There is, however, a growing realization of a coaching crisis in youth sports. It is a crisis created by the failure of youth sports organizations to select coaches with better qualifications. And, it is a crisis which has been sustained by many well-intentioned coaches who did not realize that coaching is, first and foremost, effective teaching. For example, one research report estimates that more than 70% of American youth are turned off to competitive sports by age 13. The primary reasons are the kids are tired of getting yelled at by coaches; and, they are given attention only if they display exceptional skills. In other words, coaching appears to be ineffective in motivating youngsters to participate.

Motivating participation is a teaching function and should be a hiring qualification. Returning to the interview question, what quality would best distinguish a coaching candidate? It could easily be the candidate who proposes to "coach to the reasonable expectations of my kids' parents!" Traditionally, teachers have been held to standards established by communities of parents. Wrestling coaches, as teachers, should be measured by the same standards. **The wrestling coach who understands that the requirements of the job will be measured by the reasonable expectations of his wrestlers' parents knows he or she must be an effective teacher.**

Coaches, in any sport, owe certain legal obligations to their wrestlers. The goal of risk management programs is to identify those legal obligations for coaches, then translate them into coaching conduct or behavior.

EFFECTIVE TEACHING

Legal Obligation: Coaches are supposed to be teachers first and foremost.

Coaching Behavior: Enroll in certification and continuing coaching education programs; and, start your own reading education program in coaching and communication skills.

EFFECTIVE SUPERVISION

Legal Obligation: Coaches are responsible for team supervision wherever and whenever the team meets.

Coaching Behavior: Hire competent assistants; and, establish a plan of supervision for all team practices, meetings, games, and other events.

EFFECTIVE REACTION TO MEDICAL EMERGENCIES

Legal Obligation: Coaches are supposed to know medical emergencies when they see them; and, to know how to respond quickly and responsibly.

Coaching Behavior: Take a certification course in emergency medical procedures, or at least first aid; and, establish a plan for prompt reaction to medical emergencies.

PROVIDING SAFE EQUIPMENT

Legal Obligation: Coaches are supposed to know how to buy, fit, and maintain safe sports equipment.

Coaching Behavior: Establish equipment fitting, distribution, and maintenance plans in accordance with all manufacturer warranties, guidelines, and directions; take continuing education programs regarding equipment; and, maintain records on equipment inspection and reconditioning.

PROVIDING SAFE FACILITIES

Legal Obligation: Coaches are supposed to know when surface conditions pose a danger to wrestlers.

Coaching Behavior: Take continuing education programs regarding facility operations; establish a plan for regular mat inspections, including quick repair of defects or problems and proper cleaning.

PROVIDING SAFE TRANSPORTATION

Legal Obligation: Coaches are supposed to know how wrestlers are being transported to away events, and with whom the wrestlers will be traveling.

Coaching Behavior: Use the league and parents to help establish transportation plans which should include approved drivers, vehicles, and stops; and, establish a team code of travel conduct.

PROVIDING DUE PROCESS

Legal Obligation: Coaches have to establish fair rules and policies, and explain their reasons for suspending a wrestler from the team.

Coaching Behavior: Use the league and parents

to establish rules and policies regarding team conduct; provide written copies of rules and policies to wrestlers and their parents; never suspend a wrestler without giving the wrestler and his parents the chance to explain their conduct.

PROVIDING COMPETENT ASSISTANTS

Legal Obligation: Coaches are supposed to hire or assign assistant coaches who are as competent as the head coach.

Coaching Behavior: Start a training program just for the assistant coaches; plan and organize the staff with continuing education and training as a requirement; and, require references from all assistants.

DEVELOPING A RISK MANAGEMENT PROGRAM

Coaching can be very frustrating when it involves being constantly second-guessed. Obviously, the coaching profession is one that has always been suffered to hindsight. For that reason alone many coaches might prefer an evaluation standard based solely on their effort or time spent coaching. When dealing with volunteers, it seems more fair to be evaluated on one's willingness to work with kids. The problem is that risk management cannot be successful if it measures effort alone. A successful risk management program has to evaluate coaching performance as "effective teaching."

Volunteer coaches who accept the teaching role also accept the role of a parent. And, thereby, they assume the standards of effective teaching. **Parents have the right to assume the coach has the ability to teach the sport or activity; to teach it safely; and, to teach it with the participation of their child in mind.** Obviously, it is expected that the experience will be fun. Those are the desired characteristics of an effective coaching risk management program.

Many risk management programs are developed simply by listing or identifying the legal competencies expected of coaches. The premise is that when a coach practices those legal competencies it results in an effective risk management program.

The problem is that merely identifying coaching competencies does not mean a coach

knows how to practice them. Using "effective teaching according to the reasonable expectations of wrestlers' parents" as the risk management mission, we will develop the risk management program in three steps. First, we will identify the legal competencies required of coaches. Second, we will integrate those competencies into a management program. Third, we will offer three suggestions how to implement the management program into an effective coaching risk management plan.

THE LEGAL COMPETENCIES EXPECTED OF COACHES

Legal experts have identified as many as twelve, and as few as five, legal competencies expected of coaches at any level of participation. All agree that the foundation of coaching competency is effective teaching. This program suggests that coaches consider eight additional competencies:

- Effective supervision
- Effective reaction to medical emergencies
- Providing safe equipment
- Providing safe facilities
- Safe transportation
- Matching wrestlers according to size, skill, and maturity
- Providing "Due Process"
- Providing competent assistants

Effective Teaching or Instruction

This competency has been extensively reviewed in the first section of the chapter. It is important that coaches realize this competency is inclusive. That means many of the competencies we will discuss naturally flow from effective teaching. In other words, the effective teacher knows that instruction means a great deal more than teaching moves or conducting drills. The wrestling coach has to learn that this competency demands a great deal of sensitivity, compassion, and patience; and, some specific non-instructional abilities.

Effective Supervision

Effective teaching includes the supervision of wrestlers. Effective coaching supervision has two primary components: *when* to supervise and *how* to supervise.

When to Supervise

Supervision is not strictly limited to the mat or to practice time. Supervision may be required when parents are late to pick up kids after practice. It may be required when kids are being transported under coach's direction to a match or practice. Or, it may be required during a team picnic off the training area. Any team function where wrestlers are required to attend should be supervised. Coaches need to also be prepared, however, to supervise those functions where attendance is optional, or even where the team just happened to be present without parental supervision. The coach is expected to know that greater supervision may be needed before and after practice, as well as when wrestlers are coming to or leaving practice.

Based on our risk management mission, the risk-conscious coach will not wonder if there is a responsibility to supervise in a particular instance. Rather, he or she will act according to whether, "It is reasonable for my wrestlers' parents to expect that I will supervise in this instance."

How to Supervise

There are three elements to "how to" supervise wrestlers. The first is to have a sufficient number of assistants to supervise. If the program provides assistant coaches, then this may not be a major problem unless the coaching staff's attention is solely directed to the area of activity. The greatest need for supervision usually occurs with wrestlers not directly involved with the activity, or who are away from the center of activity. Parents expect there will be sufficient help to supervise their youngsters during any phase of the activity.

The second element is location. **This means that the staff is located on and around the training area where they can see and readily react to any situations requiring supervision.** As noted before, supervision is not limited to the training area. Location and accessibility of supervisors includes locker rooms, showers and toilets, or other areas where team members are likely to congregate.

The final element is competence. One of the coaching competencies we will discuss is providing competent personnel. **It is reasonable for parents to expect that coaching assistants or aides are as well-qualified as the coach.** It is not unreasonable for parents to expect their children to be supervised by a competent staff.

Are teenagers qualified or competent to supervise younger students or wrestlers? Age is not a legal bar to sage supervision if the teenager has experience and maturity. For example, it is common to leave public swimming pool supervision in the hands of teenagers. However, those youngsters have water safety certification, training programs, and some experience, before they are left to supervise pools. Similarly, the coach who relies on team dads or older brothers and sisters to supervise should be sure those parties possess the same degree of competence.

The failure to reasonably supervise is the primary allegation in most personal injury lawsuits filed against coaches and sports administrators. Our society has a deep-seeded belief injuries would not occur if proper supervision is provided. That surely is the attitude of many parents whether their children's injury was activity-related or caused by some risk other than wrestling.

Effective Reaction to Medical Emergency

Ideally, coaches should be certified in emergency medical treatment, or at least in first aid. Most injuries occur during practice, and safety experts have come to realize that qualified medical personnel are usually not available during the periods of greatest risk. **Many states now require that coaches have some minimal certification in emergency medical procedures.** Youth sports organizations and coaches should check for any local and state requirements regarding availability of medical personnel.

Parents expect that the coaching staff can recognize a medical emergency when it occurs. They also expect the coach to have a plan which can be immediately implemented to deal with the emergency. There was a case where a youngster suffered heat stroke during football practice. The coach, the assistants, and the other school officials immediately recognized what had occurred. Unfortunately, no one was able to determine how to treat the emergency. The youngster received no medical care for well over two hours. That type of reaction would simply be unacceptable to parents, as well it should be.

There should be a plan for notifying emergency care providers; for providing emergency medical transportation promptly; and, for notifying a wrestler's parents and family physician as soon as possible. Clearly, a coach would be well-advised to have signed medical consent forms as well as appropriate addresses and phone numbers available at all times.

Providing Safe Equipment*

Teaching a sport or activity means that the teacher knows how to use the tools of the trade. There are a number of factors that coaches have to consider with equipment.

First, if the coach is directly involved in the purchase or approval of equipment, or has agreed to exclusively utilize a certain manufacturer's equipment, then the coach may have assumed the same legal responsibility as the manufacturer. This is referred to as products liability. It means that liability can attach to the coach for any equipment which is defectively designed or manufactured.

In most instances, however, providing safe equipment means the coach should make sure that it fits each wrestler correctly; that equipment is worn during activity; and, that the coach knows how to properly re-condition and store equipment. **Plainly, it is expected that coaches will instruct their wrestlers on the proper means of equipment care and will watch for the misuse or abuse of equipment.**

A good coaching practice is to thoroughly read manufacturer instructions and guidelines. A coach can usually rely on those directions for maintenance or repair problems. Local youth leagues or associations can usually identify trade associations and journals which will provide up-to-date information regarding equipment use for their coaches.

*This is not as big a concern for wrestling as it is other sports. However, there are still pertinent issues that need to be understood.

Providing Safe Facilities

Providing safe facilities is similar to the safe equipment competency. It is based on a coach's ability to recognize dangerous wrestling surfaces and conditions. **Wrestlers should not be subjected to the risk of injury from improperly maintained mats, from unsafe surroundings, or even from poor equipment.** A coach should have a knowledge of maintenance and repair processes. For example, coaches should learn about common problems with mat surfaces, protective barriers, and equipment.

Transportation

Generally, there is not an obligation to provide transportation. Often, however, coaches find themselves planning or organizing their team's transportation. In those cases, coaches assume the obligation to plan a safe means of transportation. While the type and condition of the transportation vehicle is important, the more critical consideration for the coach is knowing and approving who will drive team members. The major liability problem here is insurance coverage for the team. In many states, wrestlers who travel with friends or other team members by private arrangements may not be covered for personal injury due to the strict limitations of guest driving statutes. It is a good idea to have an organizational plan or policy which specifies who is permitted to drive the team; or, if available, which vehicles are to be used. Parental input should be included in any policy regarding transportation. Finally, it is important that the automobile insurance policies of the parents, coaches, and the youth sports organization be reviewed to determine where liability and medical coverage will be provided.

Matching Wrestlers According to Size, Skill, and Maturity

This competency has been addressed in the first part of the chapter, but it bears repetition. Good teaching requires coaches to advise their wrestlers of the risks of injury common to wrestling. It is important that size and experience differences be considered when organizing drills and scrimmages. In the best interest of safety for all athletes, wrestlers should be separated by size and/or skill levels. **Basically, this coaching competency recognizes that safe contact drills and exercises are an important part of effective teaching.** It also recognizes that parents reasonably expect their inexperienced child will not face undue risks while learning wrestling.

Due Process

This is not easily accepted by many coaches as a competency. To a great extent, coaching has adopted the military style of command and leadership as the basis for its management method. In other words, providing reasons or explanations for coaching instructions are characteristic of the profession. Of course, *due process* is also perceived as a legal tactic encompassing attorneys and second-guessing.

In fact, due process is an effective teaching method. It does not interfere with the decision-making process, but it provides a level-headed approach to enforcement of rules and procedures. It does not, as popularly thought, mandate a forum where wrestlers will be represented by a lawyer. Simply stated, due process merely means that before a wrestler is to be suspended from a match or from the team, the coach will explain what rule was violated and give the wrestler the opportunity to explain his or her conduct. Due process requires that team rules have a legitimate instructional or supervisory purpose; and, that the coach will enforce the rules fairly and consistently. Due process does not hinder a coach's right to discipline, or to require adherence to team rules. **Due process merely means that a coach will be fair with the establishment and enforcement of team rules which is another reasonable parental expectation.**

Competent Personnel

Parents have the right to expect that assistant coaches or aides are competent. If teaching and supervision will be shared by more than just the head coach, then coaching competency requires that assistants be as competent as the head coach.

This obligates coaches to do three things. First, to recruit and select competent assistants;

second, to plan a good training program for assistants which emphasizes the goals and objectives of the instructional program; and, finally, to perform a competency evaluation of assistants. It is common knowledge that getting good assistants can be a difficult chore. However, it is an easier task than facing legal liability for failing to provide capable personnel. Coaches are urged to check the references on all assistants, and to plan and implement comprehensive training programs. Most states provide coaching competency certification programs for coaching staffs.

THE "MANAGEMENT" PROGRAM FOR COACHING RISK MANAGEMENT

The basic functions of organizational management are planning, organizing, staffing, leading, and evaluating. They are important to the risk management because they help establish a competency program for the types of legal risks we identified.

Effective management, like effective teaching, begins with goals and objectives. The processes of planning, organizing, staffing, leading, and evaluating depend on established goals and objectives. We have already identified coaching goals and objectives in the first part of the chapter. They are enhancing kids' physical skills, teaching kids how to learn, and establishing good social behavior. It is important to remember that winning was not identified as a primary coaching goal. Unfortunately, in this day and age, winning is often mistaken as the primary goal of sport. However, just as the business organization risks its health by concentrating only on short-term profits, youth sports risks its credibility if it cannot see beyond winning.

The three goals specified (physical, mental, and social) are valuable because they not only serve as a foundation for sport, but they represent what most parents expect from their children's participation in sport. Certainly winning is a desirable and motivating goal of all sports. As a teacher of wrestling, you know that there are steps along the way that need to be emphasized over outcomes. Wrestling has the ability to develop and show character. Parents expect youth sport to instill confidence, teach sportsmanship, develop physical skill, and provide fun. The three goals of sport do just that.

Planning

As noted, effective teaching requires planning. Using the three goals as a basis, a coach should plan how he or she is going to achieve those goals. A good teacher utilizes a lesson plan and a syllabus for achieving teaching goals. The effective coach should have a lesson plan which charts a path for wrestlers to achieve team and personal goals. A prudent coach will have plans for supervision, plans for reacting to medical emergencies, and plans for transportation issues. Planning is a critical function, and the planning process can be utilized as a valuable tool for training assistant coaches. From a parental point of view, most would expect that the coach has established goals or guidelines for the team and for their children.

Organization

Most organizations realize that establishing goals and objectives has little effect if the structure of the organization is not designed to meet them. Since the goals we have identified in the first part of the chapter are generally recognized in sport, you will not find many diverse organizational structures in youth sports. Many organizations have structured themselves along the traditional lines of the military command structure. A means of insuring that your team's organizational structure is effective is to examine how well you communicate the goals and objectives. For example, a principal means of good planning is to get feedback. In other words, how well a coach has planned can be gauged from the feedback of athletes and parents. By the same token, organizational effectiveness can be gauged from team and parental feedback regarding communication within the team structure.

Staffing

This again refers to the competent personnel issue. Since physical, mental, and social goals of sport serve as the basis for your planning and organization, they also determine who you should hire. Will a candidate who sees winning as the primary goal of sport be a person who is likely to fit within the team organization? We already realize that planning and organization issues have to match the goals which have been established. From a staffing point of view, a coach is much better off hiring or accepting assistants who share the same goals and objectives.

Leading

This management function looks at leadership from two sides. First, why do people in an organization follow a leader? Second, how does a leader motivate people to perform with their best effort. There is no trick to understanding how this function works. When parents recognize that the coach can help their children achieve goals which the parents believe are important, they will support the program. When wrestlers see that their participation is more important to the coach than merely winning or losing, they will follow the program. Finally, when a coach, like the effective teacher, can show how those goals help the wrestlers become better, they will be motivated to perform better. Again, the emphasis is on the goals and objectives. A coaching manner may be charismatic, or it may be relatively passive. **Whatever manner or method is used to coach a team, adherence to goals and objectives will be the mark of the good leader.**

Evaluating

This management function is really called controlling, however, that term does not best describe the function. The purpose of controlling is to evaluate or measure how successful an organization has been in accomplishing its goals and objectives. Some coaches will measure success based on winning and losing percentages. Other coaches, like effective teachers, will measure success on the basis of retention. That is, did most of the kids retain an interest in the sport and return to play the next season. In risk management, the measure of success is the safety of the program.

Again, this function is based on the physical, mental, and social goals of sport. From a risk management perspective, when an evaluation indicates that these goals have been largely met, then it is a good and safe indication that the coaching risk management program has been effective. By the same token, you cannot assume a coaching risk management program has been effective, if winning is the only measure of success.

IMPLEMENTING THE COACHING RISK MANAGEMENT PROGRAM

Implementing is the most difficult part of any management program. Many people who consider themselves "idea people" lack the ability to execute their plans. Experience persistently reminds us that ideas have little value if there is no capability to implement them.

We know that risk management starts with risk identification. Risk identification, however, has little effect in a risk management program if the program itself is not properly implemented. Often, organizations leave implementation to a risk manager whose function is to coordinate risk identification and elimination. In coaching, however, all coaches have to be risk managers. They cannot leave that function to others. That means that all coaches must have the ability to implement risk management goals and objectives.

There are three essential elements for the successful implementation of a risk management program: communication, working through people, and accepting change.

Communication

Like most of us, coaches probably would not admit they don't communicate well. As a matter of fact, many coaches exaggerate their oral communication skills. Since coaches rarely have their writing critiqued, many might also assume their writing skills are satisfactory. The reason for these false assumptions is that people believe that effective communication is in the message itself. In other words, if what is spoken or written is good, then the communication is good. That may be true in literature, but it is rarely true in organizational communication.

We now know, of course, that the key to effective communication in any organization is not the message, but the receiver. In other words, it does not matter how good the message may appear. If the message is not received and understood by the receiver, the communication has been ineffective. Coaching communication is compounded by the different ages, backgrounds, and experiences of other coaches and wrestlers. Therefore, it takes a very strong and understanding effort by a coach to be an effective communicator. The first step is to learn how to listen.

Be an Emotional Listener

The first lesson for the coach who wants to improve his or her organizational communication skills is to become a more effective listener. According to organizational management experts, there are two types of listening: rational listening and emotional listening. Most of us are rational listeners. That means that we tend to evaluate or judge what others have said to us. It is exemplified by our responses which either agree or disagree with what the speaker said. The rational listener judges others' communication, and is not prepared to change his mind or behavior as a result of what the speaker said. Emotional listening, on the other hand, means that you view things strictly from the speaker's point of view. It means that you can be influenced to change your mind or behavior. For the coach, it means the coach puts himself or herself in the shoes of the speaker, whether assistant coach or wrestler. This is a tough characteristic to learn because most of us are more interested in communication as it affects us, not how it affects the speaker.

Effective Teaching Requires Emotional Listening

The effective teacher knows that children see and understand things in different ways than adults. The teacher who is an emotional listener views things from the child's perspective. It is that ability which enables the effective teacher to communicate with children. The first step in effective communication for the coach is not speaking or sending a message; rather it is learning how to listen.

Teamwork: The Ability to Work Through People

Another organizational concept which has proved successful is teamwork. Teamwork, of course, is recognized as a critical element of success in sports. It is a quality upon which many coaches evaluate their team's performance. Also, it is a personal characteristic that coaches look for in their athletes. Unfortunately, it is not always altogether clear that coaches understand how to build teamwork, or how to participate as a team member.

Effective Teamwork Requires Commitment to Training

A goal of teamwork is to make your members as good as they can be, and to help them develop a feeling of satisfaction in what they do. Often, that goal depends on a leader's commitment to training. Today's effective organizations emphasize continuous training for their members, as well as cross-training to help members develop new skills and specialties.

Training is not merely something one learns to start a job, or a sport. It is a way of working; it never ends. It is a commitment which requires a willingness to train, retrain, and then train some more. Do the training practices of organizations have a place in youth sports? If organizations know that teamwork based on a commitment to training creates job satisfaction, it's safe to assume that wrestler satisfaction and retention will result from the same commitment to training. Can coaches become committed to that concept? It is difficult to gauge. For example, coaches often respond to losses in the following ways: "We did not execute" or, "We need to work harder" or, "We weren't ready to compete." The blame is placed on the failure of the wrestlers rather than the coach. It would be novel to hear a coach say, "I did a lousy job of preparing you for this match."

Successful organizations know failures in team performance usually reflect problems at the top, not the bottom. Likewise, the coaching commitment to training would require that coach to reflect on team performance from the top first. The training ethic is intended to make assistant coaches more competent, help wres-

tlers continuously improve, and thereby create a sense of team satisfaction. If the training program is not doing that, the coach needs to first evaluate his or her performance. As noted, however, the popular excuse is that poor team performance is a result of player failure, not coaching failure.

Effective Teamwork Requires Emotional Listening

Working through people, like communication, requires emotional listening. Teamwork and the training ethic are based on the willingness to listen. Effective training requires input and feedback from the participants. A coach, therefore, must be an emotional listener to recognize whether or not the training is working. If the coach does not actively listen, it means the coach is making his or her own assumptions about the team. That is how the blame game starts.

The basis of teamwork is the capability to influence others, adapt to others, and be influenced by others. It is easy to see that emotional listening is its foundation.

The Ability to Accept Change

Many coaches model their coaching style on their own experiences. In management, it is an axiom that we manage as we were managed. In sport, many coaches coach as they were coached. There is nothing wrong with adopting some of your past experiences in sport. After all, the principal objectives (mental, physical, and social) are time-honored values. However, the effective teacher realizes that teaching those values requires change and adaption. The ability to change does not mean that you sacrifice values, it means you learn how to teach them more effectively than before.

Unfortunately, it is not easy to change even when team performance may be at stake. If your coaching experience is rooted in rational listening, as opposed to emotional listening, and team direction has always been simply left to the determination of the coach, then change will be difficult. Coaches, however, should consider that they utilize change all the time. Any special preparations for a specific opponent are changes. While many coaches may fear to change how they coach, they are, nevertheless, engaged in change and its effects every day.

The effective teacher seeks change. He or she is constantly searching for new methods and approaches to teaching. The effective teacher knows that "effective" is not a stationary concept. Effectiveness requires constant evaluation. Similarly, the coach must be able to adapt his or her methods in order to remain effective. And, the coach must be able to recognize that the role of sports has changed just as the wrestlers' abilities have.

Figure 3-2. A coach must know how to handle potentially dangerous situations by making correct decisions for the athlete.

4
Interpersonal Relations

QUESTIONS TO CONSIDER

- Who are the key individuals with whom the coach must communicate?
- What basic messages must coaches communicate to principals, directors, parents, teachers, athletes, and maintenance workers?
- What are the key elements of effective interpersonal relations?

The ability to effectively communicate to many different groups is a common trait of the best coaches.

INTRODUCTION

Why do some coaches who have only mediocre win/loss records have so much support from parents and students, while others who win championships have little or none? How do some coaches get so many students to participate, while others struggle to field a team? How do some coaches get their facilities maintained spotlessly, while others can't get the custodian to change a light bulb? There are many reasons why these situations exist. There is a good possibility, however, that interpersonal relations play a major role in each scenario.

An extremely important aspect of coaching is the development of positive working relationships with people who support you and your program. These positive relationships generally do not occur by accident; they are components of a coaching style. Some relationships take days to develop; most take months or years. Every coaching situation is unique. However, you control one common element: the amount of effort you are willing to make to create and maintain positive relationships with others.

Interpersonal relationships are part of one's coaching style. Whether or not they are effective depends on the coach.

While positive results may not appear immediately, the long-term results of effective communication ultimately pay great dividends. The following tips about interacting with specific individuals and groups will serve as a good starting point toward effective communication and the development of positive interpersonal relations that should serve you well throughout your coaching experience.

COMMUNICATION WITH IMPORTANT OTHERS AND GROUPS

The Principal

The principal is the educational leader of the building. He/she is concerned with the total school environment and the well-being of all students and staff. Get to know the principal and make it a point to keep him/her informed of events and experiences relative to your team, both positive and negative. The principal may already be aware of what you are communicating, but it is important to hear it from you.

Coaches should share the principal's concern about the total welfare of the athlete.

Show an interest and awareness of other school programs. Scan the local newspaper to become familiar with such key issues as standard test scores, a redistricting proposal, the upcoming millage or school board election, the school's recent success in the Science Olympiad, or the recent National Merit Scholarship winners who also happen to be athletes. It is beneficial to be able to discuss topical items that demonstrate your interest, concern, and support for the school and school district.

The Athletic Director

The athletic director leads the athletic program and shares many of the same concerns as the building principal. Dialogue regarding athletics with the principal may be general in nature. However, conversations with the athletic director will most likely be specific. Be sure to communicate with the athletic director about the positive, potentially positive, negative, and potentially negative situations that you face in your sport. He/she may be able to provide sound advice and assist you in alleviating problems and achieving program objectives. Read the school's literature on policies and procedures. Comply with deadlines and end-of-season responsibilities.

Frequent communication with the athletic director will eliminate many problems during the season.

Once the season is over and the athletes have gone on to other things, much remains to be done. The collection and storage of equipment, completion of end-of-season reports, and identification of needs for next season are extremely important to the athletic director. While these duties are not always as enjoyable as working with student athletes, they require your attention. When promptly completed, they will greatly assist you in establishing a positive working relationship with the athletic director.

The Parents

Communication is the key to a good relationship between the coach and parents. Many coaches have encountered problems due to "meddling parents." However, other coaches have discovered how much more meaningful coaching can be by effectively communicating with the parents. Parents want to know who is working with their sons or daughters. They want to know what your philosophy is, and if you really care about kids and their social, emotional, intellectual, and physical development. Parents may want to know how knowledgeable you are about the sport and what your goals are.

The parents' primary concern is the welfare of their child. Coaches who communicate effectively about students' welfare are practicing good interpersonal communication.

Unfortunately, the image of coaches in most movies and comic strips is rarely positive. Coaches are commonly portrayed as self-serving, insensitive, and single-minded. Sports highlights on the evening news aren't much help, as they often feature brawls, ejections, and other unsportsmanlike behavior demonstrated by a few coaches. These displays work against the credibility of coaches and athletics in general. As a result, you should make a conscious effort to meet the parents of your athletes and establish an open line of two-way communication.

If you discipline an athlete or issue a warning regarding future problems, tell the parents. If your actions are interpreted to parents by the athletes, the dinner table version is not always the same one that you would give. If, at a later date, you call these parents for support on an issue, you may find defensive parents who would rather discuss how unfairly their child was treated on that earlier occasion.

Many coaches have found that a pre-season "Meet The Team Night" helps parents get to know them and their programs. A pre-season evening practice during which the coach introduces the team and talks about his/her coaching philosophy, the potential for injury, and team policies in a concise manner, followed by a few drills and an intrasquad scrimmage, serves many purposes. It shows the coach in action (estab-

lishes credibility). It allows the coach to say something positive about each athlete (displays an interest). It illustrates to the parents exactly what their sons/daughters will be doing for the next few weeks. Being "on stage" before the season starts may also help relieve first game jitters for the athletes.

The Student Athlete

Sydney Harris, in his poem, *Winners and Losers,* wrote "a winner would rather be admired than liked, although he would prefer both. . . ." In Harris' poem the word winner could easily be replaced with coach to emphasize the point of striving to maintain high ideals, a responsible work ethic, and the qualities of good sportsmanship. To the curiously impressionable teenage mind, the coach is a role model who can have a tremendous influence. Coaches may be friends to their wrestlers, but must keep in mind that they are not peers. All teams must be governed by rules of conduct. Be firm but fair, and follow the basic rule that we should treat athletes as we would want to be treated. Have as few team rules as possible, and enforce them in a consistent manner. Use positive terminology to replace the time-honored negative ones—"sudden victory" in place of "sudden death," or "pro sprints" in place of "suicide sprints." While many of us used these terms while growing up, times have changed and so have coaching techniques. Remember, not long ago it was considered acceptable for coaches to provide salt tablets and keep athletes away from drinking water to "Get them in shape."

Conduct fair team tryouts and have a genuine concern for all who try out. If your team has a limited membership, and reductions are necessary, "cuts" should be the most agonizing experience of the season. There is nothing pleasant about eliminating aspiring members from a team, especially at a time in their lives when acceptance is so important.

Eliminating aspiring athletes during "tryouts" requires great sensitivity on the part of the coaches.

The Number 1 rule of eliminating athletes from teams is *Never Post A List.* Regardless of how many have tried out, take the time to let them know personally that they did not make the team. If you consider that athletes have invested time and money in physical examinations, possibly purchased new equipment such as shoes and practice clothing, had parents fill out emergency and insurance forms, taken the risk of trying out, and cleared other hurdles just to be a member of your team, they deserve to be told by you the reasons why they did not make the squad this season. They should be complimented and thanked for their interest and encouraged to work on those aspects of the sport you identified as weaknesses so they might try again next year. If possible, offer roles as managers, statisticians, or timers to students who do not make the team.

Most will accept that they did not make the team, and your encouragement will be greatly appreciated. However, occasionally an individual may be devastated by the rejection, and additional counseling may be needed. If you sense a problem, contact the parents and explain exactly what has taken place and provide the same encouragement for their child's future development. Do not hesitate to contact the parents about their child's current and future status as a member of the team; the athlete may be concerned about further rejection or embarrassment at home and not tell his/her parents about the team selections. He/she may even decide not to go home after school each day and wander off while the parents think that the child is at practice.

In communicating with your athletes use simple, direct language and be a listener who is objective and concerned. Young people need guidance, direction, consistency, and genuine concern from their coaches. When you fulfill these basic needs, you develop a solid foundation for a successful coaching experience.

The Faculty

At the beginning of the season, consider sending a note to the teachers of your athletes, stating your concern about each athlete's academic progress, citizenship, and attendance. Ask teachers to contact you if the students are not meeting their expectations. Keep in mind that not every member of the faculty is a supporter of the athletic program, but avoid being discouraged by those who consider athletics a necessary evil of the extracurricular school day.

If you are not a teacher in the building where your athletes attend school or you are a non-faculty coach, communication with the faculty will be more difficult, but equally as important. Having a mail box in the school and attending selected school functions will help you to communicate with the faculty.

Coaches who are genuinely concerned about the academic progress of athletes will receive general support for athletic programs from teachers.

A coach who is a strong "teacher" of a sport and who cares about students as total individuals will earn the respect and support of most faculty members. The significance of staff attitudes toward your program should not be underestimated, because they ultimately filter into the student body through classroom communication. A program that has faculty support looks for creative methods to encourage the teaching staff to get involved. Statisticians, ticket takers, scorers, and timers are always needed. Consider a "faculty appreciation night" in conjunction with a game to recognize faculty support.

The Officials

It is important to have a positive mind-set regarding officials. They are hired to enforce the rules of the game. Coaches who choose not to see them as human beings who are hired to enforce rules to the best of their ability make officials a greater part of the game than they were ever intended to be. Throughout the history of athletics, officials have never had a win or a loss; that statistic is always reserved for the athletes and the coaches. Treat officials courteously and fairly. Get to know them by name and never embarrass them. They will make mistakes just as wrestlers and coaches do, but the vast majority do a good job. Those who don't will eventually have difficulty being selected as officials. Just as officials develop reputations among coaches, be assured that coaches develop reputations within the community of officials.

The Coaches of Other Sports

Show your colleagues that you care about their programs as well as your own. Inquire about the progress of their teams and, if possible, attend a few of their contests. In general, demonstrate a genuine concern for your fellow coaches. One of the surest ways to alienate yourself from other coaches is to talk down or discourage students from participating in other sports. Another way is to encourage specialization and a total year-round commitment to the sport you are coaching. These actions deprive athletes of well-rounded educational experiences through participation in other sports and should not be tolerated.

The Custodians and Maintenance Workers

Regular care of the facilities and locker rooms is extremely important and sometimes taken for granted. Go through the proper channels when making requests for maintenance or custodial service. Whenever possible, submit your requests early. Hot water in the showers, toilet paper in the restrooms, and changed light bulbs generally tend to be maintained better when you have a positive rapport with maintenance people.

The Professional Organizations

Memberships in professional organizations can be extremely beneficial. Information on coaching clinics, books, periodicals, videos, and in some cases, liability insurance are some of the benefits provided by the professional organizations at minimal expense. Organizations welcome coaches from all levels to participate. It's also a way to keep your finger on the pulse of the action in your sport and have the opportunity to bring about change through organized efforts, if you are so inclined.

SUMMARY

Through effective communication and positive interpersonal relations we reinforce the total team concept that coaches often refer to, thereby creating the environment for a successful coaching experience. As a constant reminder of this concept, view the word "TEAM" as an acronym meaning, "Together Everyone Accomplishes More." The coach is the key ingredient in formulating that togetherness as he/she establishes the tone by which the team and the program functions and the way in which they are perceived by others.

5
Relationships with Officials and Other Coaches

QUESTIONS TO CONSIDER

- What are the coach's administrative responsibilities to the officials?
- How can knowledge of the rules reduce potential conflicts?
- What are the key points of good public relations with officials?
- How might you implement a sportsmanship campaign?
- How effective is your communication with other coaches?

Forming friendships and respect for your colleagues will enhance both your success and enjoyment of coaching.

INTRODUCTION

Coaching requires communication with many different groups: athletes, parents, maintenance and equipment personnel, officials, other coaches, administrators, support staff, fans, and the media. Your working relationships with all of these people are extremely important. However, coaches frequently take for granted their relationships with officials and other coaches.

Take the initiative to establish rapport with officials and other coaches.

The competitive environment of a key contest can lead to reduced and/or negative communication with officials and opposing coaches. Establishing rapport with people who might influence the outcome of your team's performance isn't easy and will not happen overnight, but make a consistent, positive effort. You must take the initiative and set a good example for building positive relationships with officials and other coaches.

Good communication leads to better understanding between coaches, athletes, and officials. In the event of a conflict or emergency, decisions and actions depend on the coach's ability to communicate with other coaches and officials. Negative relations with coaches, athletes, parents, fans, and/or officials frustrate everyone. Officials and coaches thrive in a positive working environment. The longterm results of good working relations will be productive and satisfying for you and your program.

RELATIONSHIPS WITH OFFICIALS

Working effectively with officials requires more than greeting them and escorting them to the dressing room on the day of competition. Officials often take the brunt of our frustration, but their role is essential to the success of any athletic program. They share your goals— to provide a safe and fair contest within the rules. They have a job to do and so do you. Let them officiate; your job is to coach.

Treat officials with respect and fairness.

Officials will make mistakes, and so will you. Treat them with respect and fairness. Get to know them by name and be sensitive to their needs before, during, and after the contest. Establish a positive reputation with the officials. Your athletes will follow your example. Athletes and officials will concentrate on their roles if they do not worry about the other's responsibilities. Let your positive behavior set the tone for the entire event.

PROPER CONDUCT OF ADMINISTRATIVE DUTIES

Working effectively with officials involves proper conduct of administrative duties, knowledge of the rules, positive public relations, and proper conduct during competition.

Contracting of Officials

Every contest should be conducted by officials who have signed contracts. A contract provides reassurance for you and scheduling information for the official. An officials' association is better able to assist you with problems if you have completed the proper paperwork involved in issuing a contract.

The contract also serves as a binding legal document in case of injury to officials. An official who is registered with your state athletic association most likely is a recipient of catastrophic insurance. The officials are usually protected by their association insurance only if under a contractual agreement. Without a contract, the case is weakened. Check with your state athletic association about liability policies and procedures.

Have a copy of the officials' contracts with you at all competitions, and ask for proof of rating and association affiliation (whatever is required by your program or state high school athletic association) if you do not know whether the official is registered with your state association.

Hosting of Officials

Establish a routine for courteous hosting of your officials. Reserve comfortable, clean, and secure dressing facilities for the officials to use before, during, and after the contest. Separate the officials from the athletes so that the officials can dress privately and without confrontation. Privacy will allow them to prepare appropriately for the coming contest. Have someone available to escort the officials to the dressing room when they arrive. For highly competitive matches, it might be prudent to have officers safeguard the exit of the officials.

Courteous treatment of officials includes clean, private dressing facilities, refreshments, and prompt payment according to contract terms.

Refreshments are always appreciated by the officials. Drinks and snacks should be available in the dressing room before, during, and after the contest.

If possible, have payment available at the site and pay the officials prior to the competition. This depends on your administrative policy. Whatever the case, follow through with prompt remuneration for the officials' services.

Evaluation of Officials

Evaluation is an important aspect of your responsibilities to the officials and the conference officers. Constructive feedback is important not only to the official, but to the officials' association as well. Be conscientious and consistent with your evaluations. Evaluate all officials, not just the ones you think have done an inadequate job. Rate them objectively based on all aspects of their performance. Using proper channels for criticism is more productive and conducive to change than inappropriate sideline comments or demonstrations.

Officials should also have the opportunity to report derogatory circumstances to high school, conference, and state association administrators. Such circumstances might include problems with the facility or equipment; any unsportsmanlike conduct by coaches, athletes, or fans; ejected coaches or athletes; and unusual termination of a contest by the official. Check with your local or state athletic association for evaluation procedures.

Using proper channels for evaluation of officials is more productive and conducive to change than inappropriate sideline comments or demonstrations.

KNOWLEDGE OF THE RULES

Learn all the rules of your sport. Many adversarial situations occur because the coach does not know the rules or misinterprets a rule. It is important that you understand rules interpretations and changes, and how to use the rule book. Know the particular rules which apply to the competition in which you are coaching.

Understand the responsibilities of the officials. Learn the mechanics of the contest; know where the official needs to be to make the appropriate call. There is a big difference between a judgment call and a miscalled rule. Know your association's protest policy and the appropriate method of resolving conflict on the field. Misinterpretation or misapplication of rules or judgment decisions of officials are not grounds for protest.

Knowing the rules benefits your team at practice and during competition. Take time to attend a preseason rules interpretation meeting. Read the rule book. Understand new rules and new interpretations of old rules. Teach these to your staff, athletes, and parents. Being informed will preserve your dignity and increase your credibility with officials, administrators, athletes, and fans.

Know the rules! Being properly informed is your responsibility.

PROPER CONDUCT OF PUBLIC RELATIONS

Rules meetings provide an opportunity for communication between coaches and officials. Your relationship with officials can have a positive or negative effect on your program. Be prepared to greet each official by name. It is comforting to an official to feel recognized and welcome. Treat your officials courteously and maintain a professional working relationship at all times. Knowing how to approach each individual may positively effect the effort that an official puts forth during competition.

Good public relations with officials can have a positive effect on your program.

Invite officials to work scrimmages as often as possible. Scrimmages provide opportunities for less formal interaction between coaches and officials. Scrimmages may also lead to situations where rule interpretations can be discussed so that coaches and athletes are in an informal but practical environment when learning the rules.

PROPER CONDUCT DURING COMPETITION

Actions speak louder than words. You are a role model for your athletes and fans. If you must discuss a call, do it diplomatically with courtesy and civil behavior. Is an outburst over an incorrect call worth the risk of ejection? What is the overall impact of your conduct? Remember, you are more useful on the sideline than in the locker room. If not, you should not be coaching sports. The level of sportsmanship which you consistently exhibit may be modeled by many who observe you.

Figure 5-1. During competition, it is important to effectively communicate with officials, your athletes and coaching staff.

Officials are expected to develop and practice courage, integrity, calmness, poise, hustle, emotional maturity, humility, common sense, politeness, and good judgment. These qualities can be reciprocally exchanged between coaches and officials. Expect the best of your officials and model the behavior you expect from them.

Take note of younger, up-and-coming officials. The longevity of their careers might depend on your attitude during their formative stages. Be patient and understanding. Concerns or suggestions should be stated privately, away from the pressure of competition. Your assistance will be appreciated if it is given in a constructive, nonthreatening manner.

Implement a sportsmanship campaign with your athletes and the student body.

Implement a campaign to emphasize sportsmanship in your athletes and student body. Discourage improper conduct by spectators. The host institution has the right to remove anyone for disruptive conduct. Reprimand your athletes for inappropriate behavior (e.g., arguing with an official, negative non-verbal behavior) and praise them when they properly handle a tough situation. Teach them respect for the officials and how to be under control in an adversarial situation.

Rewarding good sportsmanship is important and deserves more emphasis with coaches, athletes, and fans. Corporate sponsors offer various sportsmanship programs which can benefit your program and improve your relationship with officials. Try to attract such sponsors to your program (your state athletic association may have some recommendations) and publicize the names of those who exhibit good sportsmanship.

RELATIONSHIPS WITH OTHER COACHES

The contest is so much more enjoyable if you have good rapport with the opposing coach. Treat him/her with respect and courtesy. Practice good sportsmanship. Leave the competition on the floor, and communicate honestly and openly before and after the event. Be a cooperative host. If you extend appropriate hospitality, you are likely to receive the same treatment when you are the visiting coach.

Get to know other coaches. Be informed about how other teams are doing. Attend their contests when possible and lend them your support if they ask. Encourage your athletes to support other teams. A total team effort extends beyond the boundaries of your own athletes. Thriving athletic programs need the support of the entire community, especially of those within your organization.

Practice good sportsmanship with opposing coaches and support other coaches in your organization.

Good relationships with coaches and officials are vital to your program. They are the foundation of your coaching career. In a sense, as a leader of young athletes, you become a public servant. This position conveys to the community that they have "a right to know" about you and your sport. If you take the initiative to communicate with those you serve and to build positive relations, you will reap the rewards of support and credibility.

You do not become a hero by becoming a coach; you become a teacher of young men and women, a role model, and another member of the educational community. You assume responsibility for others and an obligation to act in the best interests of your athletes and their families. It is imperative that you establish a precedent for the treatment of officials and other coaches. Your influence can be powerful and widespread. Make positive, thoughtful choices.

SUMMARY

One of the coach's most important responsibilities, in addition to coaching young athletes, is to act as a goodwill ambassador for the athletic program. In and out of the presence of your young athletes you must be mindful of the image that you wish to project and conduct yourself accordingly.

Two of your most frequent guests will be coaches and officials. Before their visits, plan an agenda that can be placed into effect when they arrive. If you remember to treat coaches and officials the way that you would like to be treated, you will be setting a fine example for young athletes.

Section II
Program Development

6
Building a Wrestling Program

QUESTIONS TO CONSIDER

- What are the primary tools used in building a wrestling program?
- What is the most successful way to structure your goals?
- What are the four training phases?
- What are the seven principles of sound fund raising?

A successful program will foster enthusiastic support from all associated with it.

INTRODUCTION

Most of this country's greatest wrestlers were not only developed by excellent coaching and natural talent but were a product of very successful programs. The development of a wrestling program is a task that the greatest coaches have mastered to create an environment for their wrestlers to excel, regardless of the talent level within a room.

There are many basic principles that a coach must consider in the development and building of a wrestling program. Regardless of whether you are a club, scholastic or collegiate coach, the primary tools you will need are community support, a practice facility, a goal structure, reward system, planning, and follow-through.

COMMUNITY SUPPORT

Community support is the back bone of every successful wrestling program. This relationship creates support in every area that is important for a program's longevity and resultant success. This includes support via money, access to needed venues or businesses, numbers of fans and supporters, community pride, emotional support for the athlete, coaches and families, and kids' and parents' desire to be a part of your team which will draw the best athletes.

This type of support can only be fostered through the willingness of a coach to be able to work with several different types and levels of people in a professional and cordial manner. The coach must make the effort and take the initiative to introduce himself and work together with the community and it's constituents to best meet the needs of all concerned and not just focus on the individual needs of the athletes and program.

PRACTICE FACILITIES

Once this working relationship is established, the focus can then be turned towards the specific needs of a wrestling team. The first need is a place to practice. Depending on your respective situations, there are several options that can be sought to best meet the needs of your program. Some ideal places to use for this purpose can be found in your local Boy's and Girl's Clubs, YMCA/YWCA, Community Centers, and schools. The practice facility must be large enough to accommodate a wrestling mat for the wrestlers to practice on. The size of the room will also be determined by the number of athletes that will be involved. An ideal situation would permit all of your wrestlers to practice at the same time with enough room to account for safety. However, if this is not the case, then you can be creative in using the facilities that you have (i.e., split your practice into two, only use half of your wrestlers at a time, use buddy drills, etc.).

For beginning programs, the purchase of a wrestling mat can be a hinderance. New wrestling mats run between $4,500 for a 36' x 36', 1½" thick surface and $6,000+ for a 40'-42' x 40'- 42', 1¾"-2" thick mat. Some other options that may be available are used mats and/or the reconditioning of a damaged one. These options also cost thousands of dollars.

For schools or clubs without the funds to handle this type of purchase, there are some creative ways to work around the lack of capital. Some suggestions may be to split the cost with your athletic department or intramural clubs and share the use of the mat with other sports that would need its padded surface. This includes activities such as gymnastics, judo, tumbling, cheerleading, martial arts, dance, and many others. This option would lower the cost demand for your program and increase the demand for a school or athletic department to purchase the mat. Another possibility would be to raise the money through fundraising. There are many ways to do this which are outlined at the end of this chapter.

Upon securing a facility to practice in and a mat to practice on, it is imperative and strongly recommended that you and your program have liability insurance. If you are developing a program within a scholastic or collegiate program, your institution should already have coverage. If you are developing a club program, liability insurance can be acquired through a USA Wrestling Club Charter. This can be accomplished by contacting your respective state chairperson or the national office located in Colorado Springs, Colorado. Once all of these steps are accomplished, you are ready to set some goals and objectives for your wrestling program.

PROGRAM GOALS AND OBJECTIVES

The most successful wrestling programs are not a result of the best athletes, the most money, or the best facilities but rather a result of a specific goal structure and process to achieve it. Throughout this book you will find the specifics of training wrestlers such as practice planning, fundraising, weight training, and so forth. However, without a goal, these coaching skills are useless. Your goal structure is the most important part of a coach's job in creating success in all aspects of your program. This includes the physical, mental, and social development of your athletes both on and off the mat. It also includes creating community pride and respect for your athletes and wrestling program.

Most successful people believe that the best way to develop a goal system is from the end backwards. In this, it is meant that you must decide what is your ultimate goal, whether for one season or many combined seasons, and then work backwards. For example, if your goal was to be state champions, then you would need to put a date on when you expected to achieve it. Upon establishing that objective, it is then necessary to break that down into shorter term goals. The more detailed a coach is in his planning, the better he will be able to measure his progress towards the pre-established long-term goals.

The detail planning of the best coaches follow a very similar pattern. That is, the breakdown of goals in the following manner: year end, seasonal peaks, monthly, weekly, daily, and individually. It must also be stated that your goal structure provides a road map for your destination. However, there are many ways to get from point A to point B, and many times you must allow for variation and flexibility in your planning.

Once your goals are established, it is important to make sure that they are shared and consistent with the goals of your administration, athletes, and community. This shared vision will create the powerful dynamics of a group working together towards a unified goal

and not one coach or team working towards a goal in conflict with the necessary support group.

REWARD SYSTEM

One of the great motivators of mankind is the need for recognition. The knowledge and nurturing of this fact makes a very dramatic difference between good coaches and excellent coaches. The unified effort of parents, athletes, coaches, fans, businesses, administrations, and all support faculty are paramount in every model of excellence. This can be witnessed in the reward structure and recognition accorded the members of a winning team.

Rewarding your athletes should always be done by the achievement of specific goals. It is important that they are not given incentives and rewards for doing nothing. This will counteract the effect that this recognition is meant to have. The actual substance of the rewards you give your athletes can be as trivial as extra rest during practice all the way up to trophies and plaques presented among a large group of people. The actual reward isn't as important as the recognition among the wrestler's peers. When striving towards a worthwhile goal and the achievement of it, the recognition enhances the athletes' feelings of self-worth, self-esteem,

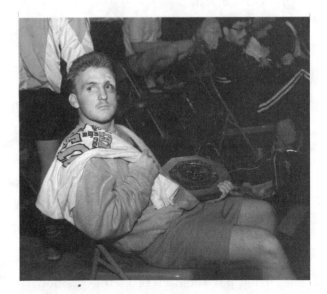

Figure 6-1. After years of hard work, this athlete's goal of winning a Junior National Championship was achieved.

and confidence. This in turn motivates the athlete towards greater achievement and resultant success. This cycle is fostered by the establishment of the aforementioned goal structure. Within that structure are the targets for the athlete to shoot for daily, weekly, monthly, and seasonal. At the end of those targets is the recognition and reward that every person needs and desires.

There are many things and ideas that a coach may institute in designing and implementing a reward system for his program. Some time-tested methods are as follows:

- Listing the names of Conference Champions, State Champions, State Placers, All-Americans, National Champions, etc., in view of the public, school, and athletes.
- Establishing records in different categories of achievement, i.e., pins/takedowns, wins/season, wins/career, tournament victories, etc.
- Developing a Hall of Fame with specific requirements to qualify.
- Having a year-end banquet for the wrestlers, their families, and fans in which the awards are presented.
- Rewarding the team members as a whole regardless of whether they were the first team members or junior varsity.
- Having a wrestler of the week, month, or particular match.

These are just a few examples of the types of rewards that the best coaches and programs use on a regular basis. The sky is the limit when a coach uses the imagination to develop a recognition system for his athletes and wrestling program.

PLANNING AND FOLLOW-THROUGH

To achieve the goals that you've set, it is very important to plan your work and work your plan. The more detailed your goal structure the easier and more apparent your planning will be. The results achieved by most successful teams and programs is not by accident. They have put themselves in the position to achieve their goals by planning their work and working their plan to peak at specific major matches and tournaments.

Figure 6-2. In 1993, with the leadership of its' coaches, the United States was rewarded with a World Championship.

As discussed earlier in goal setting, planning for your program works best when started from the end backwards. Your plan will follow accordingly with your goals for the season. Once again, you would start with a yearly or seasonal plan then break it down into monthly, weekly, and daily segments. The importance of this method cannot be stressed enough. Success is not an accident and luck does not just occur by chance. When you fail to plan, you definitely plan to fail.

Following is an example of USA Wrestling's Freestyle and Greco-Roman National Team schedule periodization plan. This should aid you in developing a competition schedule as well as outlining the times of the year for recovery, base training, and peaking.

Training Phases

1. Competition Phase: This is the actual week of competition. Each time you find a competition graph, you will also find a percentage of your maximum performance. The graph will stop at the minimum percentage of your maximum performance. For example, the first graph stops at 100% for the World Team Trials that were held in June.

We feel a wrestler should never compete at less than 70% of their maximum performance and never fall below 60% of their maximum performance at any time during the year, including the active rest stage. It is much easier to maintain a high level of fitness than it is to start over.

2. Preparation Phase: The preparation phase, or base training phase, is the key to being successful during the competition season. This phase insures adequate strength, endurance,

Table 6-1 (a-b).

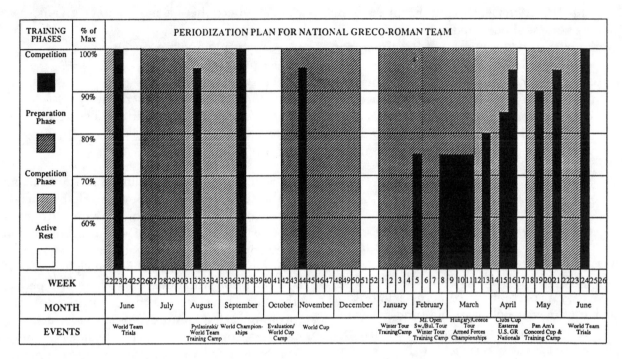

(a)

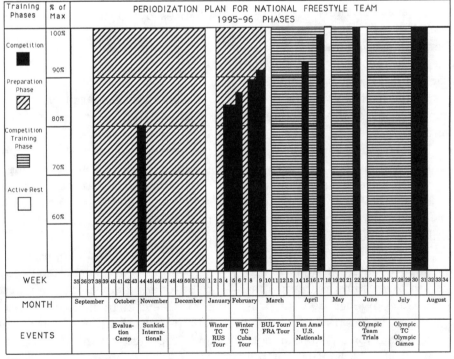

(b)

flexibility, balance, and technique for the more intense competition phase. This phase should be less intensive but high volume training. You have to prepare your body for those tough competitions.

3. Competition Phase: During this phase your training volume should gradually decrease while your intensity and technique work will increase.

4. Active Rest Phase: This should be the time of the year when your training is reduced so you can recover emotionally and physically. Your training should be low volume and low intensity but it is important for you to maintain a good conditioning base.

FUND RAISING

The successful development of a wrestling program entails many components to be fulfilled by a head coach and his staff. Beyond the obvious physical, technical, and training skills needed by a coach, it is also necessary to wear the hat of master politician and fund-raiser.

As wrestling is traditionally a non-revenue generating sport, it is crucial for the long term success of a program to have a plan and a means to generate the needed monies to run a team. The best wrestling programs have developed an extensive and detailed fund-raising plan designed to support the ever-growing needs of the athletes, community, and fans.

Though one of the most abhorred responsibilities of a coach, fund raising and promotion for your team is a vital part of creating a program that encompasses all of the components of the best programs.

The primary goal of fund raising is quite simply to raise money to pay for expenses incurred by a program that are necessary but not covered by your budget. The definition of "necessary expenses" will vary from program to program, but will grow as your program develops. For example, when starting a program from scratch, the most important items that may need to be purchased are a wrestling mat and uniforms for your squad. However, as your program develops, other "necessary" items that may be needed are promotional posters, media guides, and better facilities. Regardless of the level of your needs, it is important to understand the basics of how to go about raising money for the success of your program.

Seven Principles of Sound Fund Raising

1. Go where there is money to be given
2. Ask
3. Create a win/win proposition
4. Be professional
5. Work
6. Combine stability and creativity
7. Sincere verbal and written "Thank You"

1. *Go where there is money to be given*

With the understanding that fund raising is the solicitation of money, the first principle for a coach to know is to, "go where there is money to be solicited." This one principle, when used correctly, will save you time and generate more money than any other principle used.

In most situations, the places and people that may have money to be donated to your program are community businesses, doctors, lawyers, company presidents, business owners, community clubs and organizations, etc. Though there is no guarantee that one or all of these people and organizations will be able to meet your needs, you will greatly increase your chances by soliciting the highest percentage donor.

2. *Ask*

Though the fear of rejection inhibits many coaches from wearing the fund-raising hat, those that overcome that fear must do so by risking rejection and *asking* for money. In facing this most basic of fears, two things will happen. One, you will overcome your fear of rejection simply by doing that which you fear most; and two, you will raise the needed money for your program.

Businesses and people with money available to donate are most often happy and honored to be able to help support a worthy cause that they believe in. In many instances, the local athletic programs are one of the most recognized and respected organizations in a city or community. For a business or person to be directly associated with a winner and athletic team is a privilege and honor. Do not be ashamed or afraid to ask them to donate to your worthy cause.

3. *Create a win/win proposition*

When soliciting a business or person for a donation, one of the most important principles to remember is to put yourself in the position of the person being asked. When you do this simple task, you can better formulate your approach and sales pitch to meet the needs of that person. Regardless of how much money one may have to donate, people in general will give based on how they can benefit from the transaction. You are soliciting them for *your* purposes but they will give for *their* purposes.

In designing your fund-raising plan and presentation, always think in terms of a win/win situation. How can the money donated benefit your program and how will the donator benefit from giving you the money? Many times this may be intangible such as the mere association with your program or it may be tangible such as advertising space allotted for the donator to help increase his business. Whatever the reward, it is imperative to create a win/win situation for both you and your prospective donor. This will insure a long lasting relationship and possible repeat donations.

4. *Be professional*

When approaching any type of donor, your professionalism will speak volumes about not only yourself but your program, institution, and athletes. Professionalism is no more than presenting yourself as the ultimate representative of how you perceive your program and all those persons associated with it.

This entails the way you dress, your hygiene, your spoken words, any presentation materials, your posture, and organization. All of these traits, when presented in a professional manner, will dramatically increase your chances of being successful in your fund-raising attempts. For most prospects, the only representative they will associate with your program is you. You only get one chance to make a first impression. Make it the best representation you can possibly make.

5. *Work*

When all of these principles are applied, you will put yourself and program in a position to achieve the goals you desire. However, all of that will be useless unless action is put with your preparation. Fund raising is essentially you selling your program to a customer. One of the timeless principles of sales is that it is a numbers game. The more people you present with your product (your program) the more chances you will create in which they will buy it (donate). This can only be achieved by *working*.

One of the most dangerous mistakes a coach can make in this area is to limit the number of people you approach in hopes that those people will be able to fund your goals. When those few may be unable, for whatever reasons, to meet your needs then the likelihood that your goals will be met decreases dramatically. Put the odds in your favor and work the numbers. The most important word of that phrase being *work*.

6. *Combine stability and creativity*

Whether just starting a fund-raising program or adding to an established one, this principle will have a dramatic effect on the amount of money you will be able to raise.

Stable fund-raisers are those that are developed and can be counted on year after year to generate money. Examples of these would be the formation of a booster club, running an annual tournament, season ticket sales, wrestling camps, paraphernalia sales, etc. Creative fund-raisers are those that may not be used every year but help to generate funds for your program. Examples of these could include the sale of raffle tickets, car washes, special events, candy or food sales, specialty advertising, fan clubs, walk-a-thons, etc.

There are numerous ways to be creative in establishing fund-raising programs, and there are basically no limitations on the number of terrific ideas a club or program can use. An added benefit of creative fund raising will be the steady growth of your support group through new people and potential fans being exposed to your athletes, coaches, and program. The key is having a healthy balance of stable and creative money makers. The use of this principle will help to provide your program with both dependable "old" money (stability) and variable "new" money (creativity).

7. Sincere verbal and written "Thank You"

Upon receipt of the donation you have so diligently worked for and your donor has happily contributed, the power and effect of a simple "Thank You" cannot be emphasized enough. Too often, people are never thanked for the great job or philanthropy they exhibit on a daily basis. Do not make the mistake of putting yourself with the masses but rather separate yourself from them and sincerely thank your donors for their graciousness.

When thanks is being given in a verbal form, it is important to combine it with the physical actions of sincerity. These being a firm handshake, warm smile, and eye contact. When a written letter is being sent to a donor, it is very important to personally sign each letter and, when possible, write it yourself. This shows your donor that you respected them and their

donation enough to take the time out of your busy schedule to write them a note of appreciation and not just send them a form letter that every other donor would receive with a copied signature. When this principle is used, you will create a strong base of loyal donors that will give to your program for years to come and generate a strong predictable income on an annual basis.

SUMMARY

Fund raising, though one of the least liked aspects of a coach's job, is one of the most important components in developing a sound and perennially successful wrestling program. It's importance to a program is akin to the athlete with one weakness that he fails to develop, and, in turn, it becomes the very one that stops him from achieving his goals. The greatest coaches and programs in the world leave no weaknesses to destroy what they have so diligently worked to achieve. The use of these seven principles will put you and your program on the same level as the best.

7
Match and Program Promotion

A centered and raised wrestling mat is a tremendous way to attract and excite fans.

INTRODUCTION

It has often been said that "You don't play the sport of wrestling." Unlike other sports such as basketball, running, football, or swimming to name a few, wrestling is not an activity that you can casually "play." The physical, mental, and technical complexities of the sport demand too much for the layman to understand and perform. For those who participate in this great sport, it is precisely that aspect that attracts them. However, it is also this fact that prevents wrestling from being the spectator sport that the aforementioned sports traditionally are.

Though these facts remain true, the best coaches overcome this apparent obstacle and attract large numbers of fans and supporters. Match and program promotion is a skill that is not an accident. It must be developed with an understanding of what the public and media desires and planning to fulfill those needs. Following are some basic principles for promoting your team to the public and media.

PROMOTION TO THE PUBLIC

Promoting your program and team to the public is one of the most effective ways in which to create a tremendous following. Regardless of how good your team may be, it will not draw people to watch if the public does not know about it. The most basic principle of promotion is to *inform the public.*

There are several steps that are necessary to get this very important information out in front of the public. Regardless of the level of your program, or the amount of money you have to work with, the following steps can be carried out with a little bit of effort and planning.

One of the simplest, yet overlooked, promotional basics that can be done is to make sure a schedule of your matches is readily available and publicized. The time, date, and cost of your matches, and/or tournaments, is as important as any other promotional tool you use. Without this information, those that wish to attend your events will not do so due to the simple fact that they did not know about it.

A tremendous and potentially cost-free way in which to present your schedule is the formation of a poster/schedule. This not only notifies the public of your matches but it also gets the faces and names of your athletes in the public eye and conscience. The best way to cover the cost of this project is to solicit sponsors for the poster. In return, the sponsor's name or business can be placed on the poster which will provide them with a terrific vehicle for advertising. Many community businesses desire the advertising, name recognition, and reach that a poster/schedule of this type can provide them.

The distribution of this poster is also an important follow-up to its creation. The use of your wrestlers to distribute them to friends, family, and community businesses is a great publicity and marketing method. When this is done, people get the opportunity to meet the athletes and can then form a relationship with the team and associate the verbal and written information with the distinctive faces and personalities of your program.

The use of special events throughout the season is also another way in which to draw attention and interest to your program. This can be done be designating specific matches as those in which discounts, coupons, or souvenirs are provided for special age groups or persons. Some examples of this may be having group nights where a group receives either free or discounted admission; poster night in which the first 50-1000 spectators receive free autographed posters; parents night specifically held to honor the parents of the athletes; theme nights where those dressed according to the particular theme receive free admission; raffle nights where prizes are drawn at the conclusion of the match or during a pre-determined intermission. The creative use of your imagination is the best way in which to devise different ideas that will meet the specific demands of your program, community, and public.

PROMOTION TO THE MEDIA

Wrestling coaches are often frustrated by a lack of coverage by the media. Although individual coaches may not be able to change this problem on the national level, each coach can do his part to better promote the program in the community.

The most important thing to understand is that coaches should not expect the media to

Figure 7-1. Successful promotion to the public can result in outstanding attendance at your wrestling events.

cover wrestling on its own. Like it or not, wrestling is not basketball or football, which receives automatic coverage from the media.

Wrestling people must work to get their local media interested in the sport. It must be both easy and fun for journalists to cover wrestling, or they may not bother.

The first rule is that coaches should not try to "do it all." It is the coach's job to train the athletes and supervise his program. A different person with an interest in the media should be specifically assigned to promoting the team.

This kind of person can be found for almost any program. For a college program, it might be a student sports information assistant, a volunteer journalism student, or an active alumnus. For a high school or club program, it could include a journalism student, an interested parent, even a member of the team. The key is to find somebody who is willing to put in the time and effort to make it work.

Your wrestling promoter only needs a few basic tools to get the job done. A telephone is a must, along with a typewriter or word processing unit. Each team can design its own letterhead, for press releases and invitations. Access to a facsimile machine is also helpful .

It should be the goal of your promotions volunteer to develop a regular following for your wrestling program in the local media. They should also try to excite other media to cover wrestling on special occasions.

Basics to Get Started

Create and expand a mailing list

Find the addresses for the journalists who cover wrestling now and those who might cover it in your community. Place the addresses on a label form or in a computer database. This should include newspapers, radio, and TV stations. Make sure to get the name of the person in charge. A letter addressed to "editor" may never reach the proper person. Other information to collect includes phone numbers and fax numbers. This list should be constantly updated, as media members often change jobs or get new assignments.

Work the mailing/target list

Create pre-event press releases, results press releases and feature story press releases. Make sure that wrestling is a part of the journalist's regular mail.

Call selected journalists with story ideas and invitations to attend events. Ask them how you can better help them cover the team. Be positive, no matter how badly you are treated.

Create story ideas (find an angle)

Ask yourself: "Why should this be covered? What is interesting, new or exciting about this?" Don't expect journalists to fully research your story. Do as much of the work for them in advance. Make it easy to cover.

The best personal human interest stories are often locked in a coach's head. Tell your publicity volunteer about your athletes, team, and the competition.

Some journalists don't care about who beat who. They want feature material, interesting personal tidbits. Get to know your athletes as people and share that with the press. Wild hobbies, outstanding academics, big families, obstacles and handicaps overcome . . . the list goes on forever if you are creative.

Be available/make athletes available

Stories often die because journalists can't locate coaches or athletes for interviews in a timely fashion. Be available. If busy or traveling, let someone know where you are and how to reach you. Check in for messages. Return requests promptly. This is the biggest area of missed opportunities.

Create "The Big Event"

No matter how good or bad a team or schedule may be, there will always be at least one event which has special importance. It may be a meeting with an arch-rival, a match for a team championship, the regional or post-season qualifier, something that makes it bigger than the others. It could also be an individual match up, the two best in the league or region going for top rankings. Identify those and blow them up LARGE.

The final thing to remember is to treat the journalists well when they decide to cover your team. You must provide them a professional work situation, so the journalists will be encouraged to come again. Remember—EASY and FUN.

Journalists need a few basics to do their job correctly. A place to sit, a place to work, a place to shoot photos and video tape, and access for interviews. For large programs, that means having a press row and work room available. For others, it may just mean giving the journalist a VIP seating location.

When the event is over, the coaches and athletes must be available for interviews, regardless of whether or not the team wins. If a journalist can not get quotes after the event, which is part of his job, he/she may never cover wrestling again. The journalist may also need access to a telephone to file the story. Help them do their job.

After the event, the publicity volunteer should report the story and results to those not there. You might type up a small press release with results to FAX or mail to local media. At the very least, it includes calling in the final result and highlights of the event to the media after every match.

SUMMARY

There is no guarantee that doing this work will always result in receiving media coverage. However, if these basics are not covered, it is a good bet that there will be no coverage at all.

Most of this is not the job of a coach. Someone else should be doing the work. However, a coach must help make it easy for his promotions people to do their job. The coach should also follow up to make sure it is getting done.

8
Wrestling Club Development

QUESTIONS TO CONSIDER

- What do all successful wrestling clubs have in common?
- What are the six questions that need to be answered when starting a wrestling club?
- Is it necessary to have both medical and liability insurance for a wrestling club?

The development of a wrestling club can benefit many kids.

INTRODUCTION

Today, in one way or another, all kids face some difficult odds because they have to make daily choices about drugs, alcohol, and sex that can affect the rest of their lives. All too often, they have to make those choices when they are far too young to recognize the consequences of making the wrong decision.

Knowing that, responsible adults are willing to put in the time, effort and energy it takes to organize and run youth sports programs. They know that more often than not, kids who get turned on to sports, won't turn to drugs.

Consider the possibilities and remember that you, and adults like you, can make an important difference in the lives of youngsters in your community by giving them the opportunity to participate in wrestling.

Naturally, every town or community is different. In many communities, youngsters have very few opportunities to participate in well-organized and well-run youth sports programs. Perhaps yours is one of them. If that's the case, then it should be fairly easy to find other adults who are willing to join you in organizing a Kids Wrestling Club.

Maybe there are already several other ongoing youth sports organizations, but many kids still aren't involved in sports. Here again, it's not hard to point out how and why wrestling offers some benefits not to be found in other sports.

So, let's get specific. Answer the questions about youth sports in your community, and you'll have a better idea about how a Kids Wrestling Club can become a success in your community.

GETTING ORGANIZED

The volunteer in any wrestling program, particularly in any youth wrestling program, is the heart and soul of any club. It's what makes the wheels go round and round.

Nearly all successful wrestling clubs have several things in common. They put the emphasis on fun and fundamentals and de-emphasize winning until youngsters are emotionally ready to accept both winning and losing.

Almost all wrestling clubs have something else in common; they all started small, sometimes with a tiny, but dedicated group of volunteers taking on all the different duties and responsibilities involved in running a Kids Wrestling Club.

In many cases, the idea to start a Kids Wrestling Club begins with one individual, who must then go about getting the help he or she needs to bring the benefits of this sport to kids in the community. If you find yourself in that position, then you probably have several questions:

1. *Who will organize the team?*
2. *Who will coach?*
3. *Who will pay expenses?*
4. *Where will they practice?*
5. *What will they wear?*
6. *What are the legal responsibilities?*

In looking at the answers to those and other questions, you will soon recognize that you're going to need the help of a group of adult volunteers.

Who Will Organize the Team?

Why not you? Usually a parent, high school coach or other adult with a concern for the well being of kids in the community takes the job. And often they have little or no previous experience in organizing a club for kids or adults. With this in mind, don't let any lack of experience on your part keep you from taking the steps that will get you moving toward a successful wrestling program.

Your first step is to ask around and find other people interested in helping you.

Organizational Meeting

Find a meeting place, such as a local YMCA, church, school, recreation center, or your home, and call a meeting of people who might be interested. Then send announcements about the meeting to local newspapers and radio station. Usually the news media is happy to give you free publicity for community projects like this.

How you approach this organizational meeting depends largely on the people in your community and their current interest in and enthusiasm for wrestling. If you live in an area where wrestling is already very popular, then you will have little if any trouble "selling" the sport.

On the other hand, if you live in a community that isn't already well tuned in on the benefits of Kids Wrestling, you may need to take the time to explain them. If you aren't a former wrestler, then you might want to get someone who is to talk about their positive experiences in the sport.

The main goal of the meeting is to enlist the help and cooperation of other adults and, if possible, to elect a slate of officers.

If you have a great deal of initial interest in the club, you will probably be able to find one individual to serve in each position. Of course, smaller groups of people can double up on some of the jobs. Following are the various positions that need to be filled:

The President; runs the meeting, appoints committees and oversees all the club's business.

The Vice-President; fills in whenever the president can't make a meeting or other club business.

The Secretary; records minutes at each meeting, and maintains correspondence with other clubs and with USA Wrestling's state or national officers.

The Treasurer; has responsibilities that grow with the size of the club. In the beginning, with a very small club, operating on a small budget, one of the other officers might handle the money. But clubs can quickly grow to the point where keeping accurate accounts of revenues and expenditure becomes a time consuming job, and one best handled by someone with experience.

Depending on the size of the club, you might also need to set up committees to secure a place to practice, provide transportation to out-of-town matches, find equipment, and conduct your own tournaments.

Who Will Coach the Team?

This can be a tricky question. The goal of this book, along with the USAW Video Syllabus, is to give people with limited experience the guidance they need to run a successful wrestling club. If you need to find a coach, start by seeing if any parent has experience in wres-

tling. Look around the community for an ex-wrestler willing to accept the responsibilities involved in coaching youngsters. Just be sure to find an individual whose goals are consistent with those of the club. Someone who understands the importance of emphasizing fun, fitness, and fundamentals.

Don't be afraid to ask for help, but don't underestimate the time and effort the coach will need to spend on the job. Depending on the number of youngsters, you might also need to find people, possibly parents, to serve as assistant coaches. You also need to make arrangements for the club to pay the expenses that all too often wind up being paid by the volunteer coach.

Who Will Pay the Expenses?

One of wrestling's great advantages is that it really doesn't cost much for a youngster to participate. And most clubs strive to keep it that way, by keeping individual member costs as low as possible and at times by arranging for the club or its financial supporters to pay membership costs for disadvantaged youngsters.

Naturally, travelling to events can start getting expensive, especially if and when a club wants to begin attending state or national tournaments. Clubs use a variety of means to raise money.

Sponsors

Many organizations and civic-minded clubs regularly make funds available for youth activities. Businesses certainly can create a lot of good will, while putting their name in front of the public, by sponsoring youth sports teams. Don't be shy about asking for financial help, but be prepared to answer any question from how the money will be used to how it will benefit the kids in the program. As clubs grow, their revenues and expenditures can climb rapidly.

You don't necessarily need the local business community to pick up all your expenses. Most clubs sell concessions, including food and drinks and even T-shirts, to raise money. Turning over the job of managing concessions to one individual who will work closely with the treasurer to account for the money spent and earned is a very efficient and professional method. The person in charge of concessions also gets volunteers to work different booths during matches or tournaments.

Booster Clubs

After some clubs reach a certain size and level of popularity, they can turn over the entire fund-raising effort to a boosters club, which will organize in much the same way as the Wrestling Club itself.

With or without one, a Wrestling Club can generate funds with some traditional methods such as car washes and bake sales (see Chapter 6). These days you can also rely on some more high tech money makers by having a parent with a home video camera tape matches or events and then sell copies to parents, grandparents, and other fans.

Where Will the Club Practice?

Here you may need to enlist the help of local high school or junior high coaches. Again, don't be shy about asking for their help because junior and senior high school coaches certainly understand how kids wrestling can help their own programs.

If the high school or junior high gyms aren't available, look for a YMCA, community recreation center, or church with a gym or auditorium. You need to make certain that your facility has plenty of mats. Because of the additional safety they offer, try to buy mats designed specifically for wrestling.

If you can't afford a wrestling mat, use smaller and less expensive tumbling mats. You must be sure to fasten or tape them together so that the mats don't slide around, allowing a youngster to fall on a hard floor.

What Will They Wear?

Like mats, proper clothing enhances safety. Wrestlers can use gym shorts, tee shirts, and tennis shoes. The only special equipment used consists of elbow and knee pads and headgear.

Uniforms for your wrestlers are optional. You really don't need them in the beginning. If the kids want them, and if their parents or the club can afford them, uniforms are well worth the price. Wearing a team uniform is important to most youngsters; and it certainly helps your athletes think and act like a team when they're dressed as one.

What kids cannot wear

Because they greatly increase the risk of injury, no youngster should practice while wearing . . .

- Any jeans or slacks with zippers
- A leather belt with a buckle
- Rings, watches or other jewelry

LEGAL RESPONSIBILITIES

Anyone starting a wrestling club is going to have questions about their possible legal liability. This is an area where you can get an enormous amount of help when your club applies for a Charter under USA Wrestling. Despite the relative safety of kids wrestling, there's always some risk of injury.

Clubs need both medical and liability insurance, which is available at very low rates through USAW. The details about medical and liability insurance, club charters, and memberships can be obtained by contacting USA Wrestling at (719)598-8181. The issues concerning legal responsibilities are covered in greater detail in Chapter 3 entitled *Effective Teaching and Risk Management.*

Section III
Psychology of Coaching

9
Positive Coaching

QUESTIONS TO CONSIDER

- What approaches are there to coaching?
- What are the benefits of using the positive approach?
- What problems can occur when using the negative approach?
- How do I develop a positive approach?
- How do I cope with losing when using the positive approach?

Positive coaching can make the difference in whether a young athlete remains in wrestling or not.

INTRODUCTION

Any time sport psychologists are asked to discuss motivation and positive reinforcement, one gets the feeling that coaches are looking for a "quick fix" for a specific athlete. Motivation is one of those elusive concepts that coaches learn about through experience, through what our coaches did, or through the media. Because a college coach gave a blistering intermission speech to a team that went on to win the match, other coaches assume that the speech changed the motivation level and performance of the team. Should coaches deliver similar speeches to their athletes when they need to be motivated? This approach may work once during a season or a career. However, to be effective in motivating athletes, coaches must not adopt techniques blindly.

The essence of motivation is knowing your athletes and understanding what they want from sport. In other words, do you know why your athletes are participating in this sport? A recent study conducted by the Youth Sports Institute reported that young people participate in sport: 1) to improve skills and learn new ones, 2) for thrills and excitement, 3) to have fun, 4) to be with friends and make new ones, and 5) to succeed or win. When elite hockey players, ages 13 to 18 years, attending a player development camp were asked why they played hockey, the most frequent responses were: 1) to go to a higher level of competition (e.g., Olympics, pros), 2) to improve skills and learn new ones, and 3) to win. The similarity between youth sport and elite participants is readily apparent; both groups want to improve their skills.

Perhaps the most important point for us to recognize is the desire of athletes to improve their skills and to learn new skills. Coaches can help athletes meet this goal by providing a good learning environment whereby athletes can practice new and old skills without a fear of failure or the risk of losing self-esteem when practice attempts are unsuccessful.

It is significant that young athletes did not report winning as the most important reason for participating in sport. Coaches often get caught up in the "winning is everything" philosophy. That is what we hear constantly from the radio and TV announcers of professional sports.

The key to motivation is knowing your athletes and understanding what they want from your sport.

Recently, the announcers of a college football game expressed dismay at the number of games ending in a tie score. They wanted overtimes to determine a winner. While this change might enhance the network's rating, there is no evidence that athletes or coaches experience psychological stress from a game ending in a tie. We must not get caught in the trap of having former professional athletes and coaches, or uninformed announcers, telling us that the only thing that matters in sport is winning. While winning is important, it is not the reason that motivates athletes to practice or to continue participating in sport.

Although striving to win is important, winning is not the most important reason why athletes participate in sports.

The purpose of this chapter is to focus on how coaches can be more effective in meeting the participation motives of athletes. We will discuss how to create a good learning environment in which your athlete can acquire the technical skills needed to be successful in sport. A related purpose is the creation of a social environment in which athletes can experience positive interactions with each other.

THE POSITIVE AND NEGATIVE APPROACHES TO COACHING

When working with athletes, young or old, it is important to remember that we are dealing with people. The Number 1 rule to keep in mind is that we should treat athletes as we would want to be treated. Most of us respond better to a person who is empathetic with our shortcomings and who is patient with us while we learn.

There are two basic approaches to coaching: the positive approach and the negative approach. Each approach is capable of influencing the behavior of athletes. Both approaches are based on the assumption that an individual's behavior is influenced by the consequences each behavior produces.

The positive approach focuses on *desired* behaviors or consequences by asking athletes to behave or perform in a specific manner and by reinforcing the athlete when the desired behaviors occur. For example, if you ask an athlete to compete at a higher weight class for the benefit of the team and the athlete does so (desired behavior), then you reward or reinforce the athlete for attempting or executing successfully the desired behavior. With young athletes or beginning athletes, you reinforce attempts to produce the desired behavior.

A positive coach concentrates on desired behaviors and rewards players who display the desired behaviors.

The negative approach to coaching involves eliminating *undesirable* behavior through physical and verbal punishment and criticism. This negative approach is based on fear. Although we do not advocate this approach, there is evidence that this approach can eliminate poor performance in certain athletes. There is also evidence that this approach can eliminate athletes as well!

Often we hear coaches tell athletes, "The team that makes the fewest errors will win." Obviously, there is much truth to the saying. Because errors are often easier to see than steady, unspectacular performance, coaches tend to focus on eliminating errors. To eliminate errors, coaches simply punish athletes who make them. These coaches assume that if wrestlers are scared enough of making errors, they will be more likely to perform better.

It is not hard to find examples of coaches who use the negative approach. Many highly successful coaches scream at their athletes for every mistake, grab athletes by their uniforms during timeouts and publicly humiliate them, and may actually hit athletes who are not meeting expectations. For inexperienced coaches, these successful negative coaches serve as role models. Negative behaviors are imitated, with the naive coach thinking this abusive behavior causes athletes to perform correctly. These inexperienced coaches do not realize that the

negative coaches' success may be due to their effective teaching techniques.

While punishment and verbal abuse may change the behavior of some individuals, there are some undesirable side effects. Perhaps the most serious is the fear of failure that results when athletes are criticized or punished excessively for making mistakes. Closely associated with a fear of failure are decreased enjoyment of a task and increased likelihood of more errors. This cycle of fear, leading to more errors and less enjoyment, may cause wrestlers to become hesitant and uncertain, experience high anxiety about performing in critical situations, or be more vulnerable to injury during competition.

A negative coach focuses on errors and punishment for athletes who make errors.

A negative approach often results in an unpleasant teaching situation. Athletes who are exposed to verbal criticism, punishment for errors, or sarcastic comments about their performances will often withdraw socially and emotionally. When this happens, the group becomes very quiet during practices and matches. In addition, there is a sense of resentment or hatred by the team members for the coach. With older athletes, these negative emotions may draw the team together and actually strengthen team cohesion. For younger athletes, the negative environment may cause them to drop out.

The environment created by negative coaching may cause young athletes to drop out of sports.

One of the questions frequently asked by coaches is whether they should avoid criticizing or punishing athletes. The answer is no, because these techniques may be useful in maintaining discipline. However, in order for these techniques to remain effective they must be used sparingly. Unfortunately, we often see coaches who are very successful using the negative approach. This may result because these coaches have very good athletes and/or they are exceptional teachers and strategists.

The technique employed by most coaches is a combination of the positive and negative approaches. There is evidence that a mixture of both positive and negative reinforcement is likely to produce the best results. Athletes know when they have made mistakes, and your credibility rests on your honesty in evaluating their performances. However, a coach can be honest and help athletes learn from their experiences or a coach can punish athletes who make errors and create athletes who "fear failure." The key is your intention. The effectiveness of a coach's reinforcement may depend on the coach's intention in giving the praise or punishment. There is little doubt that most athletes, and adults, respond best to the positive approach.

STRIVE FOR THE POSITIVE APPROACH

The positive approach aims at strengthening the desired behaviors through the use of encouragement, positive reinforcement, and technical instruction. Young athletes are generally highly motivated to learn a sport, and the use of positive reinforcement strengthens their enjoyment.

All of us spent hours practicing sport skills and, even though we try to repress the memories, many of our early attempts were failures. However, friends provided us with positive support, plenty of encouragement, and the reassurance that we'd "get it" soon. Our persistence may have been directly related to our friends' support. When friends stopped giving us support and encouragement or ridiculed our attempts, we often withdrew from the activity. A coach's feedback works the same way.

The positive approach fosters a positive learning environment for youth sport participants. In this positive environment mistakes become "stepping stones to achievement." Athletes learn from their mistakes. They know that positive coaches will provide them with the technical information to change their performances plus the encouragement and support to try again.

Most coaches of sport teams want to be respected and liked by their teams. This mutual respect results in improved communication and fosters a willingness to work together to resolve individual and team problems. This result was reported in a study of Little League coaches.

One group of coaches was taught to be positive and encouraging by increasing the frequency of positive reinforcement by 25 percent. A second group of "untrained" coaches continued to coach as they normally had. At the end of the season, the athletes who played for the trained coaches reported that 1) they liked the coach more, 2) they thought the coach was a better teacher, 3) they were more attracted to the team, and 4) they had better self-concepts. This latter finding was especially true for athletes who had low self-concepts.

Athletes with low self-esteem are likely to benefit most from a positive approach.

Low self-concepts are often the result of being told directly or indirectly how bad we are at a task. If told often enough that they are not very good, athletes begin to believe that they are not very good. Athletes with low self-concepts are particularly vulnerable to failure because they interpret failure as "proof" that they are not very good. To turn this negative thinking around, coaches must be positive and help these athletes see errors as temporary states that can be corrected. The fact that coaches can be effective in improving self-concepts by increasing their positive reinforcement to athletes by 25 percent is powerful evidence of the effectiveness of the positive approach.

In addition to helping kids feel better about themselves, the positive approach increases the athletes' learning of skills. Part of this learning may be a result of viewing a positive coach as a better teacher. Additionally, the positive approach creates an atmosphere whereby athletes are willing to try new and different skills. There is no fear of failing. Thus, young athletes will ask more questions and practice more.

DEVELOPING THE POSITIVE APPROACH

Implementing the positive approach begins with the coach's awareness of effective reinforcers, how often to use these reinforcers, and what behaviors should be reinforced. Each of these aspects of the positive approach will be discussed below.

Figure 9-1. Effectively communicating a positive approach to overcoming match situations separates the best coaches from the rest.

Choosing Effective Reinforcers

When working with athletes, it is important to know what rewards are effective in changing behavior. In other words, what are athletes willing to work for? Surprisingly, research has shown that the best rewards are free. For example, a pat on the back, smile, friendly nod, and verbal praise are all effective, free reinforcers. In this respect, young athletes react to these reinforcers in much the same way as adults do. All of us appreciate this simple acknowledgement of a job well done.

These free rewards are effective with athletes of all ages. Specifically, research has shown that verbal praise and the coaches' attention are particularly effective with athletes 13 to 15 years of age compared to 9- to 12-year-old athletes. The effectiveness of coaches' attention was compared to giving candy and money to 9- to 15-year-old swimmers and was found to be comparable in terms of the number of laps the athletes were motivated to swim. One drawback that should be noted with regard to using food or money to reward performance is the decline in intrinsic motivation. Practically, coaches may not be able to afford the use of food or money as rewards. Certainly it is not necessary because free rewards are as effective.

The most potent rewards that coaches can use are free—a smile, a word of encouragement, a pat on the back.

The use of free reinforcers should be combined with an instruction or instructional reminder to improve their effectiveness. For example, as you pat the wrestler on the back for winning a match, you can tell him that he did a good job of executing the single leg takedown that won it. This instructional reminder provides a cue for the athlete that will help him be successful in the future.

Select and Reinforce Specific Behaviors

In addition to choosing effective reinforcers, coaches must identify the specific behaviors they want to reinforce. In other words, what must the athlete do to earn a reward from

Figure 9-2. Losing is winning when positively approached. This attitude will foster more success among your athletes.

the coach? For starters, use your reward power to strengthen skills that a player is learning. For example, a wrestling coach tells his team that the team that scores the most takedowns will win the upcoming tournament. Therefore, the focus of the day's practice would be on singles and doubles. Unfortunately, the coach chose to teach takedowns by having the top wrestler in the referee's position try to hold the bottom wrestler down. If the bottom wrestler escaped, he/she could then try to execute a single or double leg takedown. Although this drill resulted in many takedowns, the coach never commented on how well the takedowns were executed but instead focused on the top man holding his opponent down. This behavior resulted in a mixed message for the young athletes: coach says it is important to get takedowns but only talks about the top man's riding ability. Thus, the wrestlers conclude that riding is more important than takedowns.

Along the same lines, coaches should break down complex skills into component subskills and concentrate on one subskill at a time. Most wrestling skills are complex in that many body parts are involved to execute a skill. The coordination of the body parts is critical as is the ability to integrate another person into the skill.

Positive coaches reduce complex skills to subskills, then reward the parts that were performed correctly.

For example, executing a single leg involves starting in a good stance, moving your opponent out of position, lowering your elevation, penetrating, and lifting to finish. Each of these actions could be defined and practiced as a subskill (basic) of a single leg.

Using this approach provides the athlete a chance to experience success doing smaller parts of the skill. In addition, the coach has the opportunity to positively reinforce subskills performed correctly while providing pointers on how to improve the next subskill. For example, after you have been working with your wrestlers on executing a single leg, your lightweight has a chance to demonstrate the skill in a match. He maintains a good stance, moves his opponent out of position, lowers his level, and then takes a terrible penetration shot. As a coach,

you have choices: reject the entire attempt based on the bad penetration, or acknowledge and reinforce the subskills performed very well. The final subskill can be practiced more during the next practice.

If a coach chooses to reject the entire performance, the young athletes are led to believe that nothing was done right, rather than to understand that they performed sections of the skill correctly. By selecting and reinforcing specific behaviors, athletes gain confidence that they will improve with more practice. This outcome alone should result in your feeling successful as a coach.

When, and How Often, Should Reinforcement Be Given?

The answer to this question depends on how proficient the athlete is at performing the skill. When athletes are *learning* a skill, coaches should reinforce every desired response. Until inexperienced athletes have had a lot of practice, they cannot always tell whether they performed a skill correctly. When first learning a knee-over-toe penetration step, most wrestlers have difficulty forcing their lead leg knee down. Therefore, to determine whether the penetration was good or not, athletes look at the result. If they shoot incorrectly and score a takedown, they assume the technique was correct. The emphasis in the early stages of learning a wrestling skill should be on technique and correct decision making, not just outcome.

As athletes become more proficient, coaches should reinforce the correct behavior intermittently. Research has shown that continuous feedback following a learned skill is not as effective as intermittent feedback. As athletes come to know the difference between correct and incorrect technique, the coach's feedback is redundant, and athletes tend to ignore it. However, intermittent feedback either supports or refutes the athlete's own perceptions. Differing perceptions provide the coach with the opportunity to discuss the finer points of the skill—which gives athletes new information to use. Environments must be conducive for athletes to accept and incorporate information that results in performance changes. The positive approach creates this type of environment.

Coaches should reinforce a desired behavior as soon as it occurs.

The question of when reinforcement should be given is an easy one to answer. Specifically, coaches should reinforce a desired behavior as soon as it occurs. This is equally true during contests as it is during practices. Waiting to tell athletes their faults at the conclusion of a drill often results in athletes not remembering what they did initially. The feedback is neutralized by time.

Reinforce Effort and Other Desirable Behaviors

Coaches, parents, and even athletes tend to focus most of their attention on outcome—scoring a takedown, getting an escape, pinning your opponent. This focus may be fine for elite athletes who are relatively consistent. For young athletes, and for most of us, who are not consistent in the performance of a skill, coaches should reinforce effort, or the attempt to perform a skill correctly. Thus, when we ask a wrestler to pin his opponent and the wrestler tries, using good technique, we should acknowledge the effort. This positive reinforcement tells the wrestler that his or her technique is basically correct and that the effort is appreciated.

Young athletes must be reinforced for their efforts as well as the outcome of those efforts.

The only thing that athletes have control over is the amount of effort they make. As mentioned earlier, the negative approach often results in athletes attempting to protect their self-esteem. One way to protect self-esteem is to give only "token" effort. Thus, when they fail, they can save face by acknowledging that they could have gotten a takedown if they had tried harder. We do not want to cause athletes to lose the motivation to try because we, as coaches, have challenged their self-esteem.

We have all experienced situations where we gave our very best effort, only to be denied a job, a promotion, or a victory in sport. Effort is the key to success in sport, and coaches must be ready to reinforce that effort. A pitcher who pitches a great game but loses on an error by a teammate (á la Roger Clemens in the 1986 World Series) should not perceive himself as a loser. His effort and subsequent performance were excellent. We must help young athletes understand that they control effort; the outcome is out of their control.

A coach can control the interpersonal relationships on a team merely by choosing the kinds of behaviors that are reinforced.

Finally, coaches can effectively change the behavior of athletes toward their teammates and opponents by reinforcing exemplary conduct. Reinforce young athletes who help pick up the equipment after practice. Acknowledge instances of good teamwork and athletes encouraging one another. The relationships among the athletes are a direct result of what the coach chooses to reinforce. If athletes are not discouraged from blaming one another for losses, this behavior will escalate to the point that athletes are afraid to try. Athletes will learn quickly to make excuses. To change this environment, or to prevent it from occurring, coaches must state the desired behaviors of athletes to each other and reinforce the occurrences of desired behaviors.

POSITIVE LOSING: A HEALTHY ATTITUDE

The goal for most athletes and coaches is to be successful. Success has generally been defined as winning. While this is a goal for participants, it should not be the only goal. The fact remains that in every match only 50 percent of the participants will be winners. If we use winning as the only criteria for success, then we must conclude that the non-winners were losers. There is a problem with this approach to defining success. The problem revolves around the attitude that results from this definition. Specifically, this approach suggests that winning, regardless of how poorly the athlete or team played, is good. Likewise, losing, regardless of how well or poorly the athlete or team played, is bad. This definitional approach to success and failure fosters an unhealthy attitude in athletes.

This attitude promotes the notion that athletes, and coaches, cannot learn from their mistakes. As most of us have learned, we can learn a lot from our mistakes and our losses. Losing is not a lot of fun, but losing should be viewed as "water under the bridge." In fact, the key to viewing losing as positive is to learn from the loss. Even in losing, certain skills or strategies were executed correctly or better than they had been in the past. Athletes should understand which of their performances were good.

In addition, athletes should learn which of their performances needed improvement. Perhaps the loss was due to the other team's superior size and speed. This is particularly evident in youth sport and high school sports, where athletes must compete with older and bigger athletes. While learning and growing, athletes must know that losing is often the result of mismatches in size and experience, and *not* the result of them being unskilled at their sport. This latter conclusion can result in young athletes dropping out of sport before they develop fully the skills necessary to compete with older athletes. However, if the athletes did misperform skills or *known* strategies, they need to learn what the mistake was and what they must do to correct it.

The coach is the key in developing a healthy attitude toward losing. Your attitude will be mimicked by the athletes. Even though you may understand that your behavior is the result of disappointment or frustration, the athletes may not. They could view your behavior as the correct way to cope with loss. Rather than learning from the loss, they associate a negative affect and self-perception with losing.

To foster a healthy attitude toward losing, coaches and athletes should analyze the loss, determine what was done right and what was done wrong, and then forget the loss, but continue to work on improving performance.

The coach's behavior is a powerful example in helping athletes to know how to deal with losing a contest.

The positive view of losing does not lessen the disappointment. However, it does provide insight into one's performance. The value of a positive losing attitude may best be summed up in the following quote from a youth sport participant. "When I was a kid I had a great coach. He taught me how to bounce back when things were tough. I wish I could thank him now, but I can't remember his name."

Figure 9-3. After losing a tough match, positive support for your athlete is critical.

10
Effective Communication

QUESTIONS TO CONSIDER

- How can you send clear messages to your athletes?
- What is the positive approach to communication?
- What are the characteristics of a good listener?
- How can good communication skills improve your ability to coach?

Even the best wrestlers in the world continue to learn by being good listeners. (Pictured from l-r, Olympic and World Champions, Dave Schultz and Mark Schultz).

71

INTRODUCTION

The most important skill you must have in coaching is the ability to communicate with your athletes. It is critical to effectively carrying out your roles of leader, teacher, motivator, and organizer. Effective communication not only involves skill in sending messages, but skill in interpreting messages from your athletes and their parents.

As a coach, the most important skill is the ability to communicate with your athletes.

Sending Clear Messages

Any means you use to convey ideas, feelings, instructions, or attitudes to others involves communication. When communicating with your athletes, your messages may contain verbal as well as nonverbal information. Nonverbal messages can be transmitted through facial expressions, gestures, and body movements.

When you send messages to your athletes, you may, without thinking, send unintentional nonverbal information as well as your intentional verbal message. If your nonverbal message conflicts with what you say, your message will probably be confusing. For example, when you compliment your athletes on a good job and then let your shoulders slump and heave a heavy sigh, your athletes may be less receptive to your next attempt at praise. Another mixed message occurs if you tell your athletes they should never question officials' calls and then you denounce an official's decision. If the need arises to question an official's call, you should ask for clarification in a professional manner.

Using a Positive Approach to Communicate

Communication between you and your athletes is more effective when you use a positive approach, which involves establishing:

- mutual trust,
- respect,
- confidence, and
- cooperation.

Essential Factors In Sending Clear Messages

Getting and Keeping Attention

Getting and keeping your athletes' attention can be accomplished by making eye contact, avoiding potential distractions, being enthusiastic, and emphasizing the importance of what you have to say.

The positive approach is an essential element of good coaching.

For example, when you want to instruct your athletes on a new skill, organize them so everything you do is visible to them. Be sure they are not facing distractions. It also helps to use a story, illustration, or event that highlights or reinforces the instruction that is to follow.

Using Simple and Direct Language

Reduce your comments to contain only the specific information the athlete needs to know. For example, when an athlete makes a mistake in a drill make sure your feedback is simple, focuses on one error at a time, and contains only information that the athlete can use to correct the mistake. Keep information simple and specific.

Checking With Your Athletes

Make certain that your athletes understand what you are trying to say. Question them so you will know if they understood the key points of your message. For example, let's say you are trying to explain a complicated drill. After showing them the drill, ask them for information you perceive they should have acquired from your explanation, before you send them to practice the drill.

Being Consistent

Make sure your actions match your words. When a discrepancy occurs between what you say and what you do, athletes are affected most by what you do. "Actions speak louder than words," and you need to practice what you preach if you wish to effectively communicate with your athletes and avoid the loss of credibility that comes with inconsistent behaviors.

Using Verbal and Nonverbal Communication

Your wrestlers are more likely to understand and remember what you have said when they can see it and hear it at the same time. Demonstrating a drill, while explaining the key points, will result in your wrestlers having a clear understanding of what you want them to know and do.

BEING A GOOD LISTENER

Remember, too, that you must be a good listener to be an effective communicator. Communication is a two-way street. Being receptive to your athletes' ideas and concerns is important to them and provides useful information to you.

Part of coaching involves listening to your athletes.

By listening to what your wrestlers say and asking them how they feel about a point, you can determine how well they are learning. This often provides you with opportunities to teach them what they do not understand.

Essential Factors in Good Listening Skills

Listening Positively

Athletes want to be heard and to express themselves. You can encourage this by using affirmative head nods and occasional one- to three-word comments (e.g., "I understand.") while you're listening. The quickest way to cut off communication is by giving "no" responses or negative head nods.

Listening Objectively

Avoid prematurely judging the content of a message. Sincerely consider what your athletes have to say. They may have good ideas! A good listener creates a warm, nonjudgmental atmosphere so athletes will be encouraged to talk and ask questions.

Listening With Interest

Being a good listener means being attentive and truly interested in what your athletes have to say. Look and listen with concern. Listen to what is said and how it is said. Establish eye contact and make sure your body reflects your interest in your athlete's message.

Being receptive to your athletes' thoughts and comments is important to them, and it provides you with essential information.

Be receptive to comments that are critical of you or your coaching. Criticism is the most difficult communication to accept, but it is often the most helpful in improving our behavior.

SUMMARY

The ability to communicate with your athletes is critical in your role as a coach. It is a skill that involves two major aspects: speaking and listening. Coaches who are effective communicators get and keep the attention of their wrestlers, send clear and simple messages, and check to make sure their messages are consistent with their actions. They also have good listening skills, which involve listening positively, helpfully, objectively, and with concern.

11
Maintaining Discipline

QUESTIONS TO CONSIDER

- What is the best way to prevent misbehavior?
- Should athletes be involved in establishing team rules?
- How should team rules be enforced?
- What are the key points of an effective plan for handling misconduct?

INTRODUCTION

Coaches often react to their wrestlers' misbehavior by yelling, lecturing, or using threats. These verbal techniques are used because we often do not know what else to do to regain control. Many discipline problems could be avoided, however, if coaches anticipated the occurrence of misbehavior and developed policies to deal with it.

Harsh comments may prevent misbehavior, but they often create a hostile, negative environment that reduces learning and motivation.

PLAN FOR SOUND DISCIPLINE

Although threats and lectures may prevent misbehavior in the short term, they create a hostile and negative atmosphere. Typically, their effectiveness is short-lived. Moreover, this type of relationship between a coach and team members does not promote a positive environment in which it is fun to learn the sport nor does it motivate the wrestlers to accept the coach's instructions.

A two-step plan for sound discipline must be in place before misbehavior occurs. The steps are: 1) define team rules, and 2) enforce team rules.

Athletes want clearly defined limits and structure for how they should behave. This can be accomplished without showing anger, lecturing the athletes, or threatening them. As the coach, it is your responsibility to have a systematic plan for maintaining discipline before your season gets underway. Coaches who have taken the time to establish rules of conduct will be in a position to react in a reasonable manner when wrestlers misbehave.

Athletes want clearly defined limits for how they should behave.

Define Team Rules

The first step in developing a plan to maintain discipline is to identify what you consider to be desirable and undesirable conduct by your wrestlers. This list can then be used to establish relevant team rules. A list of potential behaviors to consider when identifying team rules is included in Table 11-1.

Your wrestlers should be involved in establishing the rules for the team. Research has

Table 11-1. Examples of desirable and undesirable behaviors to consider when making team rules.

Desirable Behavior	Undesirable Behavior
Making every effort to attend all practices and contests except when excused for justifiable reasons	Missing practices and contests without legitimate reasons
Being on time for practices and contests	Being late or absent from practices and contests
Listening to instructions	Talking while the coach is giving instructions
Concentrating on drills	Not attending to demonstrations during drills
Treating opponents and teammates with respect	Pushing, fighting, and/or using abusive language with opponents and teammates
Giving positive encouragement to teammates	Making negative comments about teammates
Bringing required equipment to practices and contests	Habitually forgetting to bring required equipment or uniform to contests and practices
Reporting injuries promptly	Waiting till after the team roster is set to report an injury
Helping to pick up equipment after practices	Leaving equipment out for others to pick up

shown that athletes are more willing to live by rules when they have had a voice in formulating them. This can be done at a team meeting, early in the season. Smoll and Smith (1979) suggest the use of the following introduction to establish rules with athletes:

> "I think rules and regulations are an important part of the game because the game happens to be rules and regulations. Our team rules ought to be something we can agree upon. I have a set of rules that I feel are important. But we all have to follow them, so you ought to think about what you want. They should be your rules, too."

Rules of conduct must be defined in clear and specific terms. For instance, a team rule that athletes must "show good sportsmanship" in their contests is not a very clear and specific rule. What, exactly, is showing good sportsmanship? Does it mean obeying all the rules, calling one's own fouls, or respecting officials' decisions?

Athletes are more willing to live by rules they had a voice in formulating.

Remember, you are a part of the team and you should live by the same rules. You should demonstrate the proper behaviors so the athletes will have a standard to copy. As a coach, you must also emphasize that behaviors of coaches as seen on TV (such as screaming, throwing chairs, and belittling and embarrass-

ing athletes) are also examples of undesirable conduct!

Enforce Team Rules

Not only are rules needed to maintain discipline, but enforcement of those rules must be carried out so recurrences are less likely. Rules are enforced through rewards and penalties. Wrestlers should be rewarded when they abide by the rules and penalized when they break the rules. The next step, therefore, in developing a plan to maintain discipline, is to determine the rewards and penalties for each rule. Your wrestlers should be asked for suggestions at this point because they will receive the benefits or consequences of the decisions.

The best way to motivate athletes to behave in an acceptable manner is to reward them for good behavior.

When determining rewards and penalties for the behaviors, the most effective approach is to use rewards that are meaningful to your athletes and appropriate to the situation. Withdrawal of rewards should be used for misconduct. Table 11-2 gives a list of potential rewards and penalties.

The best way to motivate athletes to behave in an acceptable manner is to reward them for good behavior. When appropriate behavior is demonstrated, comment accordingly or be

Table 11-2. Examples of rewards and penalties that can be used.

Rewards	Penalties
Being a starter	Being taken out of a competition
Playing a desired position	Not being allowed to start
Leading an exercise for part of practice	Sitting out during practice until ready to respond properly, for a specific number of minutes, or for the rest of practice (sent home early)
Praise from you in team meetings, to the media, to parents, or directly to the individual	Dismissed from drills for half of a practice, for the next practice, for the next week, or for the rest of the season
Decals, Medals, or Certificates	Informing parents about misbehavior

ready to use nonverbal interactions such as smiling or applauding.

For Example:

"I know you are all very disappointed in losing this match. I was real proud of the way you congratulated and praised the other team after the match."

"Do you realize that for our first five practices everyone was dressed and ready to wrestle at 3:00, our starting time? That helped make the practice go better! Keep it up. Let's see if we can make it a tradition!"

Penalties are only effective when they are meaningful to the athletes. Examples of ineffective penalties include showing anger, giving an athlete an embarrassing lecture, shouting at an athlete, or assigning a physical activity (e.g. running laps, pushups). These penalties are ineffective because they leave no room for positive interactions between you and your athletes. Avoid using physical activity as a form of punishment; the benefits of sport, such as learning skills and gaining strength, are gained through activity. Athletes should not associate this type of activity with punishment.

Sometimes it is more effective to ignore inappropriate behavior if the infractions are relatively minor. Continually scolding athletes for minor pranks or "horseplay" can become counterproductive. If team deportment is a constant problem, the coach must ask, "Why?" Misbehavior may be the athletes' way of telling the coach they need attention or they do not have enough to do. Coaches should check to see if the athletes are spending a lot of time standing in lines while waiting a turn to practice. Try to keep your wrestlers productively involved so they don't have time to misbehave. This is accomplished through well-designed practice plans. A lack of meaningful activity in your practices could lead to counterproductive or disruptive behavior.

Misbehavior may be the athletes' way of telling a coach that they need attention or do not have enough to do.

When the rules for proper conduct have been outlined and the rewards and penalties have been determined, they must then be stated clearly so the athletes will understand them. Your athletes must understand the consequences for breaking the rules and the rewards for abiding by the rules. Violators should explain their actions to the coach and apologize to their teammates. You must also follow through, consistently and impartially, with your application of rewards for desirable conduct and penalties for misconduct.

Nothing destroys a plan for discipline more quickly than its inconsistent application. Rules must apply to all athletes equally and in all situations. Thus, if your team is in the championship game and your star wrestler violates a rule that requires that he or she not be allowed to start, the rule must still be enforced. If not, you are communicating to your athletes that the rules are not to be taken seriously, especially when the championship is at stake.

It is impossible to predetermine all rules that may ultimately be important during the season. However, by setting up several rules early in the season, standards of expected behavior will be established. Positive and negative behaviors that are not covered by the rules can still be judged relative to these established standards and appropriate rewards or punishments can be given.

Key Points to an Effective Discipline Plan

- Specify desirable and undesirable conduct clearly in terms of rules.
- Involve athletes in establishing the team rules.
- Determine rewards and penalties for rules that are meaningful to athletes and allow for positive interaction between you and your athletes.

- Apply rewards and penalties consistently and impartially.

SUMMARY

Although threats, lectures, and/or yelling may deter misbehavior in the short term, the negative atmosphere that results reduces long-term coaching effectiveness. A more positive approach to handling misbehavior is to prevent it by establishing, with input from your athletes, clear team rules and enforcement policies. Use fair and consistent enforcement of the rules, primarily through rewarding correct behaviors, rather than by penalizing wrong behaviors.

12
Developing Psychological Skills in Young Athletes

QUESTIONS TO CONSIDER

- What psychological skills are major objectives in your program? Can you define each skill?
- Identify five major strategies or methods that can be used to develop psychological skills in young athletes.
- What are the important elements of the positive approach to communication?
- What strategies will you use to develop the psychological skills that are the objectives for your program?

Three time World Champion Lee Kemp was a master of the psychological skills that are developed in World Class athletes.

INTRODUCTION

In the last decade attention to the development of psychological skills in elite athletes has increased. Today most athletes of international caliber are able to obtain assistance in developing and maintaining psychological skills such as confidence, communication, stress management, and other forms of mental preparation. While such training programs for elite athletes are badly needed and have been long overdue, alone they are not the total answer to producing more successful and satisfied athletes. A critical need also exists for a planned, systematic approach to the development of psychological skills in young athletes.

Developing psychological skills in young athletes is important for several reasons. First, participants in youth sports involve a large and important segment of North American society. It is estimated that 20 to 30 million young athletes between the ages of 6 and 17 take part in a variety of school and nonschool sport programs. Moreover, research has shown that sport is one of the most highly valued activities in the adolescent subculture. From a practical standpoint, then, a large and important portion of society has much to gain from the development of positive psychological skills and much to lose if psychological skills are ignored or inappropriate skills are developed.

Young athletes learn psychological skills with more ease than seasoned athletes.

A second reason for the systematic development of psychological skills in young athletes is the ease with which psychological skills are learned by children. As experienced coaches know, it is much easier to teach proper sports skills and techniques to young athletes than to attempt to modify well-learned and regimented skills in seasoned athletes. This is true for not only physical skills but for psychological skills as well. Thus, it is more effective for coaches to foster proper psychological skills in athletes just beginning participation than to attempt to modify inappropriate skills later in those athletes' careers.

Psychological skills like physical skills need to be learned.

Why is so little time spent developing psychological skills in young athletes? First, psychological skills are believed by some to be inherent and nonmalleable. This is not the case, however, as psychological skills can be learned and modified. Second, people often feel that psychological skills are automatic by-products of athletic participation. For example, many coaches indicate that their athletes develop such skills as good sportsmanship, leadership qualities, positive self-image, and confidence. However, when asked what specific coaching strategies they used to develop these skills in their athletes, the coaches have few, if any, answers. Thus, many coaches have the development of positive psychological skills in athletes as objectives of their programs, but they do little to foster the development of such skills. Finally, consultants in sport psychology have not done an effective job of disseminating information about the most effective methods of developing psychological skills in young athletes. Therefore, many coaches have recognized the need to foster psychological development, but have not known the most effective methods of doing so.

The purpose of this chapter is to examine methods and strategies coaches can employ to develop psychological skills in young athletes, ranging in age from 6 to 17 years. It is based on the premise that positive psychological development occurs only if coaches systematically plan, develop, and initiate strategies designed to foster its development. It should also be recognized that the techniques discussed in this chapter are effective means of developing many psychological skills (e.g., confidence, achievement orientation, and leadership) and are not limited to the development of one specific skill.

Coaches can use a number of strategies to develop psychological skills in young athletes. These include determining and defining the psychological skills that are the objectives of the program, initiating individual and team discussions, implementing goal-setting procedures, effectively using role models, employing a positive and sincere approach to communication, and developing educational programs for interested adults.

DETERMINING AND DEFINING THE OBJECTIVES FOR PSYCHOLOGICAL SKILLS

Determine the psychological skills that are most needed and most appropriate for the athletes' level of maturation and experience.

The first step in developing psychological skills in young athletes is to determine what skills to develop and what exactly constitutes these skills. For example, the youth coach could teach psychological skills ranging from relaxation training and imagery to positive mental attitude, leadership, and sportsmanship. A decision, then, must be made about what skills are most needed and most appropriate, given the athletes' experience and level of maturation. A coach, for example, may determine that developing a positive attitude and sportsmanship are the major psychological instructional objectives for his or her youth team. Another coach, involved with a high school team, may decide that leadership and imagery are the psychological skills needing emphasis.

Define identified psychological objectives.

After the major psychological objectives are delineated, they must be defined. For instance, a coach may determine that developing a positive attitude in his or her young athletes is the major psychological objective of the program; but what is a positive attitude? Components of a good attitude include always giving maximum effort, using only positive statements in practices and matches, never talking while the coach is giving instructions, hustling between drills, and providing only positive statements and constructive criticism to teammates. The components of a good attitude can only be conveyed, discussed and reinforced in young athletes if they are identified and defined. It is, therefore, important that the coach defines what constitutes a good attitude, good sportsmanship, or any other psychological skill he or she has as an objective. Examples of defining identified psychological objectives is provided in Table 12-1.

INDIVIDUAL AND TEAM DISCUSSIONS

After the psychological objectives of the program are identified and defined, they should be conveyed to the young athletes through individual and team discussions. Meetings held throughout the season provide opportunities for the coach to better understand the athletes' objectives for the season and thereby help the coach set realistic goals. By giving the young athletes the opportunity to make decisions about their participation in sport, meetings can also be used to increase intrinsic or self-motivation.

Important and appropriate topics for discussion include the meaning of winning and

Table 12-1. A sample of psychological coaching objectives for youth wrestling.

Objective 1 — Positive Mental Attitude	Objective 2 — Healthy Perspective on Winning	Objective 3 — Good Sportsmanship
• Don't make negative statements at matches or practices.	• Learn that winning means more than beating your opponent.	• Don't argue with officials, opponents, and teammates.
• Change "I can't" statements to "I can."	• Learn that winning means always giving your best effort.	• Don't swear.
• Always give 100% effort.	• Learn that winning means achieving your personal (or team) performance goals.	• Don't make negative or sarcastic remarks.
• Don't talk while coaches talk.		• Obey all league rules.
• Hustle between all drills.		• Treat officials with respect.
		• Question officials in an appropriate manner (e.g., have only team captain address official).

success, realistic expectations, sportsmanship, and dealing with mistakes and losses. Bell (1980) presents excellent information about mental preparation, dealing with pain and discomfort, and coping with fear of failure which are presented in terms understandable to young athletes and could easily be adapted to any sport.

Several important points about implementing discussions designed to present psychological information to young athletes must be recognized. First, coaches must remember that the purpose of these sessions is to make the young athletes more aware of psychological factors in sport and to convince them that they can make these psychological factors work for them. Second, coaches should emphasize that psychological skills are not mystical or magical, but are like physical skills that can be developed through hard work and practice. Third, coaches must remember to introduce discussions of psychological information slowly and at a level appropriate to the age of the child. Too much emphasis too soon on the psychological aspects of sport only bores and confuses the child. Finally, one pre-season meeting or informal discussion of any psychological topic will not be effective in changing the attitudes and behavior of a young athlete. Coaches must realize that attitude change and the development of psychological skills take time.

Psychological objectives presented at individual and team discussions should be reemphasized throughout the season at practices and competitions.

Use discussions to outline your psychological skills program by making the young athletes aware of the important psychological ideas. During practices and at opportune times throughout the season reemphasize these important principles. For example, a coach could talk to his or her young athletes about the role of positive thinking and confidence in athletic performance. In addition, the principles should be incorporated into practices whenever possible. For example, a team rule forbidding griping or nonconstructive criticism by anyone, goal attainment charts prominently displayed to show the athletes that they are improving, and day-to-day positive reinforcement by the coach are all strategies that directly or indirectly could be used to emphasize the importance of psychological skills.

IMPLEMENTING SYSTEMATIC GOAL-SETTING PROCEDURES

Goal-setting, systematically implemented, can be effective in developing psychological skills in young athletes.

One of the most effective ways to develop psychological skills such as confidence, independence, and self-motivation, as well as actual performance improvements, is to set goals. Goal-setting is not new to wrestling as most wrestlers have engaged in some form of goal-setting in the past. Wrestlers have set goals concerning win-loss records, winning championships, making teams and beating particular opponents. However, while most wrestlers have set goals to some degree in the past, many have not been systematic in the way they have done so and this often resulted in less than maximum performance. Common mistakes include setting goals which are too general, setting unrealistic goals, not establishing series of interrelated goals and setting goals but not following through on them. Thus, if a wrestler is going to make goal-setting work for him, he must take a systematic approach to the goal-setting process and consider a number of important factors.

Most wrestlers set general long-range goals such as breaking into the starting line up in their weight division, winning the regional meet, or becoming an Olympic champion. It must be remembered, however, that these are only one type of goal and by themselves are not always effective. A wrestler cannot break into the line up, win the regional meet, or become an Olympic champion unless other more immediate goals are established and achieved. These more immediate goals include such things as improving one's double leg takedown or executing a duck under from a new set up. In fact, when setting goals it is good to remember the coaching adage "matches are not won or lost during the meet, but are won or lost during the week in the practice room." If a wrestler wants to achieve a certain long-range goal, he had better set a number of more immediate technique goals to shoot for in practice.

When actually setting goals it is best to think in terms of a staircase, with a long-range goal at the top of the stairs, one's present level of ability representing the first step, and each succeeding step representing a progression of more immediate short-range technique goals. For example: a young wrestler's long-range goal may be to win a certain championship. To accomplish this goal, however, the young wrestler must achieve a sequence of more immediate technique goals. An appropriate sequence of technique goals may include being able to execute a good single leg takedown with proper penetration and elevation in a drill situation, being able to execute the single from both the left and right sides and being able to successfully employ the single in competition.

Another common goal-setting mistake is "shooting for the stars" by setting unrealistic goals. It is foolish and frustrating, for example, for an inexperienced wrestler to focus undue emphasis on becoming a champion when he has not yet made the varsity team. Goals *should* be hard, but they *must be realistically* based on the wrestler's current level of ability and experience. Thus, at the end of the staircase we may have a difficult, even lofty, long-range goal (e.g., winning a particular championship) but between the first and last steps are a number of progressively more difficult, realistic short-range goals (Figure 12-1).

The best way for a wrestler to set goals is to talk to his coach or some other knowledgeable wrestling source who is familiar with his ability and experience. This discussion should be open and honest and the wrestler's long-range goals, individual potential, commitment

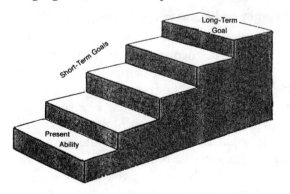

Figure 12-1. Goal-setting staircase. To experience long-term success, one must experience short-term success or failure.

and opportunity of practice should be considered. Goals should also be set in what psychologists call specific behavioral terms. Ineffective goals are often stated in general and vague terms and include such things as becoming a better wrestler or improving one's takedown. Examples of precisely stated observable goals include being able to successfully execute a good double leg takedown in 8 out of 10 attempts in practice with proper penetration, elevation and pivoting techniques, or improving conditioning by reducing one's heart rate recovery time after running 20 sets of stairs. Finally, stating appropriate goals is not enough! The coach and athlete must outline specific strategies for achieving the stated goal. For instance, if a wrester's goal is to execute a double leg takedown as described above, then a specific plan for achieving this goal must be developed. In this case, the wrestler may want to stay after practice every day and shoot 20 correct double legs.

While goal setting appears to be very simple, difficulties often arise. For example, it is relatively easy to set goals, but like New Year's resolutions many goals are soon forgotten! The difficult part comes in mustering up the day-to-day follow-up effort and evaluation procedures needed to insure that one achieves his goals. There are several techniques, however, that can be used to insure that the wrestler follows up on and evaluates progress towards his goals. First and foremost, all goals should be recorded and placed where they can be seen everyday (e.g., posted on the mirror in the wrestler's room at home). The wrestler should then develop the following routine. At the start of each day he should look at his goals and think about what he will do on this day to accomplish them. At the end of the day he should evaluate his progress by asking himself what he did today to become a better wrestler—"What did he do to accomplish his goals?" Coaches can also help by conducting follow-up meetings where progress toward goals is discussed with the individual wrestler. In addition, practice and match related statistics which reflect progress toward goals can be posted.

Finally, if a wrestler finds that he is not achieving his goals despite putting forth full effort, the goals should be reevaluated and adjusted. This does not necessarily mean that a certain long-range goal will never be achieved and that the wrestler should throw in the towel. Rather, the stairsteps may be too steep and the distance between them too far. What is needed is some step remodeling where more realistic short-range goals are determined.

THE EFFECTIVE USE OF ROLE MODELS

The verbal and nonverbal behavior of coaches becomes a model for young athletes.

Another way coaches can develop psychological skills in young athletes is by means of modeling. Young athletes hold their coaches in high esteem and look to them as sources of information about skills, attitudes, and behavior. They learn not only by listening to what the coach says but also by watching what the coach does. For example, if a coach constantly extolls the importance of confidence, emotional control, and positive attitude to his or her athletes, but lacks confidence, loses control, and seldom has anything positive to say, the athletes receive conflicting information. On the one hand the coach is emphasizing the importance of these skills, but on the other hand he or she exhibits the opposite behavior. Moreover, since actions speak louder than words, the lessons learned are just the opposite of those the coach intended.

A good example of a coach using modeling to develop psychological skills in athletes is Jim "Doc" Counsilman, famed Indiana University and former United States Olympic Team swim coach (Counsilman, 1977). Coach Counsilman strongly believes in developing confidence and positive self-image in his swimmers and tries to build these skills throughout the season. However, he also makes a concerted effort to practice what he preaches by looking and acting confident at meets even when he is somewhat anxious or nervous himself. In essence, Coach Counsilman has learned that modeling is an effective way to help foster confidence in his athletes.

Not only can coaches use themselves as models, but they can also use outstanding athletes within their sport to foster positive psychological states in their athletes. For instance, the coach can post selected quotes and stories that emphasize how outstanding athletes have

learned to cope with anxiety or how they often lost and made mistakes early in their careers but were able to overcome setbacks by hard work and training. Coaches can also invite a former athlete or outstanding athletes from local universities or colleges to speak to his or her team about psychological issues.

USING A POSITIVE AND SINCERE APPROACH TO COMMUNICATION

The communication style of the coach may be the most important strategy to developing positive psychological skills in young athletes.

While team and individual discussions, goal-setting, and modeling are all effective strategies for developing psychological skills such as confidence and increased self-worth in young athletes, the communication style of the coach may be the most important strategy. The positive approach is especially effective in developing psychological skills in young athletes. In youth sports, the coach is not working with highly-skilled adults who have experienced a great deal of success in sports and have established, stable self-concepts. Rather, the coach is involved with children who are just developing their skills. Constant criticism, sarcasm, and yelling often frustrate young athletes, lower their self-image and self-confidence, and decrease their motivation. When you are coaching young athletes, a positive, supportive approach is essential.

The positive approach to coaching consists of a number of important principles (Smoll & Smith, 1979):

Use praise and encouraging statements frequently.

1. Reward, encourage, and praise players. The most important principle in the positive style of coaching is the frequent use of encouraging statements and rewards. The frequency with which coaches use nontangible rewards such as a pat on the back, a smile, or verbal praise influences the psychological state of the young athlete. The greater use of encouraging statements and rewards by coaches, the more confidence and feelings of self-worth will be developed in the athlete.

Be positive but sincere.

2. Give encouragement and rewards with sincerity. For beneficial results to occur, rewards must be given sincerely. It means little to a young athlete to say, "You played well," if he or she played poorly. When coaches are not sincere, they risk losing the respect of their players. This does not mean, however, that we should punish or chastize young athletes for their mistakes. Rather, acknowledge they did not play up to their potential, but be sure to praise them for the things they did well and reassure them that you will help them improve.

3. Have realistic expectations. It is very difficult for coaches to give rewards sincerely unless they have realistic expectations about their athletes' capabilities. After all, if there is one thing youth sport coaches are sure of, it is that young athletes will make mistakes. Consequently, don't expect your players to play like professional or college athletes or even the local high school team. Formulate realistic expectations based on the players' experience and ability. Realistic expectations are essential if the positive approach to coaching is used to develop positive psychological states in young athletes.

4. Reward effort, not just outcome. It is easy to be positive when a young athlete makes the winning free-throw, hits a home run, or scores the winning fall; but sometimes we forget to reward and encourage children when they do not win or perform well despite 100 percent effort. All we can ask of children is that they give their best effort. Therefore, reward effort as much as outcome.

5. Reward performance, as well as outcome. One of the primary responsibilities of a coach is to teach fundamental skills and correct technique. The use of proper fundamentals and correct technique, however, does not always have positive outcomes. This is especially true in youth sports. How many times have you seen a wrestler use correct technique but not score because his opponent was just too strong. Conversely, a wrestler may do a move poorly but still score because his opponent made mistakes in countering. In such cases, the coach should reward performance and the use of correct technique, not just outcome.

6. Use a positive approach to mistakes. The positive style of coaching rewards and praises players for what they do correctly, but it does not mean that mistakes should be ignored. Athletes must be told when mistakes occur to help them make necessary corrections.

Can one correct errors with a positive approach? The answer to this question is yes, provided three basic steps are followed. First, when correcting mistakes, begin with a compliment or encouraging statement like "good try" or "way to hustle." Praise aspects of the skill that the player performed correctly. Next, tell the young athlete what was done incorrectly and how it can be corrected. Last, end on a positive note by encouraging the player with a statement such as "stick with it, you'll get it" or "keep up the good work." The order of these steps is important. The complimentary and encouraging statements offset the frustration that resulted from the athlete's mistake, and the instruction tells how the error can be corrected.

Thus, the coach using the positive approach provides corrective feedback that is necessary to improve performance and, over time, develop confidence and feelings of self-worth in the young athlete. It is recognized, however, that there is a need to provide plenty of sincere compliments and encouraging statements to offset the immediate frustration a young athlete experiences after making a mistake and maintain his or her self-worth.

EDUCATING INTERESTED ADULTS

Many times coaches plan and initiate strategies designed to foster psychological development in young athletes, but find that their efforts are unknowingly undermined by parents and other adults. These individuals often set unrealistic goals for the young athlete, place undue emphasis on winning, demonstrate poor sportsmanship, have unrealistic expectations, make a number of pessimistic and sarcastic remarks about young athletes, and are not aware of the positive approach to communication. Because such actions can have severe depressing effects on the psychological development of young athletes, many coaches conduct orientation workshops on youth athletics at the beginning of the season.

Conducting educational workshops for the parents of young athletes and other interested adults improves their understanding of youth sports and thus may contribute to the development of positive psychological skills in young athletes.

Such workshops typically last for one to two hours and are designed to facilitate communication among all parties. For example, a sample agenda for an orientation meeting for parents of youth wrestlers is shown in Table 12-2. In these meetings parents and other interested adults can meet the coaches and voice any concerns, and coaches can state their goals for the psychological development of the young athlete and specify strategies planned to achieve the goals. Issues such as realistic expectations, goal setting, the meaning of success and failure in sport, positive mental attitude, parental conduct at matches, the importance of self-motivation, and the positive approach to communication should all be addressed. Moreover, the coach can write letters containing much of the same information to parents unable to attend the meeting.

CONSIDER THE AGE OF THE ATHLETE IN DEVELOPING PSYCHOLOGICAL SKILLS

While psychological skills can be developed in young athletes of all ages, coaches must remember that, to be effective, the objectives and strategies identified for developing psychological skills must be appropriate for the developmental level of the athlete. It is essential that the developmental level of the athlete be considered since children of varying ages have been found to vastly differ in their ability to attend, comprehend, and retain information. Thus, attempting to develop the same psychological skills and employing the same strategies with all athletes, without considering their developmental level, will often create frustration, confusion, and seldom achieve the desired effects.

Goal-setting, for example, is an appropriate strategy for developing psychological skills in young athletes. However, the manner in which goal-setting is used with athletes of different ages varies greatly. The coach of elementary school aged athletes may focus sole attention on defining what a goal is, deriving a specific goal for each athlete, and assisting each athlete in achieving his or her goal. In contrast, the coach of high school aged athletes may assist each of his or her athletes in identifying a number of diverse goals, for which each athlete independently works. Similarly, team talks and discussions are appropriate for young athletes of all ages. However, the coach of younger athletes (ages 8-9 years) may emphasize one or two key points (e.g., success is not synonymous with winning, winning is giving 100% effort) through a series of five-minute informal discussions interspaced throughout the season, while the coach of older athletes (ages 15-16 years), may hold 50-minute weekly discussions on a number of psychological issues.

In summary, if coaches are to be effective in developing psychological skills in their young athletes, the general skills and strategies identified in this chapter must be modified and used in a manner which is appropriate for the developmental level of the child.

Table 12-2. A sample agenda for an orientation meeting for parents of youth wrestlers.

Topic	Time Allotted
Introduction of Coach or Coaches	5 minutes
Coaching Philosophy • benefits of wrestling participation • teaching methods—typical practice • emphasis on winning, fun, and development • team rules—coach's expectations	10 minutes
Wrestling Demonstration • meet film • conduct, scoring, and rules of the game • equipment needs	30-35 minutes
Details of Program • length of practices • practice and match schedules • expenses • insurance • physical examinations	10 minutes
Question and Answer Period	30-45 minutes

SUMMARY

Although specific procedures for developing psychological skills in young athletes have been outlined, it is unrealistic to think that coaches will always be completely successful in attaining this objective. Psychological development takes time. Moreover, the development of psychological skills is affected by individuals outside the current athletic setting (e.g., former coaches, parents, siblings, peers). However, when coaches make conscientious, continual, and concerted efforts, they can and do have enormous effects on athletes, although it is not always apparent which young athletes they are influencing. For this reason, every coach in youth sports programs must plan, develop, and initiate coaching strategies designed to foster psychological development in the young athlete. Individual and team discussions, systematic goal-setting, the effective use of role models, the positive approach to communication, and educational programs for interested adults are all strategies coaches can use to foster psychological development in young athletes.

Adapted from: N. Wood (ed.), *Coaching science update.* Ottawa, Canada: Coaching Association of Canada, 1983.

SUPPLEMENT A: Goal Setting Worksheet

Long Range Wrestling Goal(s): _____

Short Range Wrestling Goal(s): 6 mos. _____

1 yr. _____

Area-Wrestling Skill	Specific Goal	Strategies to Achieve Monthly Goal
Basic Skills		
— stance		
— motion		
— change of level		
— penetration		
— lifting		
— back step		
— back arch		
Basic Attacks on Feet		
— single		
— double		
— head to outside series		
— fireman's		
— drag		
— duck under		
— headlock		
— hip toss		
— arm throw		
— body lock		
— salto-souplesse		
— lateral drop		
Contact-Action		
— pummel-push		
— pop-chop		
— shuck-drag		
— snap-block		
Counter Attacks on Feet		
— re-throw		
— front-headlock		
— hip bump		
On Mat — Tilts and Turns		
— quick tilts		
— far crotch		
— gut wrench		
— arm bars		
— leg series		
Psychological Skills		
— goal setting		
— relaxation		
— imagery		
— mental preparation		
Fitness Tests		
— 40 yard dash		
— 400 meter run		
— 2400 meter run		
— strength		
— muscular endurance		
— flexibility		
— weight control		
— injury		

13
Helping Wrestlers Cope with Stress

QUESTIONS TO CONSIDER

QUESTIONS TO CONSIDER

- What is the critical factor affecting a wrestler's performance?
- When does a wrestler perform best?
- What two factors create heightened stress states in athletes?
- What is the most important principle to remember when helping wrestlers cope with stress?

Major events such as the Junior National Championships can tremendously heighten competitive stress in a wrestler.

INTRODUCTION

A wrestler sits in a chair awaiting his up-coming match. He has warmed-up for an hour, but just cannot get loose. His palms are sweaty, he has a queasy feeling in his stomach, and his hands are cold and clammy. He gets up and paces. He cannot sit still. The time for his match arrives, he crosses the circle and shakes hands with his opponent. Questions immediately flash into his mind. Will I be able to set him up? Will my single work? How can he be that strong? What will my parents and coach think if I do not wrestle well? The match begins and contact-action is initiated. The opponent shucks and shoots. His opponent's shot is not that good. It is not as deep as it should be. The wrestler, however, does not react in his normal fashion. He is still tight, despite his lengthy warm-up. The result is a takedown for the opponent.

What happened to the wrestler in this match? Why did he not react in his normal fashion and counter the takedown? A likely reason for his poor performance is his inability to cope with competitive stress. Coping with competitive stress is not only a problem specific to this particular wrestler, but has been found to be a problem faced by many wrestlers, at all levels of competition. In fact, a U.S.A. Wrestling study (Gould, Horn & Spreemann, 1982) of junior elite wrestlers revealed 53% of the wrestlers sampled indicated that heightened anxiety sometimes hurts their performance. Thus, coping with stress is an important issue that wrestlers and coaches need to better under-stand.

Thus, a wrestler performs best at his optimal level of emotional arousal.

While any wrestler who has ever stepped on the mat has experienced competitive stress, the critical factor affecting performance is the manner in which a wrestler deals with that stress. Why is it that some wrestlers make stress work for them and rise to the occasion, while other wrestlers buckle under the pressure and exhibit poor performance? Additionally, what can coaches and parents do to help wrestlers cope with stress? This chapter will address these issues. Specifically, the purposes of this chapter

are threefold and include: (a) an examination of the stress performance relationship; (b) the identification of factors which have been found to heighten competitive stress in wrestlers; and (c) the presentation of coaching strategies that can be used to help wrestlers cope with stress.

THE STRESS-PERFORMANCE RELATIONSHIP

Both sport psychologists and experienced coaches have learned that the stress perfor-mance relationship is not simple. It has been found, for example, that wrestlers do not per-form well when they experience little stress or emotional arousal. In essence, they are not mentally or emotionally ready to wrestle. They are not psyched-up! It has also been found, however, that too much stress or arousal re-sults in wrestlers who are overmotivated or psyched-out, and in turn, perform poorly. Just what is the answer, "psych-up" or "psych-out"?

Research has shown that an inverted-U best explains the relationship between a wrestler's level of emotional arousal (stress) and perfor-mance. This relationship, depicted in Figure 13-1, reveals that best performance results when a wrestler is optimally (usually moder-ately) aroused. Specifically, as a wrestler's level of emotional arousal increases, performance improves until an optimal level of arousal is reached. It is at this time that a wrestler exhib-its his best performance; wrestling up to his capabilities. After reaching this optimal level of arousal, however, any further increases in

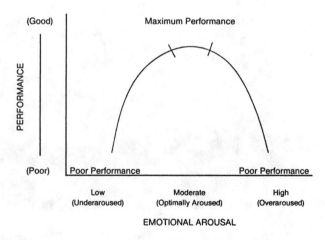

Figure 13-1. Arousal-Performance Relationship.

arousal results in performance decrements. Thus, a wrestler performs best at his optimal level of emotional arousal and demonstrates poor performance when he is under or over aroused.

Unfortunately, research has not developed tools that allow us to precisely specify what an individual wrestler's optimal level of arousal should be. Wrestlers and their coaches must learn this through awareness and experience. However, it has been found that all wrestlers do not have the same optimal level of arousal. Figure 13-2, for example, depicts the emotional arousal-performance relationship for two wrestlers. Inspection of this figure reveals that both wrestlers have an inverted-U relationship between their emotional arousal and performance. However, the optimal level of emotional arousal that results in best performance for wrestler A is very different from the optimal level of arousal that results in best performance for wrestler B. Consequently, substantial differences between wrestlers exist in terms of what specific optimal levels of emotional arousal lead to best performance.

FACTORS WHICH HEIGHTEN COMPETITIVE STRESS IN WRESTLERS

If a coach is to help a wrestler cope with stress, he needs to understand what factors create heightened stress states in athletes. Generally, two factors have been identified as major sources of stress in wrestlers and other athletes, as well (Martens, 1978). These include the importance the wrestler places on his performance and the uncertainty the wrestler has about his capabilities and personal relationships with others. For example, it has been found that the greater the importance the wrestler places on the event, the more likely he will experience heightened arousal. Thus, a wrestler will experience more emotional arousal prior to the finals of the state championship, than before a local dual meet. It must be recognized, however, that the importance of an event is not exclusively defined in terms of the caliber of competition or size of the event. Parents, coaches and other important individuals in the wrestler's life influence event importance by their actions. For instance, a coach who repeatedly emphasizes how important a match is for a particular wrestler, increases the wrestler's perception of the importance of that match. Similarly, a wrestler may feel that it is more important for him to win when his parents and friends attend a meet, than when he knows few people in the crowd. In essence, the greater the wrestler views the event's importance, the more stress he will experience.

Just what is the answer. "Psych-up" or "psych-out"?

The second general factor related to increased emotional arousal in wrestlers is uncertainty about capabilities and relationships with others. That is, the greater the uncertainty, the more stress experienced. For example, a wrestler will experience more stress when he has little confidence in his ability to execute needed moves, than when he is confident in his skills. Similarly, if a wrestler is uncertain about his relationships with others (e.g., he wonders whether his coach or parents will still like him if he loses), heightened stress will result. Thus, uncertainty about abilities and relationships with others is an important source of stress that must be recognized by parents and coaches.

While feelings of uncertainty and perceptions of event importance are major sources of stress for any wrestler, it is also important that

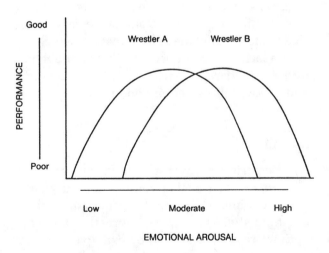

Figure 13-2. Wrestlers specific optimal levels of arousal. Wrestler A—Gets up quick; but fades fast. Wrestler B— Takes longer to get up; but stays at a higher level longer.

coaches and parents recognize those wrestlers who are especially susceptible to heightened anxiety states. Specifically, psychologists have identified certain types of individuals who have an especially difficult time coping with stress. These individuals are characterized by high-trait anxiety and low self-esteem. High-trait anxious wrestlers are those individuals who want to excel so much that they perceive competition to be very threatening and because of this become very nervous and perform poorly. Similarly, low self-esteem wrestlers have so little confidence in their abilities they become over-anxious, which causes them to perform poorly. In essence, because of their personalities, these wrestlers have an especially difficult time coping with stress. These wrestlers are not doomed to failure, however, as they can benefit the most from coaching strategies designed to reduce stress.

COACHING STRATEGIES FOR HELPING WRESTLERS COPE WITH STRESS

Based on an understanding of the stress-performance relationship and factors related to stress in wrestlers, a number of coaching strategies can be used to help wrestlers cope with stress. These include: (1) recognizing the unique psychological makeup of each wrestler; (2) identifying wrestlers who have problems coping with stress; (3) individualizing coaching styles; (4) reducing event importance; (5) reducing wrestler uncertainty about relationships with others; and (6) developing confidence in wrestlers.

Why is it that some wrestlers make stress work for them . . . while others buckle under pressure?

RECOGNIZING THE UNIQUE PSYCHOLOGICAL MAKE-UP OF EACH WRESTLER

The most important principle to remember when helping wrestlers cope with stress is to realize that each wrestler is unique. Some wrestlers have a very low optimal level of arousal and perform best when they seem almost too lackadaisical to wrestle, while other wrestlers have higher optimal levels of arousal and must

pump themselves up to perform well. For example, Gene Mills, a former member of the national free-style team, must be pumped up to wrestle well. However, Lee Kemp, a three-time world champion, is just the opposite. In fact, when asked how he likes to mentally prepare for competition Lee indicated that " . . . I do not like to psyche myself up. I try to relax myself as much as possible. I am not a 'rah-rah, fire-up' guy—at least wrestling isn't that way to me." Thus, if coaches are to help wrestlers reach optimal emotional readiness, each wrestler must be viewed as unique.

IDENTIFYING WRESTLERS WHO HAVE PROBLEMS COPING WITH STRESS

Because each wrestler is unique it is especially important that coaches learn to identify those wrestlers who have difficulty coping with competitive stress. For example, a wrestler who consistently performs better in practice than in major competitions, has trouble getting loose before matches and demonstrates marked personality changes before competition is exhibiting the symptoms of heightened anxiety. If, after observing these symptoms, the coach suspects that a wrestler is having problems handling competitive stress, he should talk to the wrestler and verify that stress is, in fact, the problem. If so, efforts should be made to identify the specific factors causing the heightened stress (e.g., worry about what parents will think or say). Similarly, coaches should be very sensitive to statements made by wrestlers which reflect a lack of confidence and threat of evaluation, both characteristics of high-trait anxious and/or low self-esteem individuals.

INDIVIDUALIZING COACHING STYLES

Because each wrestler is unique and has his own optimal level of emotional arousal, it is of utmost importance that coaches adjust their coaching styles to help each wrestler reach his optimal readiness state. For example, a coach may give an emotional pep talk to all his wrestlers before the big meet. This practice often backfires, however, as many of the wrestlers become overpsyched, exceeding their optimal level of arousal. A more effective coaching strategy is to deal with each wrestler individually. While a few may need to be psyched-up, many need to relax and others will want to be left alone. In essence, coaches must recognize that mental preparation in wrestling is specific to the individual wrestler.

REDUCING EVENT IMPORTANCE

As previously stated, the greater the importance placed on the wrestler's performance, the greater the stress created. While there is little a coach can directly do to control the importance of a big meet or match within the season, a number of indirect strategies can be employed to reduce stress. For instance, the coach can play down the importance of a big match by treating it like any other competition. Similarly, when discussing the match with his wrestlers, the coach can refer to it without constantly informing the athletes of how important it is. Finally, the coach may want to explain the significance of taking a low-key approach to the upcoming competition with parents and other influential adults.

REDUCING WRESTLER UNCERTAINTY

It must also be recognized that since feelings of uncertainty about relationships with influential others can create heightened stress in wrestlers, uncertainty should be reduced by creating a supportive atmosphere. This is especially important when coaching a wrestler who is high-trait anxious and/or low self-esteem. Practically speaking, then, it is important that the wrestler understands that others will not base their liking of him on his won-loss record. It should also be made clear that when others provide constructive criticism, they are criticizing only the wrestler's performance, not the wrestler as a person.

DEVELOPING CONFIDENCE

One of the most effective means of helping a wrestler cope with stress is to instill confidence in him. This can be accomplished in several ways. First, realistic practice and match goals should be set for each wrestler. Moreover, these goals should not be defined in terms of win-loss record alone. Rather, technique (e.g., points scored, number of reversals made) and fitness goals should be emphasized. Coaches should then continually encourage the achievement of these goals. Second, emphasis should be focused on positive feedback regarding goal attainment, while at the same time correcting performance errors. After all, it is extremely difficult for a coach to instill confidence in a wrestler if he only focuses on the wrestler's mistakes and errors. Lastly, considerable time should be spent on skill instruction and learning, since the most effective way to develop confidence in a wrestler is through positive changes in behavior.

SUMMARY

While a number of strategies for helping wrestlers cope with stress have been discussed in this chapter, it must be recognized that there are no magical or quick-fix approaches to stress management. Like physical skills, psychological skills take time to develop, and coaches must have realistic expectations regarding their development. Thus, it is unrealistic to expect a wrestler to effectively cope with stress after using the strategies presented in this chapter on only one or two occasions. Consistent, long-term efforts on the part of coaches are needed. Those coaches who systematically employ these procedures over time will find that they can reap the benefits of the program and produce wrestlers who can more effectively cope with competitive stress.

14
Relaxation Training for Wrestlers

QUESTIONS TO CONSIDER

- What is relaxation?
- What are the four phases in learning relaxation?
- What steps are important to understand about relaxation?
- What are the key points to remember about relaxation training?

A wrestler who understands relaxation will have as much fun in a big match as he does rolling around.

95

INTRODUCTION

A keen understanding of the relationship between performance and the ability to control ones mental and physical anxieties is a trait common among wrestling champions at every level. It is a well-known fact that a relaxed physical state will respond much better to mental signals sent to the body than will a tense state. Many times, this ability to relax and focus characterizes the "pressure wrestler" or one who seemingly always performs well in big match situations.

The following chapter will outline the importance and concepts behind relaxation training for wrestling.

WHAT IS RELAXATION?

Relaxation is a state where one is physically and mentally free from uncontrolled tension, anxiety, and thoughts. It is characterized by feelings of ease, looseness, tranquility, and rest.

PURPOSES OF RELAXATION TRAINING

The purposes of relaxation training include: (A) the physiological calming of the body, and (B) the shift from anxiety–provoking thoughts to a relaxation set.

WHY LEARN RELAXATION TRAINING?

Wrestlers should learn relaxation training to help achieve proper mental preparation (i.e., help achieve an optimal level of emotional readiness) before or during a match; to help one sleep the night before a major event; and as a mechanism for helping develop concentration and imagery skills.

PHASES IN LEARNING RELAXATION

Phase 1: *Tense–Relax Cycle*—tense and relax various muscle groups throughout the body focusing on the feelings associated with tensed and relaxed states / Time (7-10 days; 20 minutes a day).

Phase 2: *Relaxation Only Cycle*—relax muscle groups individually without tensing. Begin to use a cue word to signal relaxation (e.g., relax) / Time (7-10 days).

Phase 3: *Full-Speed Relaxation*—begin to add speed by learning to relax the individual muscle groups more quickly. The ultimate goal is to learn to relax deeply in the time it requires to take a deep breath, inhale and exhale slowly / Time (20 times a day).

Phase 4: *Utilization Stage*—begin to use relaxation in anxiety provoking conditions. Practice first under low stress conditions, then under moderately stressful conditions, and finally employ relaxation under highly stressful conditions.

STEPS IN LEARNING RELAXATION

- Lie down and relax your entire body. If you hear noises don't try to block them out, but focus on your breathing—inhaling, then exhaling slowly. If you want to move slightly, that's OK. Close your eyes, take it easy and relax.
- Tense the muscles of your right lower leg and foot by pointing your toe. You will tense for 5-6 seconds and then relax. You should be able to feel the tension in the foot and the calf and then totally relax. When you relax feel the warmth in the muscles. Repeat this procedure again on the right leg and then repeat it twice for the left leg.
- After tensing and relaxing the lower leg and foot, tense (for 5 seconds) and relax the thigh and buttocks region (twice for each leg). Tense the buttocks and thighs by pushing down with your butt.
- Tense and relax the forearm and hand by making a fist. Do this twice for each arm.
- Tense and relax the bicep of each arm by bending at the elbow and pretending you are doing a chin up. Repeat twice for each arm.
- Tense (for 5 seconds) and relax the back muscles by arching the back up. Tense and relax the back twice.

- Tense the stomach and chest muscles by breathing in and releasing—relaxing. Do this twice.
- Tense the neck and shoulders by shrugging your shoulders (pulling them together) and then releasing them and relaxing. Repeat this twice.
- Tense the face and forehead by gritting your teeth and pulling your eyebrows together, then relax. Do this twice.
- (Optional Step): Rehearse—concentrate and view yourself perform. Try to focus on the details—clearly and vividly. Focus on doing the move correctly and feeling the move as you execute it.

KEY POINTS TO REMEMBER ABOUT RELAXATION TRAINING

Psychological skills are like physical skills. They must be *practiced regularly* before they are learned.

As with physical skills, wrestlers have different psychological skill abilities. Some wrestlers will be more effective at relaxing than other wrestlers. All wrestlers, however, can learn to improve their ability to relax.

The same relaxation training procedure is not best for everyone. Individual wrestlers often modify the technique to fit their own individual preference and style.

15
Visualization and Imagery Training for Wrestlers

QUESTIONS TO CONSIDER

- What is imagery?
- What steps are used in preparing to practice imagery?
- What are the phases of sport imagery development?

WHAT IS IMAGERY?

Imagery is a basic psychological skill which involves the ability of a wrestler to mentally re-create objects, persons, skills, and situations while not actually being involved in these environments. Athletic imagery not only involves visualization, but all the senses, with kinesthetic or muscle sense being especially important.

WHY DOES IMAGERY WORK?

Imagery is effective in improving performance because the human mind cannot distinguish between perceptual and real stimuli. Thus, imagery allows the wrestler to practice physical skills, without having to actually perform them. Mental imagery also gives you a chance to deal with a problem or event in your head before you are confronted with it in the real world.

Relaxation + Imagery + Concentration = Better Performance

STEPS IN PREPARING TO PRACTICE IMAGERY

- Select the right setting—quiet, dark, comfortable and free from distraction.
- Be relaxed (see relaxation training steps).
- Be motivated—to be effective, imagery must be consistently practiced.
- Be realistic and patient—imagery works, but it must be practiced.

PHASES IN SPORT IMAGERY TRAINING

- Develop sensory awareness—focus on all the senses, not just the visual.
- Develop *vivid* and *clear* images—hear the crowd, feel the mat, feel the movement.
- Practice *controlling* your images—start with simple skills and move to more complex ones; correctly execute them.

- Use *internal* imagery—see yourself from your own mind's eye.

PHASES OF SPORT IMAGERY DEVELOPMENT

- Begin with guided practice—instructor guided imagery.
- Practice self-directed imagery.
- Employ imagery during practices.
- Begin using imagery in competitive events.

ATHLETIC IMAGERY GUIDELINES

- Use short imagery practice situations (5 minutes).
- Imagine good performances and positive outcomes.
- Feel the move as you visualize it.
- Use slow motion imagery for skill analysis.
- Follow images of incorrect performance with images of correct performances.
- Use triggers to strengthen imagery (e.g., a color, your shoe).
- Practice, practice, practice.

16
Self-Control Skills for the Elite Wrestler

QUESTIONS TO CONSIDER

- What is centering?
- How can this help your wrestlers?
- What are the three phases of centering skills?

Understanding centering skills enabled the U.S. to capture the 1995 World Championships and athletes Terry Brands, Bruce Baumgartner, Kevin Jackson, and Kurt Angle to earn gold medals.

CENTERING

Centering is the act of focusing your attention on a single point in your body, your center of gravity. For most people this point lies somewhere right behind the navel. It is less important that one knows exactly where their true center of gravity is than it is to learn to focus attention on a single point within the solar plexus region.

HOW CAN CENTERING HELP WRESTLERS?

In the martial arts, centering is used as a method to reduce unwanted tension and increase concentration powers for body control. Likewise, wrestlers can use centering to stay loose under pressure and to focus attention on their center of control. Remember that whoever controls the center of gravity controls where the body moves. If it's your opponent, he controls you. Learning to center helps keep you in control.

The act of centering has both physical and psychological effects. These effects are REAL and can truly aid wrestling performance.

Physical Effects of Centering:
- decreased heart rate, decreased respiration rate, increased oxygen to muscles, decreased negative tension
- better control of hips, better balance
- movement from center of gravity allows more strength, better timing, better coordination

Psychological Effects of Centering:
- feel more in control, stronger, more confident
- focuses attention to an important element of wrestling, the center of gravity
- directs attention *away* from negative thoughts or other distractions

TRAINING CENTERING SKILLS

Everyone can center to some small degree right now. However, like all psychological skills, centering under the pressure of high-level competition requires practice.

Phase 1: *Progressive Relaxation and Breathing Skills.* Along with relaxation training, spend some time focusing on the easy, natural rise and fall of your stomach as you breathe. Let the stomach muscles totally relax. Proper breathing comes from the diaphram, *not* the chest. (5 min./day along with relaxation training)

Phase 2: *Breathing Skills and Centering of Attention.* Focus on a point just behind your navel. Concentrate on this point and then feel your entire body in relation to it. Remind yourself: Your strength, power, balance, and control all come from this point.

Build in a mental cue for centering. One method is to breathe in through your nose and out through your mouth on every breath. As you breathe in, say a cue word (e.g., "center") to remind yourself to center, and as you exhale say another cue (e.g., "relax") to remind yourself to stay loose. At the end of one breathing cycle, many athletes like to cue their attention toward their opponent while staying centered (a word like "attention" or "action" works well). The entire sequence might be:

Breathe in (nose)   Breathe out (mouth)
"Center" → "Relax" → "Attention"

Phase 3: *Centering During Workouts.* Practice centering between drills or between periods of workout matches. Later, make it a habit to center each time you enter your stance. Use breathing and cue words to reinforce the centering drill. As your skill improves, try centering in low-pressure competition, gradually working up to more important matches.

The more automatic your centering skills become, the more they can be used in important competition. The better centered wrestler will have more strength, speed, and balance, and better timing, concentration, and confidence.

Section IV
Developing Wrestling Skills

17
Basic Skills:
Contact and Action

QUESTIONS TO CONSIDER

- What are the seven basic skills?
- What are the five major areas of concentration in USA Wrestling's training program?
- What is the importance of mastering the basics?
- What are the eight "action" upper body movements?

Two of the United States' greatest wrestlers, Dave Schultz and Lee Kemp, attained complete mastery of the basic skills.

INTRODUCTION

USA Wrestling's National Training Program has been developed with the direct input of its National Instructional Staff.

The primary goal of the Instructional Staff has been to establish a "system" whereby a coordinated and uniform approach to teaching the international styles of competition can be implemented.

This systematic approach to teaching and training both wrestlers and coaches has already been initiated at coaching clinics presented by the national staff, at USA Wrestling's National Developmental Camps, in the USA Wrestling film, "Successful Wrestling—Seven Basic Skills," in the publications *USA Wrestler, Link,* and *The Complete Coach,* and in USA Wrestling's Freestyle and Greco-Roman Video Syllabus.

THE "BASIC CONCEPT"

The concept of "Total Wrestling" as advocated by FILA relates to the intent and interpretation of the present international rules. The concept of the "TOTAL Wrestler" as advocated by USA Wrestling's National Training Program relates to the fact that a successful wrestler is the product of many disciplines brought together in a coordinated and meaningful manner.

The following presentation has been put together to provide coaches and wrestlers useful information for implementing a program that will help develop the "TOTAL Wrestler."

THE "WHOLE IS EQUAL TO THE SUM OF ITS PARTS"

What makes a champion? An intricate combination of many factors! The champion of today must be made aware of more than just technique and general body conditioning. He must come to know all aspects of himself and how to improve on each of them.

The USAW's National Training Program covers a wide gamut of disciplines including the following:

Successful Technique—"A Systematic Approach"

Mental Toughness—"The Psychological Edge"

Cardiovascular Endurance—"The Most Important Muscle"

Flexibility—"Key to Reducing Injuries"

Nutrition—"Our Source of Energy"

Weight Training—"Strength Plus Endurance"

Mat Strategy—"Know the Rules"

SUCCESSFUL TECHNIQUE

There are five (5) major areas of concentration in the USA Wrestling's Training Program that deal with technique. These areas are the following:

Basic Skills
Contact
Attacks
Counter Attacks
Tilts

BASIC SKILLS

The sport of wrestling involves a myriad of moves and counter moves, all intended to eventually take one opponent from his feet to his back.

The successful execution of any of these moves is dependent upon the athlete having mastered a series of very specific, yet basic skills.

The wrestler must first and foremost develop control and movement of his own body. Too often the coaches and wrestlers concentrate first on various holds and maneuvers that are executed against an opponent. Before such maneuvers can be successfully executed, however, a wrestler must have disciplined himself to know where his own body is in space and the relationship of certain key body parts to each other.

There are seven (7) basic skills that emphasize this discipline. When combined in the proper sequence, they provide the wrestler both MOBILITY and POWER.

1. stance—ability to keep the head, neck, back, hips, elbows, and legs in a prescribed position to each other.
2. motion—ability to move the body from one position on the mat to another in a lateral or circular direction and remain in a good position (stance).

3. changing levels—ability to move your hips up and down in relationship to your opponent while remaining in a good position (stance).
4. penetration—ability to move your hips directly into, under and through your opponent while remaining in a good position (stance).
5. lifting—ability to move your opponent's body mass in an upward direction, up and/or off the mat.
6. back step—ability to move your hips into and under your opponent while twisting backwards into his body.
7. back arch—ability to control your body parts and remain in balance while driving your hips into and under your opponent as you go from your feet into a high arching back bridge.

The ultimate result of mastering each skill and executing them in the proper order is the wrestler's ability to lift. It is this skill, lifting, that most clearly distinguishes the international styles of wrestling from our own American "folk style." A good Greco-Roman or freestyle wrestler must be able to lift. The prerequisites to lifting, however, are penetration, changing level, motion and good body position (stance).

POSITION → MOTION → LEVEL →
PENETRATION → LIFT

(Lift: Back step and back arch are special forms of lifting)

If we are in agreement that "lifting," above all other skills, is the major difference between our folk style and the international styles, then the following concept applies.

To lift (Skill 5) you must have your hips and legs under the center of gravity of your opponent.

To be in this position requires that your movement into your opponent, penetration (Skill 4), be of such a nature that it gets you to the right spot at the right time.

Successful penetration must always be preceded by a change in the level of the hips (Skill 3) of the wrestler attacking his opponent.

The ability to change your level (vertical motion) and then penetrate (horizontal motion) is preceded by your ability to keep your feet, hands and body free, and in a position for fluid motion (Skill 2).

Having disciplined your body parts to remain at a specific position in relationship to each other (Skill 1) will enable the body as a whole to move in a free, fluid manner.

Basic Drill Series

1. Stance
In & Out 10 Cues

2. Movement
Shuffle in Place
Circular Motion
Lateral Motion

3. Change of Levels
Shuffle & Change
Circle & Change
Lateral & Change

4. Penetration
Stance, Change/Level, Drop Step
Stance, Change/Level, Step In
Stance, Change/Level, Double Knee Drop

5. Lifting
a. Low Level Lift
   Stance, Change/Level, Drop Step
   Butt on Heel, Lift, Arch
   Double Carry
b. Low to Mid Level Lift
   Follow Up Step w/Trail Leg
c. Mid Level Lift
   Stance, Change/Level, Step In
   Arms, Squeeze, Body-Lower C of G, Hips
      -Thrust, Hi-Crotch
   Double, Hi/O Single, Low Single, Hi Single, Duck, Lift & Arch
d. Crotch Lift
e. Waist Lift

6. Backstep
Shadow: Step, Backstep, Pivot
Head & Arm: Step, Backstep, Pivot

7. Back Arch
Knee—Back Arch
Low Squat—Back Arch
Standing—Wall Walk-Back Arch
Standing—Two Hand-Back Arch

Standing—Single Hand-Back Arch
Standing—Solo-Back Arch

Verbal Cues for Seven Basic Skills

1. Stance

a. Feet Spread
b. Knees Bent to Power Angle
c. Hips: Flexed, Set & Square
d. Back Rolled Slightly
e. Shoulders Rolled In & Over Knees
f. Elbows: In, Inside Knees
g. Forearms: Rotate from Inside
h. Weight: Slightly Forward
i. Hands: From the Crotch, Palms Forward, Fingers Up
j. Be Able to Move Forward, Backward, Right & Left

Into stance 10 times checking above cues

2. Movement

Motion & Position
a. Shuffle Holding Stance Together
b. Lateral Movement
c. Circular Movement

3. Changing Levels

a. Change Levels Holding Stance
b. Lateral—Change
c. Circular—Change
d. Change—Penetrate

Position

4. Penetration

Drop Step
    Change Levels
    Power—Plant Take Off Foot
    Step—Sprint Deep to Foot Placement
    Knee—Drive Lead Knee to the Mat
    Balance—Keep Knees Spread—Trail Leg Slightly Back
Step In
    Change Levels
    Power—Plant Take Off Foot
    Step—Strike Deeply to Foot Placement
    Stance—Return Immediately to Stance
Double Knee Drop
    Change Level
    Power—Push Drive with Legs/Block-Post Shoulders

Step—Double Knee Drop or Squat
Drive—Explode from Squat/Lift—Low Level Lifting Skill

5. Lifting

Arms: Secure—Squeeze
Body: Lower Your Level
Hips: Drive Under & In
Legs: Lift by Extension—straightening

a. Low Level Lift
    Stance, Change/Level, Drop Step
    Butt on Heel, Lift, Arch
    Double Carry
b. Low to Mid Level—Follow Up Step w/Trail Leg
c. Mid Level Lift
    Stance, Change/Level, Step In
    Arms, Squeeze, Body Lower C of G, Hips-Thrust, Hi-Crotch
    Double, H/O Single, Low Single, Hi Single, Duck, Lift & Arch

    i. Crotch & Waist Lift
    ii. Body Lock w/Arm & wo/Arm
    iii. Rear Standing w/Waist Lock
    iv. Body Lock—Throw—Rethrow w/Partner

6. Back Step

Lift Requiring Sharp Hip Rotation
Lead Foot: Step Forward and Slightly Across Opponent
Trail Foot: Back Step to Heel of Lead Foot
Feet: Close Together
Hips: Pivot 270 to Thrust Hips in Front of Opponent (Pivot on Trail Foot)

a. Head & Arm: Step, Back Step, Pivot
b. Shadow (w/o Partner): Step, Back Step, Pivot

7. Back Arch

Stance to High Arching Bridge
Stance: Feet Spread, Toes Outward
Knees: Bent
Center of Gravity: Lowered & Over Base of Support
Hips: Forward Thrust
Head & Shoulders: High Arching, Backward to Side of Head & Shoulder

a. Knee—Back Arch
b. Low Squat—Back Arch
c. Standing—Walk the Wall
d. Standing—Two Hand Back Arch

e. Standing—Single Hand Back Arch
f. Solo—Back Arch

CONTACT

In an effort to reinforce the intent and interpretation of the international rules, USA Wrestling's Training Program has concentrated on certain terms that may be new to most coaches; CONTACT is one of those terms.

"CONTACT!" implies that the wrestlers must come closer to each other to initiate a hold or undertake such contact with the body that provides an opportunity for performing a hold.

Traditionally the "tie up" and "set up" would be used to explain what is being emphasized. Unfortunately, both of these terms imply an excessive amount of holding, controlling or manipulating of an opponent, which is not consistent with the present FILA rules.

In fact, FILA goes on to say that "contact" must be immediately followed by "ACTION!" (even to the point where the wrestler must take a "risk" by performing an "action"). Such action is to be rewarded! On the other hand, to make "contact" with your opponent and use up time with a hold or not to make contact at all, even though you may be repeatedly diving or attacking him, is to be prevented by issuing a warning.

In describing the various types of holds or grips you can secure once you have made "contact," the Training Program tries to concentrate on identifying specific parts of the body:

As an example:

head and bicep (collar tie up)
both biceps (traditional inside position)
shoulder and wrist (underhook position)
wrist and elbow (2 on 1 or Russian tie)

The "action" that follows the "contact" has been broken down into eight (8) characteristic upper body movements:

Pummel—rolling the arms for an inside position
Push—drive with the legs, block with the chest/shoulder
Pop—quick, short upward movements against opponent's arms (elbows)
Chop—quick, short downward movement against opponent's arms (wrist, elbows)

Shuck—pushing opponent's arm (elbow) from the outside so as to drive it across between his body and yours
Drag—pulling opponent's arm (tricep) from the inside so as to move it across between his body and yours
Snap—an extended downward motion on your opponent's head
Block—to secure part of your opponent's body (elbow) and hold it in a specific position while you move your own body past it

ATTACKING THE "ATTACK ZONE!"

Attacking the "attack zone" is the basic offensive maneuvers from which points will eventually be scored and referred to as "attacks." This term is specifically used to emphasize the constant, aggressive approach a wrestler must take in attempting to score against his opponent.

Besides trying to develop this type of an attitude, the USA Wrestling's Training Program also concentrates on where the "optimum" point of attack should be initiated.

To reduce your opponent's power and mobility, you must be able to move and control his hips. Therefore, your most successful attacks will be those that are initiated directly to the "attack zone," his hips.

If you imagine your opponent's hips are the center of a target and each concentric ring out from the "bulls eye" is of a lesser value, you can effectively analyze which type of an attack is most likely to score the highest points.

To attack the wrist, ankles or top of the head will usually be less effective than to attack the waist, hips or thighs. If, however, you attack the extremities of your opponent's body and can bring them in toward his center of gravity, you increase your chances of success (i.e., armdrag, head and heel).

Lifting your opponent is also more likely accomplished if you are lifting up through his center of gravity (hips). The further out from the "attack zone" the more you must rely upon motion to score your points.

SUMMARY

In summary, the USAW has developed and is proposing a "system." We are not advocating any new or unique maneuvers. We are providing a coordinated, consistant approach to teaching coaches and wrestlers the underlying principles that make all maneuvers work.

The seven (7) basic skills represent the foundation to this program. Every attack can be analyzed as to whether the skills were executed properly and in the right sequence. As a coach or a wrestler, you have a reference line (i.e., sequence of skills) to go back to in order to see where your attack was unsuccessful.

The term "contact" and "attack" emphasize the attitude and the strategy that must become a "built-in" part of every wrestler.

We identify the contact with specific parts of our opponent's body. The ensuing "action" can be characterized by eight (8) basic upper body movements.

The ULTIMATE result of an attack should be a LIFT (either a straight lift or a special form of the back step and back arch).

If for some reason you cannot lift, then you go back to the beginning of the sequence of skills and start over.

Usually by changing your direction (i.e., Skill 2—Motion) or getting a "new angle," you will be able to score on your opponent.

SUPPLEMENT A: Freestyle Syllabus

The following outline is in accordance with USA Wrestling's Freestyle & Greco-Roman Video Syllabus. This is the written outline to both follow and reference the video that can be purchased along with this text.

It is recommended that this chapter be read and used alongside the video syllabus for the best understanding of its content. USA Wrestling will continue to offer its member coaches the most advanced and best technical instruction available.

Basic Skills

I.   Position (*Stance*)
    A. Square
    B. Staggered

II.   Motion

III.   Change Levels

IV.   Penetration
    A. Inside step
    B. Outside step
    C. Knee Spin

V.   Grips
    A. Knuckle Lock
    B. Hand Clasp
    C. Forearm Grab or Hook
    D. Butterfly Lock

VI.   Lifting

VII.   Sprawl

VIII. Backstep

IX.   Back-Arch

X.   Contact (*Tie-Ups*)
    A. Head tie
    B. Head and Biceps
    C. Biceps tie (*one or two*)
    D. Elbow tie (*one or two*)
    E. Two on One
    F. Underhook (*one or two*)
    G. Wrist tie-up (*one or two*)
    H. Forearm Hook

XI.   Set-Ups
    A. Pop
    B. Chop
    C. Shuck
    D. Drag
    E. Pummel
    F. Any fake or feint
    G. Post

XII.   Hip heist

XIII. High Turn (*Head Post*)

XIV.   Swisher

XV. Granby
    A. Tri-Pod
    B. Over the top
    C. Turn in (*off head post*)

XVI. Sit out, turn

XVII. Bridging

Takedown Techniques

I. Double leg
    A. High Level Finishes
        1. Tackle
        2. Flair (*Make an L*)
        3. Run the pipe
    B. Low Level Finishes
        1. Lift & Flair
        2. Cut across
        3. Trip (*Inside and outside*)
        4. Trap the wrist on the waist
        5. Trap the wrist on the ankle

II. Single leg
    A. High Level Finishes
        1. Flair
        2. Run the Pipe
        3. Block the far heel
        4. Flank
        5. Change to two (*Low double leg, below the knee*)
    B. Single leg Tree-top Finishes
        1. Roll your shoulder and trip far side
        2. Tree-top, slap the head and trip the far leg
        3. Lift and turk
    C. Single leg (*Low Level Finishes, head inside*)
        1. Post and Circle
        2. Post and Duck between the legs
        3. Pull the knee, step and put your head across your opponent's body (Cut Across)
        4. Far side carry (*Dump*)
        5. Trap the wrist (*On the ankle or the waist*)
        6. Bring the far knee down and change to double leg (Low Level Flair)
        7. When opponent covers your head, peek your head out by throwing your elbow and change to a double leg

III. High Crotch
    A. High Level Finishes
        1. Change to double leg
            a. flair
            b. run the pipe
        2. Lift
    B. Low Level Finishes (*Low level finishes, head outside*)
        1. Transfer the weight to the far leg and attack a double leg
        2. Hook the ankle, head behind the knee, go backside
        3. Bring the far knee down and hook the far leg at shin or flair
        4. Post and elevate (*When your opponent has the angle on your shoulder*)
        5. Set him on his hip
            a. pull back
            b. post the head and cartwheel across opponent
            c. lay back and take the head when opponent uses a half
            d. trap the wrist that is around the waist or crotch and roll to the head

IV. Duckunders
    A. From wrist tie-up
    B. From underhook
    C. From overhook
    D. From open position

V. Fireman's Carry
    A. Carry to both knees
    B. Near arm far leg
    C. Over and under (*head outside carry*)

VI. Arm Drags
    A. Drag to a double
    B. Drag to a single
    C. Drag to a trip
    D. Fake fireman's and drag

VII. Ankle Picks (Hook)
    A. Head and Heel
    B. From an underhook
    C. From a two on one
    D. From a front headlock

VIII. Knee Picks (Hook)
    A. From head and bicep tie-up
    B. From underhook

C. From two on one
D. From elbow control

IX. Inside Trip
    A. From an over and under
    B. From a two on one
    C. From a front headlock
    D. From a headlock position

X. Front Headlocks
    A. High Level Finishes
        1. Cross ankle pick
        2. Inside trip
        3. Head trap, bridge through
        4. Arm trap, bridge through
    B. Low Level Finishes
        1. Snap and butt drag
        2. Snap and knee drag
        3. Circle to single
        4. Circle to craddle
        5. Roll through Head Trap
        6. Roll through Arm Trap
        7. Shuck off circle
        8. Knee block

XI. Throws
    A. Head and Arm
    B. Hip toss
    C. Lateral Drop
    D. Arm spin
    E. Shoulder throw
    F. Salto

XII. Two on One Techniques
    A. Reach around & capture the far hip
    B. Single leg
    C. Foot sweep
    D. Fireman's carry
    E. Double leg
    F. Ankle pick or knee pick
    G. High crotch
    H. Arm drag
    I. Duckunder
    J. Head & arm or Shoulder throw

XIII. Breakdowns From Behind (*Tri-Pod*)
    A. Gut Wrench
    B. Crotch Lift
    C. Lift and Turk
    D. Pick up Ankle and leg lace
    E. Pressure down on the knee

F. Heel Block and sag back
G. Spiral

Counter Attack Techniques

I. Five Lines of Defense
    A. Head
    B. Hands
    C. Arms
    D. Hips
    E. Technique (moves or tricks after opponent has gotten past your head, hands, arms, and hips)

II. Forearm Block
    A. Opponent's head is down
        1. Block and reroute
        2. Block, post and spin
        3. Block and shuck
        4. Block and knee drag
    B. Opponent's head is up
        1. Block, post and hit double leg
        2. Block, post and hit ankle pick
        3. Block, post and hit single
        4. Block, post and hit high crotch
        5. Block, post and hit a duckunder

III. Forearm Shiver Block
    A. Front headlock
        (low level front head lock finishes, same as X. B)

IV. Sprawl
    A. Opponent's head is inside
        1. Butt drag
        2. Front body lock
        3. Front ¼
        4. Waist block and knee block
        5. Spladle
    B. Opponent's head is outside
        1. Roll the hip and sprawl
        2. Crotch lift
        3. Switch
        4. Neck Wrench

V. Counter the Single Leg When Opponent Has the Angle
    A. Kick out
    B. Reverse Spin
    C. Step over crotch lift
    D. Hip Lock (*Whizzer*)
    E. Lat Pull

Clearing Tie Ups With Counter Offense Techniques

I. Clearing the Head Tie Up
  A. Double knee drop
  B. High Crotch
  C. Circle away and single leg
  D. Duckunder
  E. Arm drag
  F. Change to a two on one
  G. Arm spin
  H. Shoulder throw

II. Clearing Underhooks
  A. Control the elbow and duckunder
  B. Change levels and double leg
  C. Change levels and single leg
  D. Fireman's carry
  E. Inside Trip
  F. Arm spin
  G. Post, limp arm and high crotch
  H. Post, limp arm and single leg
  I. Shoulder throw
  J. Set em in the lap and lateral drop
  K. Head and Arm

III. Clearing the Two on One
  A. Change levels and single leg
  B. Control far elbow and high crotch
  C. Shoulder throw
  D. Step behind knee
  E. Control the wrist and hip toss

IV. Clearing the Wrist
  A. Duckunder
  B. Arm Drags
  C. Single leg
  D. Change to a two on one

V. Clearing Bicep Tie Up
  A. Chop to a double leg
  B. Chop to a single leg
  C. Pull the elbow high crotch
  D. Pull the elbow single leg
  E. Duckunder

VI. Clearing Front Headlock Tie Up
  A. Sucker Drag
  B. Change levels high crotch
  C. Dump
  D. Pull the wrist and leg trap
  E. Hold the wrist and high crotch

VII. Clear the Over and Under Tie Up
  A. Pummel to duckunder
  B. Pummel to hip toss
  C. Outside single
  D. Inside Trip
  E. Snap to a front headlock
  F. Footsweeps
  G. Underarm spin
  H. Shoulder Throw
  I. Knee Pick
  J. Pummel to firemans
  K. Pummel to high crotch
  L. Pummel to headlock
  M. Bodylock throws

Par-Terre Offense

I. Gut Wrench
  A. High gut wrench
  B. Low gut wrench
  C. Mid-rib gut wrench
  D. Trapped arm gut wrench

II. Leg Turns
  A. Leg Lace
  B. Double Knee Trap
  C. Inside Ankle Pick
  D. Split the Legs and Hook the far Knee
  E. Split the Legs and Turk the far Leg
  F. Near Leg Turk
  G. Step-over Near Ankle Pick and Bow and Arrow
  H. Far Ankle Pick and Bow and Arrow
  I. Figure Four the Near Leg and Turk
  J. Crossbody and Bar Half

III. Arm Turns
  A. Inside Wrist Bar and Waist Tilt
  B. Inside Wrist Bar and Block the Head
  C. Put the Inside Wrist on the Back and Crossface Tilt
  D. Put the Inside Wrist on the Back and Underhook Tilt
  E. Post the Hand and Underhook Tilt
  F. Arm Bar and Run the Head

IV. Crotch Lift

V. West Point (Chest Cradle)

VI. Cradles
  A. Crossface Cradle

B. Nearside Cradle
C. Farside Cradle

VII. Near Arm Block and Waist Tilt

VIII. Far Side Wrist Control (*under opponent's chest*)
A. Lift Far Wrist and Near Thigh and Turk
B. Lift Far Wrist and Drive or Circle the Head
C. Switch Far Wrist Control (*by reaching between the legs and capturing the wrist*) and Elbow Snatch

Par-Terre Defense

I. Basic Position
A. Hips Flat
B. Arms at 45 degree angle
C. Hands in a Fist
D. Head up
E. Chest up (*slightly*)
F. Legs Wide

II. Defense Wrist Control
A. Rolling the Wrist
B. Two on One
C. Push Back

III. Defense Gut Wrench or Body Lock
A. Blocking
B. Hip Down (*away from the turn*)
C. Leg Trap
D. High Leg Over
E. Motion, Push Back, Move Forward, Move Sideways, Move Up
F. Hip Heist on Trapped Arm Gut Wrench

IV. Defense Leg Lace
A. Base Up
B. Bring Far Knee Under You
C. Kick
D. Hand Fight
E. Catch Opponent's Foot

V. Defense the Crotch Lift
A. Turn Hip (*Hip Down*)
B. Pinch Legs
C. Trap the Wrist
D. Catch the Foot

VI. Defense Turks and Leg Traps
A. Movement

B. Hip Down
C. Push the Turk Leg
D. Lock Legs Out

Escapes

I. A. Stand-ups
1. Inside Leg
2. Outside Leg
3. Swisher
4. Tri-Pod
B. Finishes From the Feet
1. Hand Control, Isolate the Leg and Turn Outside
2. Hand Control, Isolate the Leg and Turn Inside
3. If Hands are Locked High, Chop the Elbows
4. If there is a half nelson, throw the Elbow By
C. Hip Heist
1. Low Level
2. Mid Level
3. High Level
D. Headpost
E. Switch
1. Low Level
2. Running Switch
3. Inside Switch
4. High Level Switch
F. Granby Rolls
1. Tri-Pod
2. Over the Top (*push back*)
3. Sit-out turn in Granby
G. Sit-Out and Turn
1. Sit-out and Turn In
2. Sit-out and Turn In
H. Clearing the Spiral Ride
1. Stand-up
2. Inside Switch
3. Shoe laces
I. Clearing the Ankle
1. Post the Ankle
2. Swisher
3. Shoe laces
4. Switch
J. Clear the Legs
1. Tri-pod Granby
2. Mule Kick and Shoe laces
3. Switch
4. Swim

K. Clearing the Crab Ride
 1. Post the Knee Step on the Foot and Hip Heist
 2. Take the Bottom of the Foot and Slide Down and Away

Pinning and Riding

I. Ankle to Pin or Back Points
 A. Cradles
  1. Near Side
  2. Far Side
  3. Crossface
  4. Cross Ankle
 B. Cross Ankle and Half Nelson
 C. Cross Ankle and Figure Four the Leg

II. Near Wrist to Back Points or Pin
 A. Near Wrist and Waist Tilt
 B. Near Wrist and the Underhook Tilt
 C. Put the Near Wrist on the Back and Crossface
 D. Near Wrist and Block the Head and Lace the Arm
 E. Put the Near Wrist on the Back and Switch to Arm Bar

III. Spiral to Pin or Backpoints
 A. Spiral to Half Nelson
 B. Spiral to Reverse Headlock When Opponent Steps Over Leg
 C. Spiral to Near Wrist Turn

IV. Tight Waist to Cross Wrist Turns and Pins (only use the tight waist after your opponent has been broken off his base)
 A. Cross Wrist to Waist Tilt
 B. Cross Wrist Elbow Snatch (catch the elbow when opponent tries to clear his wrist)
 C. Cross Wrist to Crossface Turn
 D. Cross Wrist to Turk
 E. Cross Wrist to and Arm Bar

V. Leg Turns and Pins
 A. Crossbody Turk
 B. Crossbody Power Half
 C. Crossbody and Capture the Far Arm (grapevine)
 D. Crossbody Capture Far Elbow and Wrist
 E. Bent Leg Turk
 F. Figure Four the Near Leg Turk

Five Basic Rules From the Takedown Position

1. Think position first and fight for your control
2. When your hands move your feet should move
3. Don't stay in the same tie-up for more than five seconds
4. Work to break your opponent's balance
5. In freestyle wrestling keep your back to the center

Five Basic Rules From the Bottom Position

1. Think position first (hips, elbows, hands, feet & head)
2. Hand Control
3. Put your opponent's hips behind yours
4. Get your hips away from your opponent's
5. Move on the whistle, hit the first move & chain wrestle

USA WRESTLING FREESTYLE SYLLABUS GLOSSARY

1. BLOCK: Cause an obstruction so something can't be moved
2. CARRY: To carry across the shoulders, like a fireman's carry
3. CHOP: Short downward blow with your hands
4. CORNER: Position where your opponent has an angle to go around you
5. DRAG: Pulling an object across the body
6. DUMP: Throw down or set down on the mat
7. FLAIR: Stepping across the body while hooking the knee and pulling
8. GRAB: Thumb spread so you can grip
9. HOOK: Keeping the thumb in and curving the hand to form a hook
10. POP: Short, quick blow upward
11. POST: Put on the mat like a pole, so you can go around or, straighten upright like a pole so you can go under
12. SAG: Bend or hang downward like you are falling

13. SHUCK: Throw across the body with a forearm
14. SNAP: Quick, short, pulling or pushing motion
15. SWEEP: Move continuously in one kicking motion
16. SWISHER: Swinging your ankles away from your opponent in one continuous motion
17. SWITCH: To change or exchange
18. TRAP: To capture, lock, prevent from moving
19. TREETOP: Clear the single leg in front of your body and lift it
20. TRIP: Cause opponent to stumble or lose balance

SUPPLEMENT B: Greco-Roman Syllabus

Basic Skills

I.   Position (*Stance*)
    A. Square
    B. Staggered

II.   Motion

III.   Change Levels

IV.   Penetration
    A. Inside step
    B. Outside step

V.   Change Direction
    A. Side to side
    B. Forward/Backward

VI.   Grips
    A. Knuckle Lock
    B. Hand Clasp
    C. Butterfly Lock
       1. Wrist
       2. Forearms
       3. Elbows

VII.   Hang

VIII.   Pull
    A. Backward
    B. Side

IX.   Push
    A. Forward
    B. Side

X.   Lift

XI.   Bridge

XII.   Backarch

XIII.   Gut Wrench

XIV.   Pivot

XV.   Backstep

XVI.   Hip Pop

XVII.   Contact (Tie-Ups)
    A. Head
    B. Bicep
    C. Wrist
    D. Elbow
    E. Underhook
    F. Two on One
    G. Head and Arm
    H. Pinch Headlock
    I. Front Headlock
    J. Forearm

XVIII.   Set-Ups
    A. Pop
    B. Shuck
    C. Drag
    D. Hook
    E. Post
    R. Pummel
    G. Any fake or feint

Takedown—Techniques—Throws

I.   Backarch Throws
    A. Basic Backarch Throw
    B. Types of Backarch Throws
       1. Straight over
       2. Whip
    C. Backarch Throws By Position
       1. Under/Over Lock

a. Step around
b. Straddle
c. Step to trapped arm
2. Bodylock-Under/Over Wrap
a. Step around
b. Straddle
c. Step to trapped arm
3. Bodylock-Double Under
a. Step around
b. Straddle
4. Bodylock-Pinch headlock
a. Slip over to the body

II. Sag Throws
A. Sag Bodylock
1. Drive thru leg
2. Pull and Pop
B. Sag Wrap
1. Drive thru leg
2. Pull and Pop
C. Sag Headlock
D. Sag Shoulder
E. Sag Spin

III. Pivot Throws
A. Under/Over Pivot Throw
B. Pinch Headlock Pivot Throw
C. Double Under Pivot Throw

IV. Backstep Throws
A. Basic Backstep Throw
B. Backstep Throws
1. Arm Throw
2. Shoulder Throw
3. Hip Toss
4. Headlock
C. Other Backstep Techniques
1. Armspin
a. Armspin series
2. Arm Throw To The Knees
3. Hip Toss To The Knees

V. Front Headlock Throws
A. Straight Over
B. Side

Takedown Techniques—Body Attacks

I. Finishes From The Body
A. Lift and Clear Legs
B. Lift, Circle Backwards and Clear Legs

C. Lift and Crackback
D. Step and Twist
E. Pivot, Turn the Corner and Hang
F. Fan
G. Backstep
H. Back-Arch
I. Change Direction

II. Arm Drag
A. Penetraton
1. Outside step, near leg
2. Inside step, near leg
3. Inside step, far leg
4. Outside step, far leg
B. Tie-Ups
1. Wrist tie
2. Forearm tie
3. Outside Two on One
4. Inside Two on One
5. Underhook
6. Pummel

III. Slide-By
A. Types of Slide-Bys
1. Body
2. Turn the Corner
B. Penetration
1. Inside
2. Outside
3. Step Across
C. Finishes
1. Turn the Corner Finishes
a. Hang
b. Lift to Back-Arch
c. Lift, Return to the Mat
2. Body Finishes
a. Back-Arch
b. Lift, and Clear Legs
c. Lift, Circle Backwards, and Clear Legs
d. Change Direction
e. Crackback
f. Twist
D. Set-Ups
1. Pummel
2. Underhook
3. Under/Over
4. Two on One
5. Forearm/Wrist

IV. Duckunder
A. Types of Duckunders

1. Body
2. Turn the Corner
B. Penetration
    1. Outside
    2. Inside
    3. Across
C. Finishes
    1. Turn The Corner
        a. Hang
        b. Lift to Back-Arch
        c. Lift, Return to Mat
    2. Body
        a. Back-Arch
        b. Lift and Clear Legs
        c. Lift, Circle Backwards, and Clear Legs
        d. Crackback
        e. Change Direction
        f. Twist
D. Set-Ups
    1. Pummel
    2. Two on One
    3. Wrist

Par-Terre Offense

I. Basic Gut Wrench
    A. Tight lock
    B. Pressure forward
    C. Block hip with knee
    D. Load hips
    E. Back-Arch, and turn thru

II. Turns
    A. Gut Wrench
        1. High
        2. Medium
        3. Low
    B. Reverse Gut Wrench
    C. Arm Bars

III. Lifts
    A. Gut Wrench Lift
        1. Swing step lift
        2. Tripod lift
        3. Snatch lift
        4. "Jump Up" lift
        5. Knee lift
    B. Finishes From The Gut Wrench Lift
        1. Sit on the leg, lift to a back arch
        2. Sit on the leg, sit through to gut wrench

3. Step out, turn hip, back arch
4. Start lift, gut wrench to the other side
5. Polish lift
6. Sit on the leg continue through to low level back arch
C. Reverse Lift

Par-Terre Defense

I. Basic Par-terre Defense
    A. Basic Position
        1. Hips Flat
        2. Arms at 45 degree angle
        3. Chest up, back arched
        4. Fingers curled under, hands slightly turned inward
        5. Legs wide
    B. Basic Movements
        1. Forward
        2. Backward
        3. Side to side
        4. Spin

II. Defending Turns
    A. Gut Wrench Defense
        1. High
            a. Push backwards
            b. Hips up
        2. Medium
            a. Chest up
            b. Pressure on lock
            c. Forward movement
            d. Roll lock down to hips
        3. Low

III. Defending Lifts
    A. Gut Wrench Lift Defense
    B. Reverse Lift Defense

Technique by Position

I. Under/Over
    A. Step Around Bodylock
    B. Slide by Bodylock
    C. Armspin
    D. Pivot/Whip
    E. Slide By
    F. Shuck

II. Pinch Headlock
    A. Attacks From The Pinch Headlock

1. Headlock
   a. Sag
   b. Backstep
   c. Reverse Headlock
2. Whip
3. Back-Arch
4. Slip-over
5. Shuck
6. Duckunder
7. Change of Direction
8. Bodylock

B. Clearing The Tie Up/Counter Attacks
   1. Pull head, underhook the opposite side
   2. Whip
   3. Hang, circle, underhook opposite side
   4. Headlock

III. Double Under
   A. Shuck
   B. Change Direction
   C. Pop and Pull Whip
   D. Back-Arch Whip Throw
   E. Back-Arch Pivot Whip Throw
   F. Double Under Pivot
   G. Most Basic Finishes From The Body

IV. Two on One
   A. Duckunder
   B. Slide By
   C. Armspin
      1. Near Arm
      2. Far Arm
   D. Reach Around
   E. High Dive
   F. Shoulder Knock Down
   G. Shovel Knock Down
   H. Back-Arch Whip

V. Underhook
   1. Snap down
   2. Shuck
   3. Slide by
   4. Bodylock
      a. Wrap
      b. Lock
   5. Sag
      a. Wrap
      b. Lock
   6. Arm Drag

7. Duckunder
B. Clearing The Tie Up/Counter Attacks
   1. Pull the head, repummel
   2. Hang and circle, repummel
   3. High arm over to the underhook
   4. Knockdown

Technique by Series

I. Armspin Series
   A. Armspin Attacks
      1. Armspin
      2. Spin thru to the body
      3. Armspin, change direction, sag
   B. Armspin Counters/Counter Attacks
      1. Step around
      2. Step around to drag
      3. Hip in, pull arm out
      4. Hip in, lock hands, drop to mat
      5. Circle toward the head, push on head, pull arm out, (or arm drag)
   C. Finishes From The Mat
      1. Continue the spin
      2. Out the back door
      3. Arm bar finish
   D. Set Ups To The Arm Spin
      1. Pummel
      2. Two on one
      3. Under over lock
      4. Collar tie

II. Bodylock Series
   A. Bodylock Attacks
      1. Step around (underhook or overhook side)
      2. Slide-by bodylock
      3. Armspin
      4. Sag (drive through or pull and pop)
      5. Headlock (sag or backstep)
   B. Bodylock Counters/Counter Attacks
      1. Sag the hips
      2. Step around post leg
      3. Step around re-throw
      4. Step off the throw
   C. Moves To The Body
      1. Pull lock high, step to the body
      2. Throw elbow back, step to the body
      3. Step around

Basic Backarch Throw

I. Definition: A *Backarch Throw* is any throw that originates from a bodylock and takes the thrower into and through a backarch position.

II. Teaching Progression
   A. Bridge
   B. Backarch Teaching Progression
   C. Three Step Throw Drill
   D. Hip Pop
   E. Throw With Crash Pad

III. Coaching Points
   A. The heart, the dynamic, the key to all backarch throws is the hip pop.
   B. The momentum of the throw should be up and back.
   C. The backarch is the follow-through.
   D. As a general rule, turn to the trapped arm side to complete the throw.

IV. Drills
   A. Backarch throws with the crash pad.
   B. Backarch throws for speed and spontaneous action: Have several partners rotating on the thrower. Work for speed as well as technique. Do 30 second to 1 minute goes.
   C. Backarch throws with the throwing dummy.

Grips

I. Definition: The way a lock is secured.

II. Coaching Points
   A. *Knuckle Lock*:
      1. The knuckle lock grip is made by clasping the hands together at the fingers.
      2. The knuckle lock grip is good when extension, reach, or maneuverability is important.
      3. The knuckle lock grip is tightened by pinching the elbows together and pulling the arms to the body.
   B. *Hand Clasp*:
      1. The hand clasp grip is made by clasping the hands together at the palms.
      2. The hand clasp grip is good when a strong lock is needed along with a certain amount of extension and maneuverability.
         NOTE: The hand clasp grip offers less extension and maneuverability than the knuckle lock grip but makes for a much stronger grip.
      3. The hand clasp grip is tightened by pinching the elbows together and pulling the arms to the body.
   C. *Forearm Grab*:
      1. The forearm grap grip is made by grabbing the forearm.
   D. *Butterfly Lock*:
      1. The butterfly lock grip is made by hooking the wrists, forearms, or elbows.
      2. The butterfly lock grip is tightened by pinching the elbows together and pulling the arms to the body.
      3. The butterfly lock grip is good for close tight locks.
         NOTE: Good grip for gut wrench.

III. Drills
   A. Gripper Squeeze: Squeese a tennis ball or other hand size object to increase hand strength.
   B. Grip Hang: Secure the desired grip from a standing position, secure grip around partner's chest, squeeze and hang for designated time period.
   C. Isometric Squeeze: Secure desired grip, squeeze for a designated time period.

Hang

I. Definition: Using some part of your opponent's body to support all or part of your body weight.

II. Coaching Points
   A. Attacker's weight should be transferred from his feet to his opponent's body.
   B. Maintain good position when hanging.
   C. Create "Heavy Hands" by securing a grip and sagging the hips.

III. Drills
   A. Underhook, Collar Hang: Partner stands erect with arms straight out. The driller hangs from an underhook collar tie position.
   B. Two on One Hang: Partner stands erect. The driller hangs from a two on one tie position.
   C. Double Under Lock Hang: Partner stands erect with arms straight out. The driller hangs from the rib cage with a high butterfly lock.
   D. Arm Drag, Hip Hang: Partner stands erect. The driller hangs from an arm drag and hip position.
   E. Free Hang: Partner takes a solid stance with his hands on his knees and a good base. The driller can grab anywhere on the back, neck, and shoulders as he moves from position to position without the use of his legs.
   F. Gut Wrench Hang: Partner takes a firm position on the mat supporting himself by his hands and feet. The driller takes a tight butterfly lock mid-way on his partner's rib cage. Once the grip is secured the driller hangs with both legs on one side of his partner's body, changing sides every 5 to 10 seconds by pulling his body to the other side using only his torso and low back muscles. No part of the driller's body should touch the mat.

Bridge

I. Definition: An arch position on the mat in which the wrestler is supported only by his head and feet.

II. Teaching Progression (Back Bridge)
   A. Begin with back and feet flat on the mat, with feet approximately 4-6 inches from the butt.
   B. Elevate hips, keep shoulders on the mat.
   C. Make the bridge by pushing with the legs, driving the hips forward and up.
   D. Return to starting position and repeat.

III. Coaching Points (Back Bridge)
   A. Keep the feet flat on the mat.
   B. Keep the knees above or behind the toes when making the bridge.
   C. Keep the hips elevated.
   D. Bend at the hip joint, not only at the spine.
   E. Make the bridge by pushing forward and up with the thighs and hips while rolling from the back of the head to the forehead. Avoid making the bridge by pushing up with the arms.

IV. Drills
   A. Forward and backward bridge
   B. Ear to ear bridge
   C. Flip flop bridge
   D. Circle bridge
   E. Timed bridge
   F. Partner bridge

Back-Arch

I. Definition: A skill used mainly with throws that takes the attacker into and thru a back-arch position.

II. Teaching Progression
   A. Backbridge
   B. Two handed back-arch
   C. One handed back-arch
   D. Back-arch with crash pad
   E. Back-arch
      NOTE: Next step in the teaching progression is to learn back-arch throw.

III. Coaching Points
   A. Momentum of the back-arch should be up and back.
   B. Feet should not leave the ground.
   C. Knees should stay above or behind the toes.
   D. Begin the back-arch from a slightly coiled position.
   E. The "dynamic" or heart of the back-arch is in the hip pop generated by an explosive lift from the quads., hips, and butt.
   F. Must commit fully to a full arch with head back. Pulling the head or flattening the back will result in a hard landing on the mat. When correctly done a counter balance takes place between the

hip pop and back-arch that creates a relatively soft impact on the mat.

IV. Drills
   A. Bridge
      NOTE: Make the bridge by pushing with the thighs and hips.
   B. Two Handed Back-arch
      NOTE: Use knuckle lock grip. Driller starts in a slightly coiled position with one foot inside and one foot outside.
   C. One Handed Back-arch
      NOTE: Use hand clasp grip. Driller starts in a slightly coiled position with one foot inside and one foot outside.
   D. Back-arch with and without crashpad
   E. Wall Walkers

Backstep

I. Definition: A penetration step that rotates the attacker's hips under his opponent's hips. Used for doing throws.

II. Teaching Progression
   A. Begin with a low stance
   B. Step and Penetrate (stay low)
   C. Toe to Heal (stay low)
   D. Pivot (stay low)

III. Coaching Points
   A. Change levels by lowering hips. Don't bend over.
   B. Pivot on the balls of your feet. Feet should not leave the ground.
   C. Maintain low position throughout pivot.
   D. Maintain good position throughout pivot keeping shoulders, knees, and toes in line. NOTE: No arch.
   E. Feet no more than 6 to 8 inches apart.
   F. Final backstep position: body coiled, weight on the balls of feet, slight lean forward, good body position, feet 6 to 8 inches apart.

IV. Drills
   A. Drill backstep in stages; 1. Step and penetrate, 2. Toe to heal, 3. Pivot.
      NOTE: Check position at each stage.
   B. Drill backstep with emphasis on "powering" the hips through.

NOTE: Power the hips like a hip check in hockey.
   C. Drill backstep with exaggerated level change.
   D. Drill backstep with ½ turn.
   E. Drill backstep with ¾ turn.
   F. Drill backstep finish with an explosive jump up and forward.
   G. Drill backstep finish with a shoulder roll forward.

Hip Pop

I. Definition: An explosive movement of the hips with the power generated by the legs. Sometimes called a "hip punch."

II. Coaching Points
   A. Hip pop is the first movement of a powerful lift.
   B. Execute the hip pop with an up and slightly backward motion rather than with a forward thrust.

III. Practical Applications
   A. Used with bodylocks
      1. Hip pop is the "heart" of the bodylock.
   B. Used when countering certain types of backstep throws.

IV. Drills
   A. Partner hip pop drills:
      Starting position: Partner stands erect with one arm straight out from his body and the other arm directly at his side. The driller then, standing chest to chest and hip to hip, lowers his level and locks around his partner's waist.
      Once the lock is secured:
      1. The driller lifts and jumps straight up with his partner, propelling both men into the air. Once in the air release partner and return to earth.
      2. The driller lifts and pops hips so as to take partner straight up and back. Finish the drill by keeping partner in the air while stepping backwards.
      3. The driller lifts and pops hips with a whip motion. Follow–through by keeping partner in the air while stepping backwards in a circular motion.

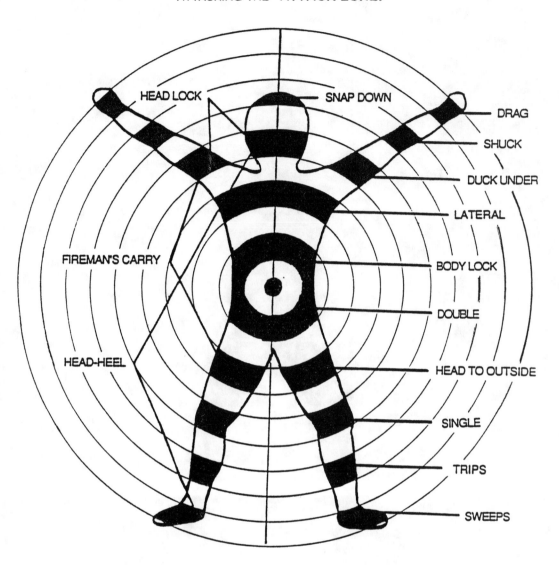

Section V
Training and Nutrition

18
Strength Training

QUESTIONS TO CONSIDER

- Is wrestling an acyclic or cyclic sport?
- What are the basic variables of training that a coach must understand?
- Why is strength training done?
- What are the stages in the periodization of strength?

INTRODUCTION

The development of a wrestler, like that of any other athlete, depends upon physical preparation, technical preparation, tactical preparation, and psychological preparation. Physical preparation must come first. Why? Because winning in wrestling comes down to generating more force at the point of attack than an opponent can resist. It's as simple as that. Wrestlers need to understand that their physical development ultimately determines their level of success. Physical development is more than important. It is necessary.

At the elementary stages of development this means that young children may be unable to execute some movements correctly simply because they lack sufficient back or leg strength, as in a double-leg with a lift. They need to get stronger. At more advanced stages of development a tremendous amount of back, hip, and leg strength may be required to execute a throw on a world-class 220 pound opponent, such as a reverse body lift and back arch in Greco-Roman.

Strength, then, is essential. This does not mean that athletes should be taken to the weight room before they are shown a single-leg. Far from it. What it does mean is that their physi-

cal development must go hand in hand with their technical development. Limited physical development will put a ceiling on technical expertise—at the least channeling it in a certain direction. This technical direction will have a similar effect on tactical ability. If an athlete's only moves are a high crotch and an arm bar, for example, then his use of tactics is going to be extremely limited. And all of these factors will impinge upon the athlete's psychological preparation. A well-trained wrestler knows he is well trained and feels confident and poised to win when he steps on the mat. On the other hand, no amount of "psych" will help an athlete with glaring physical weaknesses that have not been attended to. Much as he may want to believe that he's capable of handling a much stronger opponent, at the "moment of truth" his body will be telling him a different story. In the end the body wins most arguments.

Strength training, in one form or another, must be done.

THE PHYSIOLOGICAL CLASSIFICATION OF WRESTLING

Granted that strength training is needed, what kind of the many forms and methods must be done? The answer to this question lies in understanding completely the physiological basis for the sport. Without this understanding improper means may be employed with unintended outcomes.

First, wrestling is an acyclic sport, meaning that it is a contest characterized by great fluctuations in physical activity and rapidly changing body positions. Its demands are quite opposite those of the cyclic sports, such as swimming or running. Speed is important in wrestling, but the quickest wrestler doesn't always win. So on a speed continuum, the wrestler would be placed towards the high end but not at the top with sprinters. Endurance can also be important, but on a continuum the wrestler would probably be placed mid-way between a marathon runner at the top end and a shot putter at the bottom end. Force production is more important, and the wrestler would be placed toward the top of a strength continuum, but several notches below a weight-lifter or a thrower in track. This physiological definition of the sport is important.

When scoring movements are analyzed for their physiological requirements, it can be seen that a wide range of possibilities exist. Some scoring movements depend entirely on lateral movement and speed, such as a go-behind. Others depend upon tremendous explosiveness, such as a chest-to-chest throw. Still others depend upon maximum isometric contractions, as in a pin. Between these scoring movements a very stressful level of continuous muscular activity is ongoing. Muscular endurance is important.

The anaerobic system predominates. The ability to physiologically tolerate high levels of lactates is essential as heart rates approaching 200 and above are found in the final stages of the most demanding matches. Aerobic capacity is important for rapid recovery and for the increasing role it plays in longer matches and overtimes. All of these factors must find their proper place in the training plan.

Regarding training for strength, however, the need for power (speed-strength) and for muscular endurance (strength-endurance) are paramount. The ratio of these physical traits to the others depends largely upon the technico-tactical system that the wrestler employs, his genetic potential related to it, and his weight class. A "direct" wrestler who comes right at an opponent generally requires a much greater level of strength than an "indirect" wrestler, who depends much more on finesse for his success. Each must develop the level of strength attributes that is appropriate and necessary for the techniques that he uses and for the tactical approach that he relies on. In addition, weight class is an important consideration. For 105.5 pounders speed and muscular endurance will comprise a greater percent of the training formula, because they average nearly double the movements per match that heavyweights do. On the other hand, heavyweights must be able to manipulate 285 pounds of organized muscular resistence. A much higher ratio of strength is an absolute must.

It is important to note that the contribution of strength to the outcome changes with stages of development. For young athletes a high level of muscular endurance relative to other training factors is most important in achieving outstanding results. For elite wrestlers, however, the role of explosive strength becomes more and more important as very high levels of force must be generated in a short period of time to overcome higher levels of resistence.

STRENGTH QUALITIES

There is the mistaken notion that when a heavy object is lifted a number of times "strength" is developed. In fact there are many different types of muscular contractions that may be described as exhibiting strength and many different types of strength. The specific manner in which work is performed determines the strength adaptation that is achieved.

Based on mechanics there are four kinds of work:

1. force is produced that is sufficient to overcome the resistence
2. force is produced that is insufficient and gives way to the resistence
3. force is produced that is equal to the resistence, resulting in no change
4. some combination of the above

In wrestling all forms are present. In turning an opponent on his back, #1 is present. In losing an attack on an opponent because the hold is broken, #2 is evident. In locking up where neither wrestler can gain an advantage, #3 is present, and a stalemate may be called. Where a throw is executed followed by a hold down, #1 and #3 are combined.

Muscular contractions to perform these kinds of work may be of 3 types:

1. Isotonic—where the muscle changes length but the degree of force applied remains essentially the same
2. Isometric—muscle length remains the same regardless of any changes in applied force
3. Aucsotonic—muscle length and force applied both change (also "auxotonic")

In addition, muscular force is exhibited athletically in 8 ways: (1) Cyclic Speed, (2) Acyclic Speed, (3) Explosive-Reactive-Ballistic, (4) Explosive Ballistic, (5) Explosive Isometric, (6) Phaso-Tonic, (7) Phasic, and (8) Tonic. In wrestling acyclic speed is present when there is a quick, short-lived movement against minimal resistence—as in an elbow post. Cyclic speed is not present. Explosive-reactive-ballistic movements, where there is a sharp pre-stretch of the muscle followed immediately by concentric work, occur frequently as in a drop step and leg attack. Explosive-ballistic movements, such as in throwing a baseball, do not occur in wrestling. However, explosive-isometric movements are very important. Here a great amount of resistance is overcome, then a high level of tension is maintained as would be the case in a headlock throw to pin. Phaso-tonic work, where dynamic tension can switch rapidly to static, is very common in wrestling as in pummeling to a bodylock. While phasic work is common in cyclic sports, like running or swimming, tonic muscular tension where maximum force is applied for a long period of time is frequent in wrestling, as in a maximum effort to pin an opponent.

The strength that is needed to exhibit these athletic movements is classified in the following terms:

1. Absolute strength—the highest level of strength that can be measured, usually with a dynamometer in an isometric contraction.
2. Maximum strength—the greatest amount of weight that can be lifted in a single attempt.
3. Speed-strength (also referred to as explosive-strength or power)—the ability to generate great force quickly. It is expressed by multiplying the speed of movement times the force of contraction.
4. Strength-endurance (also known as muscular endurance)—the ability of a muscle to continue to work at a high level for a prolonged period of time.

Of these, wrestling is heavily dependent upon speed-strength and strength-endurance. Each of these traits can be classified further. Maximum levels of speed-strength depend upon the level of the athlete's absolute strength. Absolute strength correlates highly with starting strength—the ability to quickly develop force at the beginning of an effort and most particularly when there is greater than 60% of resistence to overcome, as in wrestling. Once inertia is overcome, acceleration-strength quickly raises the muscular tension to its maximum. Then absolute speed multiplies the effect. In order to develop the wrestler's highest level of speed-strength, exercises must be selected and performed in a manner that considers each of the above interrelationships.

Strength-endurance falls into two categories, both applicable to wrestling. There is dynamic-strength-endurance as when, for example, repeated attacks of high intensity must be carried out for a long period of time. There is static-strength-endurance as when one hold must be secured with a high state of tension for a long period of time, such as a front headlock. An athlete may exhibit local-strength-endurance, as in the gripping endurance of the forearms, for example, yet lack general-strength-endurance, where a large number of muscle groups are involved. Each of these can be trained independently of the others, so it is of critical importance to know exactly which strength quality is needed by the athlete and exactly how it is to be developed.

Relative strength is important for wrestlers, particularly the lighter weights, and is expressed as the ratio between an athlete's weight and his absolute strength level. For heavyweights this is not a consideration.

Another concept that is important is the concept of strength reserve, expressed as the difference between absolute strength and the strength needed to perform a skill. Obviously a wrestler with a higher level of absolute strength will experience less fatigue when performing a few repetitions of a given movement than a wrestler with a lower level of strength. Among other things this is a recognition of the fact that the development of maximum strength can have a very beneficial effect on strength-endurance.

THE VARIABLES OF TRAINING

Once the physical requirements of the sport are understood and specific strength qualities are targeted for development, the training plan can be formulated. In the beginning stages of development virtually anything will cause positive changes in the level of physical preparation of the wrestler. Untrained subjects will respond to any training stimulus. That does not mean that every training approach is "best" or even good. The correctness of a training plan can only be determined after many months or years of successful application after which the athlete being trained is able to attain increasingly higher levels of performance in a planned manner.

In order to do this the coach must understand the basic variables of training and how to successfully manipulate them to bring about the best results. These training variables are volume, intensity, and density.

The volume of training refers to the total amount of work that is done. This includes the total amount of pounds lifted, expressed in tons, or the total distance covered by running, cycling, or swimming. It also refers to the total number of repetitions performed during the training session. Relative volume is an expression of the length of time involved in practice and is nonspecific as to the activity level of that practice. A practice three hours long has a higher relative volume than one two hours long. Absolute volume, on the other hand, refers to the actual amount of work performed by an individual athlete. For example, performing 25 fireman's carries during a given unit of time is an expression of greater absolute volume than performing 15 during the same time.

Increasing the volume of training over time to reach an optimal level is an essential feature of modern training leading to advanced results. One thousand hours a year seems to be the entry volume for senior level wrestlers capable of placing at international competitions. Raising the volume of training to this level confers several benefits. The athlete's body responds to the increasing demands made upon it by elevating its ability to recover, and the higher number of repetitions greatly enhances skill development. It is best to increase the number of practice sessions per week rather than add to the length of individual workouts. A note of caution: too rapid or drastic increases in volume will result in a breakdown in the athlete's ability to adapt. Lower performance and even injury or illness will be the consequence.

In strength training absolute volume is predominantly used as the yardstick and is expressed as the total number of repetitions of a given exercise and all exercises combined. In weight training specifically the volume is expressed in tonnage and is calculated by multiplying the number of repetitions by the weight lifted and calculating in the number of sets. Thus, a hundred-pound weight pressed eight times equals 800 pounds total volume and would be written $\frac{100}{8}$. If three sets were performed, the exercise prescription would be written $\frac{100}{8}$ 3 and would equal 2400 pounds in tonnage.

Volume should be manipulated by the coach in the overall training plan in a progressive fashion. Once athletes have adapted to a certain quantity of work, a higher state of preparation can be achieved by increasing the total volume. Volume may be increased by lengthening the individual workout, increasing the number of workouts per week, increasing the number of repetitions, or by increasing the distance covered, as in road work. The usual method is adding to the total number of training sessions per training cycle, for example, going from 5 to 9 per week. This can be very effective so long as the athlete's ability to adapt is not exceeded.

The intensity of training is an expression

of the quality of work performed. It is usually expressed as a percent of maximal effort. For runners or swimmers maximal effort is expressed in time for a distance and repeats may be done at a certain percent of the athlete's best time for an event. The intensity of work can also be calculated by taking a 10-second pulse count to determine heart rate. A 10-second count is preferred, because the rapid drop in heart rate after exercise can cause inaccuracies. The resulting count is then multiplied by six to get beats per minute. The maximum value is 220 beats per minute at birth with one subtracted for every year in age. Several levels of intensity can then be set up and monitored by the coach to determine what percent of effort the athlete is expending. An excellent 7-level system would be: (1) 25-26 beats, the lowest level at which senior level athletes would achieve a training effect, (2) 26-27, (3) 27-28, (4) 28-29, (5) 20-30, (6) 30-31, and (7) 31-33, maximum training intensity leading rapidly to exhaustion. Using this method the required percent of effort can be calculated and planned for every stage of practice.

Increases in the intensity of training are a very important part of the progression that ultimately leads to peak performance. Once adaptation at a certain level of intensity is achieved the level of intensity—percent of effort—must be raised in order to create further upward adaptations. A caveat must be issued here: raising the intensity too high and too soon for the organism to adapt can bring about rapid decreases in performance and a state of overtraining. Injuries are likely to occur. Increasing the intensity too rapidly while having too little regard for the athlete's ability to recuperate is perhaps the biggest fundamental mistake that coaches make at every level. The coach should proceed with a degree of caution and a well thought out plan.

In strength training, intensity is expressed as a percent of maximum strength, the greatest weight that can be lifted in a given exercise for one repetition. This is known as the one-repetition-maximum or 1RM. Performing 5 repetitions each at 85% of 1RM would be written in this manner: $\frac{85}{5}$. A group of athletes following this exercise prescription would calculate individual weights based on each person's 1RM.

An athlete with a 200-pound 1RM would perform $\frac{170}{5}$ and 850 in tonnage, while an athlete with a 175-1RM in the same lift would perform $\frac{150}{5}$ or 750 pounds in tonnage. Both would be achieving the same training effect.

Intensity may be increased several ways, not just in terms of percent of 1RM. The speed of movement of an exercise may be increased. The rest interval between sets or between exercises may be decreased. The density or frequency of training may be increased and so may the number of planned competitions. All of these factors will raise the level of intensity of the training cycle.

The density of training refers to the frequency with which training stimuli are applied. It is used to balance work and rest in training. It can also be utilized by the coach in a progressive fashion. It is extremely important to arrive at the optimal density in training so that the amount of rest is appropriate for the amount of work. Obviously a supplementary practice conducted four hours after a hard training session is going to be much more stressful than one conducted with an eight-hour interval. The same is true within a training session. An extremely demanding bout of exercise followed by another intense effort 15 seconds later is obviously much more stressful than the same exercise prescription with a three-minute rest interval. The work/rest ratio is very important.

In strength training the density is typically expressed as the rest interval between sets. It is also expressed as the traditional "every other day" advice given to weight trainees. It is important to recognize that strength stimuli must be introduced on a regular basis or no training effect will occur due to the density being too low. On the other hand, repeated stimuli with too little rest scheduled will lead quickly to a state of overtraining due to excessive density in the training plan.

These factors are all interrelated. Each affects the others and, in turn, the body's ability to adapt during the training process. Generally training begins with a gradual build-up in the volume of work. During this time the intensity level must be kept low. Additional workouts may be added to increase the density of training and work may be repeated within a workout on fairly short rest. The level of intensity is then increased while the volume of training goes down and the density decreases, affording athletes more time to recuperate from more stressful loads. Eventually, peak performances occur when the volume of training approaches its lowest point during the training cycle and intensity reaches its highest point. This must be planned in a scientifically sound manner for the desired results to be achieved.

Problems always occur when coaches attempt to maintain a high volume of training while increasing the level of intensity. The ability of the athlete is exceeded and breakdowns occur. This fact is very difficult for many American coaches to understand. All have been reared on a 4-month season which constitutes their training "year." Competitions typically begin 2-3 weeks after the start of practices, so the level of intensity begins high and stays high. There is very little change in the volume of training and no let up in the intensity. Many athletes approach the final competitions of the year drained—physically at their weakest and psychologically most vulnerable just when the opposite outcome is desired. This approach may get thousands of high school, even college, wrestlers through their seasons, but it simply will not stand up to the rigors of international competition where clashes in training philosophy become more evident in the results that are achieved, long term. There is a better way.

A word must be said about the nervous system. Coaches typically think in terms of training the muscles and the circulatory system. It is important to recognize, however, that the nervous system also bears a very heavy load. The regeneration of a nerve cell takes seven times longer than a muscle cell. Championships are won on nerves. Therefore, it is critical that adequate rest be designed into the overall program.

PRINCIPLES OF STRENGTH TRAINING

Strength training is done for two reasons: to increase performance and to prevent or recuperate from injuries. The training plan should be scrutinized for these two objectives. Any exercises which do not contribute to these ob-jectives should be eliminated. For example, the concentration curl is a shaping exercise from the sport of bodybuilding that is designed to put a peak on the biceps. It has no place in the training of wrestlers.

The volume of training must range between 10 and 35 total repetitions per exercise in order to elicit the strength training effect. Repetitions fewer than 10 will not cause an adaptation. Repetitions in excess of 35 will cause an adaptation toward endurance and not strength. In the first case undertraining occurs. In the second case overtraining occurs. As training advances over the length of an athlete's career the volume must also advance.

The intensity of training must range between 60 to 90% of 1RM to elicit a training effect. Young athletes will experience significant strength gains with 50-60% intensities while elite athletes will have to work with 70-85%. Rarely is time devoted to 90-95% as overtraining can occur quickly.

The density of training must provide for no more than 72 hours between maximal strength stimuli, or the training effect will be lost. It is true that beginners may experience strength gains from as little as one workout per week, but the rule should be no less than three and no more than five workouts per week. Older athletes may require an increased density as a training stimulus. It is possible to train for strength every day . . . weightlifters do. The most important thing here is to change the volume within a wide range while varying the intensity of effort within a smaller range. For example, legs may be worked Monday with full squats at the following intensities: $\frac{50}{6}$ $\frac{60}{5}$ $\frac{70}{3}$ $\frac{75}{3}$ 3 for a total of 29 repetitions. On Tuesday front squats may be done at $\frac{50}{3}$ $\frac{60}{3}$ $\frac{70}{3}$ 3 for a total of 15 repetitions. Note that there is nearly a 50% change in the volume but only a 5% change in the intensity from day to day.

The principle of variety is paramount. This is little more than a recognition of the fact that the body is an adaptive organism. Frequent changes in environment and external stimuli cause frequent adaptations. Therefore, frequent variability must be built into the training program. As examples of this principle it is known that varying intensities within a training program create greater strength gains over a longer period of time than attempting to use the same intensities. The same is true of volume, and coaches will have the greatest success in their strength programs where wide range of volume is planned.

Alternating heavy, light, and moderate workouts has been shown to cause greater strength gains over a longer period of time than a constant dose of heavy workouts. They should be a part of the weekly training plan. Monthly training plans must be of different intensity weeks. The yearly plan should be composed of different intensity months, and the quadrennial plan must incorporate different levels of overall stress for different years.

It is very important, too, that a planned "light" day remain light. A common mistake is overtraining on light days. For example, the coach may plan a heavy day for Monday, so squats are done at heavy loads. Because the athlete's legs are fatigued, no running is done. Tuesday is the planned "light" day in which squats with very few repetitions and less weight are done or even no squats at all. Because the athlete's legs are not fatigued, the coach plans a three-mile run. This, in effect, turns the "light" day into a heavy day. The result is that the athlete goes hard on Monday with squats, then hard on Tuesday with running. Therefore, there is inadequate rest, and leg strength will not increase at an optimal rate. Instead squat heavy on Monday and run hard on Monday, too. Make Tuesday a light day, and greater progress will be made.

A wide range of exercises should be planned into the training program rather than a narrow range. A variety of exercises provides balanced development and forces the muscle to adapt to many different angles of pull. This promotes joint stability. In addition, it helps reduce the potential for overuse injuries. Change exercises regularly.

Lifting at various speeds has also been shown to create greater strength gains. Lifting at the same tempo (i.e., "two counts up; four counts down") should be avoided. How is speed controlled? It is easiest to tell the athlete, "Lower the weight under control. Then accelerate the weight upwards as fast as you can while main-

taining strict form." The weight of the resistance is thereby used to affect the variable of speed. With lighter weights the acceleration and resulting speed of movement will be high. With heavier weights acceleration and speed will be lower. In this manner variety in the speed of lifting is assured.

Plan to work the entire body in each strength session. It is a mistake to plan an upper body workout for one day and a lower body workout for another day. It is incorrect to think in terms of body parts. Wrestling is a sport that uses the whole body all of the time in a coordinated fashion.

SETS, REPS, AND LOADS

Properly distributing the volume (sets and reps) for a desired outcome is critical in determining the effect that the strength program will have on the development of an athlete's strength qualities. The recommended 10 to 35 total reps per exercise can be arranged in many different ways as can the percent of effort. The coach must know exactly what strength qualities will be developed with each combination, and both when and where that combination is to be introduced into the training plan or excluded from it.

Sets of seven to ten repetitions or more will develop more muscle mass than any other combination. If this regime is followed for a long period of time, however, it will actually cause a loss of strength. The same regime may also cause a loss of speed over time. Sets of ten may certainly be used, but they must be used for a restricted period of time, unless, of course, the objective in training is an increase in muscle mass or an increase in endurance.

On the other end of the spectrum sets of one to three with 75-90% loads and up generate the greatest possible increases in strength, with 85% loads being the generally accepted threshold for the development of maximum strength in mature athletes. Sets of 1-3 reps emphasizing lighter weights with 70-85% of 1RM and a faster tempo will develop the greatest degree of speed-strength. Sets of 1-3 will not cause a significant increase in muscle size.

A brief look at two classes of athletes will

readily illustrate the training outcomes described above. Bodybuilders train in the realm of 8-10 reps and develop huge muscle mass. However, they are not nearly as strong as Olympic weight-lifters who train in the realm of 1-3 reps. Weightlifters are measureably much stronger and quicker, but their muscle mass is much less. They are muscularly more efficient, and this is the attribute that is desired in wrestlers as well.

In between are sets of 4 to 6 reps which generate increases in strength, but not as much as sets of 1-3. This regimen also has a positive effect on speed of movement but, again, not as much as sets of 1-3. Finally, sets of 4-6 will cause muscle hypertrophy but not as much as sets of 7-10.

It is possible to combine elements of each of these together to achieve mixed results as well as focusing on one element at a time. For example, where the main objective is maximum strength for an acyclic sport such as wrestling the following workout may be followed: $\frac{85\%}{5}$ $\frac{95\%}{2\text{-}3}$ $\frac{100\%}{1}$ $\frac{95\%}{2\text{-}3}$. Younger athletes would perform 3-5 sets; elite athletes would perform 5 to 8 sets. Where speed-strength is the main objective explosive movements can be performed: $\frac{50}{3}$ 2 $\frac{60}{3}$ $\frac{70}{3}$ $\frac{80}{3}$ 3. Hypertrophy and strength may be increased together by using something like this $\frac{55}{8}$ $\frac{65}{6}$ $\frac{75}{5}$ $\frac{85}{3}$ 3. These are examples of what can be done. The coach can be creative in adapting these principles to the training of his athletes. There is no single formula that can be followed by all athletes at all times.

APPLYING THE LOAD

There are five main forms of applying the training stimulus.

1. The same load is applied continuously. For example, $\frac{70}{10}$ 3. [This is the least effective means as it violates the principle of variable loads.]

2. The load increases in ladder-type progression. For example, $\frac{50}{6}$ $\frac{60}{5}$ $\frac{70}{5}$ $\frac{80}{5}$ 2.

3. The load increases in a step-like fashion. For example, $\frac{60}{4}$ 2 $\frac{70}{4}$ 2 $\frac{80}{4}$ 3.

4. The load increases and decreases in a pyramid-like manner. For example, $\frac{85}{3}$ $\frac{95}{3}$ $\frac{100}{1}$ 3 $\frac{95}{3}$ $\frac{85}{3}$.

5. The load alternates in intensity in a wave-like design. For example, $\frac{60}{5}$ $\frac{70}{5}$ $\frac{65}{5}$ $\frac{75}{5}$ $\frac{70}{5}$ $\frac{80}{5}$.

THE PERIODIZATION OF STRENGTH

The development of strength is most effective when a plan is followed which attempts to bring about successive muscular adaptations by stages. Each stage has different objectives with different levels of volume and intensity of effort which are appropriate for achieving those objectives.

The first stage is the conditioning or hypertrophy stage. It is the purpose of this stage to lay the physiological base for more intense efforts later. It is characterized by the highest volume of the training year and the lowest intensity. Among the benefits to be seen during this stage is an increase in lean body mass and an elevation in the anaerobic capacity of the body. These adaptations are achieved through 3 to 4 sets of 8-10 repetitions per exercise at intensities which may approach 75% of 1RM or slightly above. The length of this training period varies with the needs of the individual athlete. A well-developed elite athlete may spend only two weeks in this regime. A younger athlete in need of greater muscle size may spend four weeks in this stage. [Remember that elite athletes may see a decrease in their 1RM during this type of training.] The following is a good example of a simple training plan during the conditioning phase: $\frac{50}{10}$ $\frac{60}{10}$ $\frac{70}{10}$ 2. A progression in intensity with a subsequent reduction in volume might look like this: $\frac{50}{8}$ $\frac{65}{8}$ $\frac{75}{8}$ 2.

The next stage is commonly referred to as the basic strength phase. It is during this stage that the broadest development of strength typically takes place. It continues for a period of four to five weeks. The volume is reduced, and the intensity level is again raised. An example might be $\frac{65}{5}$ $\frac{75}{5}$ $\frac{85}{5}$ 3. Note that the aforementioned maximal strength threshold of 85% for mature athletes is a part of the plan, and very significant increases in maximum strength will occur.

Next a brief cycle of two to three weeks is followed which emphasizes maximum strength and speed-strength development. Again the volume goes down as the percent of 1RM goes up, and the planned workload might look something like this $\frac{75}{3}$ $\frac{85}{3}$ $\frac{90}{3}$ 2. At this point the major objectives of the strength development program have been achieved for most athletes and two directions may be taken. The first is to push ahead and strive for a peak in maximum strength or speed-strength performance. The following plan might be used to achieve this: $\frac{50}{3}$ 2 $\frac{70}{2}$ 2 $\frac{80}{2}$ $\frac{90}{2}$ $\frac{100}{1}$ 3. The second course is to strive to maintain the levels of strength which have been developed while seeking to focus more energy on other elements in preparation, and tactics, for example. In order to do this, training stimuli within the maximum strength threshold must be applied on a weekly basis. For example, $\frac{65}{5}$ $\frac{75}{3}$ $\frac{85}{3}$ 2. If this is not done, strength loss will be rapid.

This typical model is more plastic than it seems on paper and can be molded to fit any strength need. For example, in a 15-week period a program emphasizing maximum strength development could devote 2 weeks to conditioning, 3 to basic strength, and 8 to maximum strength, with 2 weeks for peaking. In another 15-week plan emphasizing hypertrophy, 6 weeks could be allocated to higher volume sets of 8-10, 4 to basic strength, 3 to maximum strength, and 2 to achieving peak performance.

STRENGTH TRAINING WITHIN THE YEARLY PLAN

The periodization of strength must occur within the larger framework of the wrestler's overall yearly training plan. It is a mistake to plan for a peak in maximum strength, for example, at the end of the yearly training cycle. This would be appropriate for a competitive weightlifter, but in wrestling the championship will be won on many other factors besides strength. The dominant physical characteristics will be speed-strength and strength-endurance in addition to the role that maximum strength may play, and matches will be won or lost on the wrestler's ability to formulate a tactical plan and carry it out with technical execution.

Therefore, the special physical qualities that are essential to execute technical elements are what is needed. It is known that these special physical qualities cannot be developed to their fullest athletic potential through execution of the technique alone. It is too difficult to apply the training principles of volume and intensity, and the focus is too narrow. Instead, special abilities should be derived from a broader base of highly developed general strength which is then converted into the special strength needs of the wrestler.

A high level of general strength comes first, then, in the yearly training plan of the wrestler. This is followed by the development of specific strength and then followed by special adaptations. In developing the muscles of the neck, for example, shoulder shrugs and a headstrap may be used to develop the general strength of the muscles involved. This higher level of general strength can then be converted to specific strength in the next phase as barbell pullovers are done from the neck bridge position. Finally, special strength is developed through competitive bridging drills with a partner on top in one hold or another. So there is general strength, strength which is specific to the sport, and special strength, which applies to a narrowly defined situation within the sport.

This is not to say that during one portion of the year a single form of training is done to the exclusion of all others. Neck bridging, for example, will always be a natural part of a wrestler's activity so long as he is on the mat wrestling. It is the emphasis on each exercise or activity and the time allotted to each that is referred to in planning.

THE YEARLY PLAN

The training year is divided into two main parts: Preparation and Competition. The preparation period is further sub-divided into general preparation and specific preparation, roughly analogous to the traditional "off-season" and "pre-season." The competition period ("in-season") is also divided into pre-competition and competition. Finally, at the end of the year a period of time is planned for active rest and recuperation known as the transition period. The strength development of the wrestler throughout these periods is diagrammed (next page).

The objective of the first phase in training is the development of a broad base of general

PERIODS	PREPARATORY		COMPETITIVE			TRANSITION
	General Preparation	Specific Preparation	Pre-Competition	Competition		Transition
	1	2	3	4	5	
	Conditioning or Hypertrophy	Basic Strength to Maximum Strength	Conversion to Speed-Strength & Strength-Endurance	Maintenance	Cessation	

strength employing a wide range of exercises to strengthen the muscles and tendons and prepare them for the heavier work which lies ahead. Elite athletes may plan as little as two weeks in this phase, normally 3-4 weeks long, while young wrestlers may plan as much as 6 weeks. It is very important to begin the training year with this build-up in general strength, because it leads to fewer training injuries as time wears on.

The second phase of training shifts the emphasis through basic strength to the acquisition of maximum strength. In wrestling the ultimate goals are speed-strength (for scoring) and strength-endurance (for lasting). Neither can reach their highest potential without the development of maximum strength. The duration of this phase depends upon the maximum strength needs of the athlete but generally lasts from 6 to 8 weeks.

The third phase of training seeks to convert the maximum strength which has been developed into speed-strength (power) and strength-endurance (muscular endurance)—the specific strength qualities needed for wrestling. Roughly equal consideration must be given to both. In addition the level of maximum strength during the specific preparation and pre-competition period must be kept high or a lowered 1RM will ultimately be reflected too early in reduced power during the specific preparation and pre-competition periods. A method that has been successfully utilized in Bulgaria is to plan a strength-endurance based workout on Mondays, a maximal strength workout on Wednesdays, and a speed-strength workout on Fridays. Why this order? Because the first day of a training week is not the best time to reach maximal lifts, and the best outcome in speed-strength comes after maximal strength work.

During the fourth phase, corresponding to the competition period, the main objective is the maintenance of the maximum strength and speed-strength that has been acquired and further development of strength-endurance. The ratio of time devoted to each of these is a direct reflection of the needs of the individual athlete and the demands of the sport. Generally, weight room sessions are reduced to two in a weekly microcycle. One is a heavy day, devoted to maximal strength and explosive speed-strength. The other is a light day, devoted more to speed-strength. Strength-endurance may be developed in additional weight sessions or in more wrestling related activities, usually arranged in a circuit-like fashion.

A fifth phase lies at the end of the competition period and is the cessation phase. Approximately one week before the major competition of the year strength training ceases. This is necessary so that the athlete is fully rested and ready for a peak performance.

At the end of the competition period wrestling ends, and the emphasis is on rest and relaxation during the transition period. However, this is also the time that strength training may be performed for the rehabilitation of injuries. This period must not be longer than a couple of weeks or the athlete will rapidly begin to lose all of the gains that he has made during the last training year.

ADAPTING THE PRINCIPLES OF PLANNING

Those few coaches who have the ability to train their athletes on a year 'round basis are fortunate and can fully utilize the yearly approach for the development of strength which has been outlined here. Many coaches, however, have little control over their athletes aside from a restricted period of time.

Nonetheless the broad principles of yearly planning can be adapted to fit any situation.

Simply outline the time that is available for preparation. Then divide that time up into the appropriate training stages, maintaining the proper balance between them. Athletes can be given a periodized strength program that they are responsible for during the "off season," which will culminate in maximum strength development. If the coach can then direct them several weeks prior to the start of the season (the "pre-season"), the conversion to speed-strength and strength-endurance can begin. Once the season begins and competition occurs, the rest of the training plan can be followed as it has been presented.

FORMS OF STRENGTH TRAINING

There are many forms of strength training that can be adapted by the coach to fit the needs of his athletes. These range from highly sophisticated machines with sprockets, gears, and cables to simple calisthenic exercises such as push-ups, where the athlete's body weight is all that is needed. Here is a partial list:

- medicine balls
- gymnastics apparatus (parallel and horizontal bars, stall bars)
- rubber or spring cables, elastic bands, hand grippers
- weighted bags
- manual labor (chopping wood, "bucking" bales of hay, etc.)
- partner assisted or resisted exercises
- calisthenics
- throwing dummies
- climbing ropes, nets
- wall pulleys
- barbells and dumbbells, "free" weights
- machines

The coach must wisely make use of the best means available to him. The ideal training room for wrestling would be equipped with climbing ropes, pull-up and dip bars, an assortment of throwing dummies (optimal results are achieved when the weight of the dummy is 40-60% of the wrestler's bodyweight), medicine balls, and free weights.

Free weights are to be preferred over machine exercises. Why? The most glaring weakness of machines is that most work only one muscle, across one joint, in isolation in what is known as an open kinetic chain. In wrestling no muscle is used in isolation. Therefore, machine training is the farthest removed from the manner in which muscles are actually used in wrestling. In using machines the athlete has to accommodate himself to the limited movement of the machine, whereas in wrestling he must accommodate himself to unlimited motions requiring complex interactions between muscle groups. Machines are also a potential cause of muscle imbalances, because they do not work the assistance or stabilizing muscles. Finally, machines do not adequately provide for explosive efforts that are necessary for the development of speed-strength. For these reasons machines should not be used as the means for developing strength in wrestling.

Free weights, barbells, and dumbbells offer the wrestler the opportunity to work many muscle groups at one time (efficient use of time) in multi-joint, closed kinetic chain movements. All of the assisting or stabilizing muscles can be brought into play which insures well-rounded development, and the speed of movement can be controlled from very slow to very fast. Finally, many exercises can be creatively employed which mimick movements or postures in wrestling. This enhances the adaptation of strength to the requirements of the sport. In addition it is very critical to use climbing ropes, medicine balls, throwing dummies, and other exercises to round out the athlete's complete development.

THE EXERCISES

There are three different types of exercises typically found in strength training programs. There are exercises which emphasize the speed of movement. There are exercises which emphasize the development of strength. There are exercises which are designed to work a specific muscle or muscle group.

Though any exercise can be done fast, certain exercises have a quick component by virtue of the tempo required for correct performance. They are particularly useful in developing the quickness of athletes and their speed-strength potential. These include the snatch, the clean, the jerk, and variations of these lifts. [These quick lifts should be learned from a USAW certified club or senior level weightlifting coach.] Here are the main ones found in strength programs:

A. Power Cleans (squat or split style)
1. clean pulls
2. clean grip power shrugs
3. clean from hang or from boxes
4. combination cleans from various heights or with stops
5. dumbbell cleans
B. Power Snatch (squat or split style)
1. snatch pulls
2. snatch grip power shrugs
3. snatch grip high pulls
4. snatch from hang or on boxes
5. combination snatches from various heights or with stops
6. dumbbell snatches
C. Split Jerk (from the rack or from a clean)
1. jerk behind neck
2. push jerk, in front or behind neck
3. dumbbell jerk
4. push jerk
5. push press in front or behind neck

The benefits of these exercises accrue from the fact that a very large number of muscles are used in overcoming resistence quickly. Therefore, they mimick the energy requirements of the explosive movements in wrestling. Speed may also be enhanced by use of medicine balls, throwing dummies, or other means.

Strength exercises typically include those where a large group of muscles will have a large working effect on the body. They include all forms of squatting, pressing, and certain forms of deadlifts and rowing.

A. Squats
1. full or back squat
2. front squat
3. step-ups
4. split squats, back squats, and lunges
B. Presses
1. military press, in front or behind neck
2. dumbbell and alternate dumbbell presses
3. bench press and incline bench press
4. bench or incline bench dumbbell presses and alternate presses

C. Deadlifts/Rows
1. bent-legged or "clean" deadlifts
2. deadlifts from boxes
3. bent over barbell rows
4. dumbbell rows

Exercises for specific muscle groups allow the athlete to target weak areas and correct muscle imbalances. Very often, however, athletes get side-tracked onto these types of exercises, and they begin to dominate the training process. The coach must be firm and insist that well-chosen exercises from the speed and strength groups be done first. The saying is true, "If you develop the big muscles, the little ones will take care of themselves." Common auxillary exercises include the following:

A. Legs
1. leg extensions
2. leg curls
3. heel raises
4. leg presses
B. Lower Back
1. deadlifts
2. good mornings
3. hyperextensions
C. Upper Back
1. barbell and dumbbell rows
2. lat pull-downs and pulley rows
3. pull-ups and chin-ups
D. Shoulders
1. barbell and dumbbell presses
2. dumbbell raises—lateral, front, and rear
3. upright rows
4. dips
E. Chest
1. flyes with dumbbells, cables
2. bent arm and straight arm pull-overs, barbell or dumbbell
F. Arms
1. triceps presses, barbell and dumbbell
2. biceps curls, barbell and dumbbell
G. Forearms
1. wrist curls, in front and behind back, reverse and regular
2. reverse curls
3. plate gripping and hand grippers
H. Neck, Trapezius
1. shrugs

2. headstrap
3. 4-way neck machine
4. neck bridging

I. Abdominals, Obliques
   1. leg raises and knee lifts done lying, inclined, or hanging
   2. sit-ups, reverse sit-ups, crunches
   3. side bends and twisting movements with barbell or dumbbell

VISUAL TECHNICAL LIFTING SKILLS

Many of the lifts illustrated here are quite complicated, but an effort has been made to simplify them for ease of understanding. The main coaching points are mentioned; so that the coach will be able to direct his athletes with a degree of confidence. It is essential that athletes be coached at all times, most especially when they are in the weight room. No coach can hope to achieve great success in wrestling by giving his athletes a written practice, and then asking them to follow it on their own. The same is true in strength training. For best results the coach must be in the weight room with the athletes whenever they lift.

In Figure 18-1 the hook grip is illustrated. This grip must be used for all pulling movements, because it is the strongest grip. Approximately 50 pounds more weight can be held without slipping when using this grip. To do it properly the thumb is wrapped around the bar first. Then the index finger closes tightly over the top of the thumb and the middle finger does the same, effectively "welding" what would otherwise be an open link in the chain. The remaining two fingers wrap around the bar.

Figure 18-1

In Figure 18-2 one method for determining the proper width of the snatch grip is shown. A tape measure is used to determine the exact length from the acromio-clavicular joint of one shoulder to the second knuckle of the outstretched other arm. The tape is then stretched along the bar, and the athlete begins the grip with wrapping his thumbs at the measured points.

Figure 18-2

The Power Snatch: The starting position is shown in Figure 18-3 for the power snatch. The feet are placed hip-width apart with the toes pointing out slightly. The bar is directly above the metatarsal-phalangeal joint (where the shoelaces start), not against the shins. The legs are well bent, but the hips remain above the knees. The back is flat with the chest expanded while the head remains neutral. The eyes are fixed on a point straight ahead, 3-4 meters distant. The shoulders are in front of the bar. Arms are straight and relaxed with the elbows turned out. Hands are spaced wide in the snatch-width grip described above. The hook grip is used (see Figure 18-1).

Figure 18-3

In the lift-off (Figure 18-4) the pull begins with the legs and hips beginning to extend. The path of the bar is back somewhat as the body-weight shifts from mid-foot toward the heel. The shoulders stay in front of the bar, and the hips and the shoulders keep the same angle as the legs begin the lift, easing the weight off the platform.

Figure 18-4

As the bar clears the knees the mid-thigh or power position is achieved and the weight is rapidly accelerated with a violent, explosive muscular contraction of the lower back as well as the hips and legs as the weight shifts forward from the heels back through the mid-foot position. The shoulders remain in front of the bar as it brushes the legs where they join with the hips (Figure 18-5).

Figure 18-5

There is complete extension of the body as ears, shoulders, hips, knees, and ankles form a straight line, just like a vertical jump attempt. The athlete is up on his toes (Figure 18-6). The arms are straight but relaxed. The lift is done with the legs and back, not the arms. Coaches should watch the elbows to look for arms bent too soon. A wrist curl is done to bring the weight in close to the body, and it should move up along the body with just a fraction of an inch of space. The head stays neutral, and lifting it up or lowering it reduces the strength of pull. There should be a big shrug of the shoulders . . . shoulders move straight up to the ears.

Figure 18-6

The violent extension of the body causes the bar to continue to move upwards until the point of zero gravity is reached, where it is neither going up but has not yet started to fall. At this point the athlete must quickly go under the bar in the unsupported phase of the lift. The arms pull up, with the elbows staying as high above the bar as possible (Figure 18-7a). Dropping the elbows too early weakens the pull. The legs bend again as the feet quickly split apart to squat-width position (Figure 18-7b).

(a)

(b)

Figure 18-7

As the feet contact the floor, the arms/elbows quickly turn under the bar and lock it overhead. This is an extremely fast pull/press movement. The bar is caught behind the ears as the head moves forward under it (Figure 18-8). This is similar to a Greco-Roman duck under. At the end of this quick support phase the athlete stands erect and takes two very small steps to return his feet to hip-width position.

Figure 18-8

The Split Snatch: The split snatch is performed exactly the same as the power snatch through the entire pull phase. The difference lies in what the legs and feet do during the unsupported phase, splitting apart. The forward foot stomps on the platform with the toes pointing in (Figure 18-9) and the ankle is farther ahead than the knee. The shin is perpendicular to the floor, leg well bent, and the rear leg is flexed at the knee, toes pointing forward or pigeon-toed. A straight, perpendicular balance line should be formed through the ear, shoulder, and hip. The bar is caught behind the ear as before. During the recovery the forward leg must step back first (Figure 18-10). Then the rear leg steps forward until both feet are even, hip-width apart, bar locked out overhead.

Figure 18-9

Power Clean: In the starting position for the power clean (Figure 18-11) the same fundamentals can be seen as for the power snatch—feet hip-width apart, toes out, bar directly above the metatarsal-phalangeal joint, weight on the mid-foot (athlete should be able to wiggle his toes), legs well bent, chest expanded, back flat and locked with a neutral head. The shoulders are in front of the bar, arms relaxed and straight with the elbows turned out. The difference is that the hands are spaced shoulder-width apart. A hook grip is used.

Figure 18-11

In the lift-off the same fundamentals apply as described in the power snatch—bar travels back, body weight shifts back, the legs lift while the angle of inclination of the back stays the same (Figure 18-12).

Figure 18-10

Figure 18-12

Once the bar clears the knees, the power position is achieved and a tremendous explosion of muscular force occurs, just as in the snatch. The main point is to keep the arms straight and relaxed. The back, legs, and hips should do all the lifting (Figure 18-13). At the top of the pull there should be a big shrug of the shoulders as the body reaches complete extension up on the toes (Figure 18-14). Coaches should watch their athlete's elbows as the arms should remain straight and a wrist curl is emphasized to keep the bar close to the body. The bar should be lightly grazing the body all the way up on both the power snatch and the power clean.

The violent acceleration of the bar causes it to continue to travel upwards until the point of zero gravity is reached. At that instant the athlete must go under the bar. The elbows now lift up, staying above the bar as long as possible. If the elbows drop, the pull will not be as high or strong. Legs quickly bend and feet quickly split to the sides to squat-width position (Figure 18-5). Then the bar is racked in the support phase. The arms relax as the pull ceases and switch to quickly rotating under the bar and forward. The elbows come up to approach horizontal position in front as the bar contacts the shoulders. The bar must be supported on the shoulders, not on the wrists (Figure 18-16). The athlete straightens both legs and takes two very small steps to bring the feet back to hip-width position.

Figure 18-13

Figure 18-15

Figure 18-14

Figure 18-16

Split Clean: Exactly the same coaching points are followed all the way as in the power clean except for movement of the legs and feet. In the unsupported phase the legs split apart, one fore and one aft. Just as in the split snatch, the forward leg stomps on the platform with the tibia perpendicular, ankle ahead of knee, pigeon-toed. The rear leg is bent with the toes pointing straight ahead or in, not out to the side (Figure 18-17). It is absolutely essential that the torso be lined up so a perpendicular can be drawn through ear, shoulder, and hip. In the recovery the forward leg must push backwards and then take a step backwards first. The rear leg then moves up.

Figure 18-17

Full Back Squat: Nothing beats squats. One experiment after another has compared the strength of legs developed by squats to the strength of legs developed by other means. Squats have been shown to be consistently superior. There is something about doing leg work in the vertical plane that confers maximum benefit, and no amount of leg presses, leg extensions, etc. can come close to a simple regimen that includes squats.

To begin, the bar is placed on the trapezius, not the spine, as the shoulder blades are pinched together. The athlete should always face the rack, lift the weight off with both legs, and step backwards. It is easier to go forward when tired after a very heavy and fatiguing set of squats than to go backwards. The chest is

lifted up, and the back is locked out tightly. The head is neutral, eyes straight ahead. The feet are spaced shoulder-width apart or wider, toes pointing out (Figure 18-18).

Figure 18-18

A deep breath is taken and held while the athlete descends under control to full squat position, thighs a minimum of parallel with the floor, and hips descending between the heels. The back must remain as perpendicular as possible with no forward lean. From this position the athlete brings his hips forward as the legs extend to return to the starting position. The athlete should strive to accelerate the weight upwards and breathe out as the lift nears completion (Figure 18-19).

Figure 18-19

Front Squat: Again, the athlete should face the rack. The bar should be grasped with a clean-width grip and rested on top of the shoulders with the elbows high, just as would be the case for finish position in the power clean. The chest should be lifted up, and the spine locked out. The head stays neutral, eyes looking straight ahead (Figure 18-20). The athlete should take a deep breath of air, hold it, and descend to deep squat position, hips slightly below the knees. The hips should be lowered, under control, between both heels while the back remains flat and tight (Figure 18-21). The legs are then extended as the hips move forward and up. A key point is lifting the elbows up, and concentration on this aspect of the lift promotes the ideal body alignment. The weight should be accelerated upwards, and the athlete breathes outward as the lift is being completed.

Step Ups: This is an outstanding exercise that is being used in place of squats in certain periods of the year by many of the top track and field athletes. It has great value in wrestling, particularly during the specific preparation period, because of the emphasis on single leg extension. The athlete begins with the weight on his shoulders as for back squats. A box or bench is set so that, when the step is made, the forward leg is bent exactly at a 90 degree angle when the rear foot is extended up on the toes (Figure 18-22). The breathing pattern is the same as for squats. The athlete should push down hard on the forward leg until the body comes to an erect position. It is essential to keep the back straight. Any forward lean must be eliminated. The rear leg may come up high in front in a cycling motion (Figure 18-23) or it may just step up on the box. The required number of repetitions is usually performed with one leg first, then the other.

Figure 18-20

Figure 18-21

Figure 18-22

Figure 18-23

STRENGTH TRAINING   145

Split Squat: This is a great exercise to do after squats in the specific preparation period because of the obvious carry over to leg positions frequent in wrestling (leg attack). The bar is grasped between the legs. The feet are on boxes which allows the body to descent into a position of deeper leg flexion. The back must be kept straight. The athlete goes down and up for the required number of repetitions, then switches the opposite leg forward (Figure 18-24).

Figure 18-24

Lunges: This is another great specific strength builder and may be done in a variety of ways—on boxes, stepping onto a low box, cycling the legs, or focusing on one leg at a time. Perhaps the best way is to lunge the length of a gymnasium. This would be very close to duplicating a normal leg stride. Lunges may be done either with the bar resting on the back (back squat position) or on the shoulders (front squat position). Back position and breathing pattern are the same as for squats. The athlete should take care to lower himself slowly into the lunge position before forcefully accelerating the weight upwards, because there is a lot of stretch on the gluteal-proximal hamstring area.

Overhead Movements

A word needs to be said about the proper execution for pressing movements and movements involving the jerk. The shoulder joint is a complex one, and if exercises are done improperly joint instability and lack of flexibility can be unintended outcomes. The athlete should begin every pressing or jerking movement from a dead stop. There should be a one-second pause before beginning each repetition. This forces the body to develop starting strength, and it also prevents shoulder problems that many athletes develop from bouncing or heaving the weight upwards, which adds shock to the shoulder joint. The bar should be accelerated upwards, and the athlete should strive for a snappy lockout. In this way acceleration strength and speed-strength are developed, too, not just maximum strength. In all overhead movements the bar should be locked out behind the ears, bone on bone, and perfectly balanced above the body's center of gravity. This will ensure full range of movement and will maintain the athlete's shoulder flexibility. The lock out position should be held for one second before lowering the bar. This will provide added stimulus to strengthen the tendons and ligaments of the shoulder joint.

Split Jerk: The bar is taken off the rack or cleaned and positioned on the shoulders (Figure 18-25). The chest is expanded and the back locked out as a deep breath is taken prior to beginning the lift. The legs dip down to one quarter squat position (Figure 18-26) while the back stays perfectly vertical. Then the legs explode, driving the bar upwards. There is full and complete extension, up on the toes. The head tilts back slightly to clear the bar (Figure 18-27). Then the legs split forward and backward just as they would for a split snatch (Figure 18-28). The forward leg stomps on the platform, pigeon-toed, with the ankle ahead of the knee. The body drops under the bar to catch it overhead at the moment of zero gravity, and the bar is locked out behind the ears. There should be a crisp, snappy lock-out. In order to keep from losing the lift forward, it is essential that the athlete push off the forward leg and step back first. Then the rear leg is brought forward.

Push Jerk: The same lift can be performed as in steps 1-3 with the athlete then rebending the legs to come under the bar with no split. This is also frequently done with a sidewards split of the legs, exactly the same footwork as is used for a power clean.

Figure 18-25

Figure 18-26

Figure 18-27

Figure 18-28

Push Press: The bar is taken off the rack as it would be for a split jerk or front squat—in clean position, racked on the shoulders (Figure 18-29). The weight may also be cleaned. The legs dip down to quarter squat position (Figure 18-30) just as in the split jerk. There must be a perpendicular relationship between the ears, shoulders, hips, and ankles as viewed from the side. Then the bar is driven upwards by a forceful extension of the legs and an explosive drive from the arms and shoulders (Figure 18-31). The bar is locked out overhead behind the ears as breath is expelled (Figure 18-32) and is held there for a second before being lowered under control. As the bar is lowered for the next repetition the legs bend and give to absorb the shock.

Figure 18-29

Figure 18-31

Figure 18-30

Figure 18-32

Military Press: The military press is done from the same starting position (see Figure 18-29) as the push press, and the lock out position is exactly the same (see Figure 18-32), but there is just no bending and use of the legs.

Press Behind Neck: The bar is taken off the rack as it would be for a full back squat (Figure 18-33). The chest is lifted up, and the lower back is locked tightly as the weight is pushed overhead in a rapid, accelerating movement. The athlete should finish with a snappy lock out of the bar behind the ears (Figure 18-34), hold the weight there for a second, and then lower it under control.

Seated Military Press: The bar should be taken from the rack or cleaned to get it into position on the shoulders. The athlete is then seated. It is very important to keep one leg forward and one leg behind for balance and stability (Figure 18-35). A dangerous situation is created when both feet are forward and the athlete begins to arch back a little with a difficult repetition. This scenario can be avoided with the legs split apart. From this position the bar is pressed overhead following all the guidelines previously discussed (Figure 18-36).

Figure 18-33

Figure 18-35

Figure 18-34

Figure 18-36

Bench Press: This is the most well known of the pressing movements in America, so a photo is not needed. A few words of caution. Bench presses must be done with the same technique as other presses to avoid injury. The bar should be lowered under control and should come to a full stop for one second on the chest. Then the bar should be accelerated overhead, being pressed in an arc from the chest to above the eyes. It should be locked out overhead for one second before being lowered, under control, for the next repetition. The bar should never be bounced on the chest. This is bad for the bars, because they all become bent eventually from this, and it is bad for the shoulders because the weight of the bar plus the speed of descent creates a separating force on the shoulder joint. "Bench press shoulder" is the eventual result. It is also important to use a shoulder width grip, and to wrap the thumb around the bar as well as the fingers. The "thumbless" grip has been the cause of several serious injuries due to the bar slipping backwards off the heels of the hands. A narrower grip is recommended, because a fuller range of motion is provided by using it. A great deal of bench pressing, especially wide grip pressing, will cause a loss in shoulder flexibility over time. The overhead presses should always be a part of any program.

"Clean" Deadlift: This lift begins just as the power clean does. The same starting position is used. The same mechanics are used. The critical point is that a perfectly flat back must be maintained as the weight of the bar increases (Figure 18-37). If the athlete begins to round his back, then the weight lifted must be reduced. The athlete should be stopped whenever his technique deviates from ideal form. The main coaching point is to begin the lift with the legs and hips, while keeping the back flat and tight (Figures 18-38 and 18-39).

Figure 18-38

Figure 18-37

Figure 18-39. Finish position of deadlift.

Stiff-Legged Deadlift: The stiff-legged dead-lift is begun in a standing position with the feet hip-width apart, knees unlocked, and head tilted down (Figure 18-40). The weight is lowered slowly and under control to the floor. There should definitely be no bouncing. Then, keeping the head down, the back is extended. The athlete should try to feel the muscles of the spine work along one vertebra at a time (Figure 18-41). Only light to moderate weights should be used.

*NOTE: there are many deadlift variations—with legs bent, with legs straight, with back rounded, with back flat, with head down, or with head up, and combinations of these. The above version is used almost as a remedial exercise to loosen after a hard workout of repeated tight lower back positions.

Romanian Deadlift: This lift begins with the athlete in a standing position. Feet are hip-width apart, and the bar is grasped with a clean grip. The eyes are fixed at a point on the wall or 3-4 meters ahead. The legs are bent slightly and do not change throughout the lift (Figure 18-42). The weight is lowered slowly in a controlled fashion to a point below the knees, but it is not allowed to touch the floor, causing continuous muscular tension. Only the hip joint moves. The flat back position does not change, neither does the leg angle, and the head stays up, focused on that spot on the wall (Figure 18-43). Fighting to keep the back flat, the weight is returned in a controlled manner to the starting position. The chest should be lifted up and the back tight throughout.

Figure 18-40

Figure 18-42

Figure 18-41

Figure 18-43

Good Morning: Good mornings may be done in many ways, with the legs bent or straight, back curved or flat, and head up or down. In this version the athlete begins with the bar across the upper back similar to back squat position, and the legs are bent. Similar to RDLs, the leg bend stays fixed. The chest is expanded, and the lower back is locked out (Figure 18-44). Keeping the back flat and the head up the athlete bends at the hips only until an angle of inclination approaching horizontal is achieved (Figure 18-45). Keeping the back perfectly flat and the head up the body extends at the hips to return to the starting position.

Seated Good Morning: The athlete begins seated, usually on the end of a bench, with the bar held behind the head, similar to back squat position. The legs may be together or apart, straight or bent. In this version the legs are bent. The athlete begins with the chest expanded and a deep breath (Figure 18-46). Keeping the back flat the athlete bends over only at the waist until the torso attains a horizontal position (Figure 18-47). Then the back is extended to return to the starting position.

Figure 18-44

Figure 18-46

Figure 18-45

Figure 18-47

SELECTION OF EXERCISES

The selection of exercises is based on many factors, but in general terms the level of physical preparation of the athlete and the period of the training year are the main considerations. The level of preparation is based on a full evaluation of the athlete and determines what objectives need to be set. The period of the training year determines the degree of emphasis that is placed on the development of different biomotor abilities. The age of the athlete is considered as is his physical capacity for work and his ability to recuperate. His past training background is important as is his previous adaptation to it. An accurate assessment of the athlete's physical strengths and weaknesses must be made and any injuries or muscle imbalances noted.

All of these considerations can sometimes cause indecisiveness on the part of the coach, but decisions will be simplified if the larger principle can be kept in mind: Always do those exercises first which have the greatest working effect on the entire organism. In plain terms this means that the athlete must squat, do a major pulling movement, and do a major pushing movement during each training session. These represent the "core" lifts and are always a part of the program, because they are the "secret" to great strength. Once this core is established then auxillary exercises can be added to it, beginning with exercises for the center of the body first—the abdominal and lower back area—and radiating outwards from there. Exercises for the extremities are considered last.

Here is an example of a 3-day per week program for a developing athlete during the general preparation stage where conditioning and hypertrophy are the main objectives. The number of exercises and the volume is high while the intensity would remain low.

Monday and Friday
1. Power clean with stops [first rep from the floor, second rep from hang position below the knees, third rep from power position—hang above the knees]
2. Military press/Push press/Split jerk
3. Back squat
4. Bent over barbell row
5. Bench press
6. Stiff-legged deadlift
7. Bent-arm pull overs
8. Barbell curls
9. Lying triceps presses
10. Wrist curls
    Abdominal complex of exercises (example: leg raises + twisting sit-ups + crunches) and neck exercises

Wednesday
1. Power snatch with stops
2. Front squat
3. Good mornings
4. Military press
5. Lat pull-down
6. Incline press
7. Dumbbell pull overs
8. Cambered bar curls
9. Standing triceps press
10. End of bench wrist curls
    Abdominal complex and neck exercises

The main criteria for selection of exercises is met. There is a squatting movement on each day, back squat on Mondays and Fridays and front squat on Wednesdays. There is a big pulling movement each day with the power clean with stops done on Mondays and Fridays, and the power snatch with stops done on Wednesdays. There is also a big pushing movement done each day, with the military press/push press/split jerk done on Mondays and Fridays followed by the bench press and the military press on Wednesdays, followed by the incline press. The abdominal complex and the stiff-legged deadlifts on Mondays and Fridays and good mornings on Wednesdays serve to strengthen the center of the body. This is the heart of the program, and it is as simple as that. To it have been added some other lifts for the purposes of hypertrophy and well-rounded development. Each has to have a rationale. For example, the neck work and wrist curls are added because of the importance of these muscles to the sport of wrestling. A little more work is done on them.

Here is another sample program for use during the general preparation period, the basic strength phase. The total volume of repetitions is reduced, and the intensity is increased.

Monday and Friday

1. Power clean
2. Full squat
3. Split jerk
4. Hyperextensions
5. Bench press
6. Weighted pull-ups
7. 21's (7 lateral raises + 7 front raises + 7 rear raises)
8. Barbell curls
9. Triceps pull over press
10. Wrist roller
    Abdominal complex and neck work

Wednesday

1. Power snatch
2. Front squat
3. Seated good mornings
4. Seated press behind neck
5. Horizontal pulley row
6. Incline press
7. Curls
8. Triceps press
9. Hand gripper
   Abdominal complex and neck work

This program also meets the criteria that have been set down. Note that many of the exercises have been changed from the first program to the second, also that exercises change from Monday to Wednesday and back again on Friday. Along with changing intensities, this provides necessary variation to the training plan. Note that the squats remain a standard feature. They really can't be replaced with any other exercise, and the legs and hips with their large number of muscle fibers can be subjected to a lot more work. So the squats must stay.

As the training shifts from general preparation to specific preparation the emphasis changes to maximum strength development and the conversion to speed-strength and strength-endurance. Not all of this shift in emphasis takes place in the weight room. For example, rope climbing can be added to the training program as a means of converting to specific strength-endurance, and this is done during the wrestling practice session. Exercises may change from week to week as well as from day to day, as is the case in the following weekly examples:

Week 1

Monday
1. Power snatch
2. Power clean
3. Back squat
4. Lunges
5. Bench press
6. Seated good morning

Wednesday
1. Split snatch
2. Clean pull
3. Front squat
4. Weighted dips

Friday
1. Power snatch
2. Power clean
3. Back squat
4. Incline press

Week 2

Monday
1. Split snatch
2. Power clean
3. Split jerk
4. Back squat
5. Incline press
6. Hyperextension

Wednesday
1. Power snatch
2. Clean pull
3. Front squat & lunges
4. Weighted dips

Friday
1. Power snatch
2. Split clean
3. Back squat
4. Bench press
5. Seated good morning

Week 3

Monday
1. Split snatch
2. Power clean
3. Split jerk
4. Clean pull
5. Back squat
6. Incline press
7. Hyperextension

Wednesday
1. Power snatch
2. Clean pull
3. Front squat
4. Weighted dips

Friday
1. Power snatch
2. Split clean
3. Back squat
4. Bench press
5. Seated good morning

Week 4

Monday
1. Split snatch
2. Power clean
3. Split jerk
4. Back squat
5. Incline press
6. Hyperextension

Wednesday
1. Power snatch
2. Split clean
3. Back squat
4. Lunges
5. Bench press

Friday
Off or test

Another feature of the above 4-week mesocycle is the expansion of speed-strength exercises that are done on a daily basis. In the general preparation period the number of these exercises (clean, snatch, or jerk) done daily was one or two. In the specific preparation plan above, however, speed-strength exercises are done as many as four times in one training session (see Monday, Week 3). This is a lot of explosiveness and is very demanding work. Because of the increased level of intensity, the volume of training must go down. Fewer exercises are planned. The rule of thumb during this time is 5 to 8 (excluding abdominal work).

During the specific preparation period and pre-competition period the exercises selected change again. By the end of the pre-competition period, the goal is to have achieved maximum strength for the year and to have completed the conversion to higher levels of speed-strength and strength-endurance. The following weekly program is an example of how this emphasis is reflected in the weight program.

Monday
1. Split snatch
2. Power clean
3. Split jerk
4. Back squat
5. Dumbbell lunge
6. Dumbbell incline press
7. Seated good morning

Wednesday
1. Muscle snatch
2. Split clean
3. Clean pull from boxes
4. Push press
5. Front squat
6. Hyperextension

Friday
1. Power snatch
2. Split clean
3. Incline press
4. Back squat
5. Good morning

Use of dumbbells for some exercises creates greater instability that the muscles have to work to counteract, creating a bridge from barbell training to the movement and counterbalancing found in wrestling. Also the emphasis on split movements reflects the fact that in wrestling most often one leg is advanced in front of the other. Many more dumbbell exercises could be included, but it is very important that the reader understand that the bulk of this transition work be done in the wrestling room. Rope climbing was already mentioned, but there are many other strength exercises that must be planned as a part of wrestling practice to complete the conversion process. These would include medicine ball exercises, use of the throwing dummy, partner assisted and resisted strength exercises, strength contests against partners, and heavy repetitions in special wrestling situations. The conversion of leg, hip, back, and arm strength developed from power cleans, for example, is made more complete by the inclusion of repetitive, reverse body lifts with a partner. Calisthenic and gymnastic exercises are all important.

Finally, the competition period arrives. During this time the exercises change again. Maximum strength and speed-strength must be maintained while muscular endurance must reach its highest level. Now four to five well-selected exercises must be used.

For example:

Monday
1. Split snatch
2. Power clean
3. Full squat
4. Bench press

Wednesday
1. Power snatch
2. Dumbbell clean
3. Split jerk
4. Front squat

While much strength-endurance is developed during the course of wrestling practices, additional time may be desirable. In order to accomplish this end, a weight circuit may be designed. This may be a circuit of small muscle exercises, but it is preferable to compose a circuit of exercises that have the largest muscle groups involved. For example:

1. Power snatch X 6
2. Split clean X 6
3. Push press X 6
4. Front squat X 8
5. Squat/vertical jump X 15

Athletes must be in constant motion on this circuit and go from one exercise immediately to the next one. At the end the pulse is taken, and when it has returned to 20 counts in 10 seconds the next set is begun, usually in one to two minutes. Three or more sets may be done.

Thus it can be seen that the selection of exercises is very important and must be done with a view in mind to the training objectives for each of the training periods of the year.

BEGINNING THE PROGRAM

In beginning the strength program the coach should first develop a yearly plan. If he coaches athletes who are not yearly trainees, then he should map out a plan that is based realistically on when they will be able to train. Gradually they should be moved along toward a more yearly approach where possible.

The first decision that must be made is whether to peak once for a major competition or more often. If once (high school state championships) then a monocyclic year is planned. If twice (National Freestyle Championships and Olympic Games) then a bi-cycle is planned. This will largely be dictated by the schedule of competitions. Next, the year is planned from the main competition backwards.

The first five to seven days prior to the championship competition is boxed out. This is the period during which all strength training ceases. Preceeding this is a long period of competitions of greater and lesser importance that begins with the first "serious" match, for example, the first conference meet. This is the main competition period—the last macro-cycle within the yearly plan—during which the emphasis must be on the maintenance of maximum strength and speed-strength. These strength qualities are allotted two workouts a week while strength-endurance is emphasized, usually in a form of circuit training.

Prior to this period there is usually a competition or two of minor importance that is used simply to assess where the athlete is, so that any adjustments may be made before approaching more important competitions. This is the short period of time known as the precompetition training cycle. During this period the final conversion of maximum strength to speed-strength and strength-endurance should be seen. Before this is the specific preparation period—the second macro-cycle of the year—in which the emphasis has been on fully developing the specific strength qualities of wrestling. Preceeding that is the period of general preparation that starts in the present with the build-up of strength through general means, the first macro-cycle.

Before beginning the program there should be an evaluation of the athlete's strengths and weaknesses, done during the transition period at the end of the previous training year. Measurable goals are set for the year. Then the workload that is required to reach those goals is distributed. The total volume for the current meso-cycle (training "month," usually four weeks) is set, and then the weekly (micro-cycle) ration of repetitions is calculated. Once this is decided each training day of the week is allotted its share, and the exercises are selected, doling out the required 10 to 35 repetitions to each.

In a sample strength meso-cycle the first micro-cycle, the introductory week, starts the athlete off with a medium level of volume and a level of intensity that is somewhat high. In the second micro-cycle, the "basic" week, the volume reaches its highest and the intensity drops off somewhat. In the third micro-cycle, the "intensive" week, the volume decreases approximately to the level of the introductory week, but the intensity goes up to its highest. The fourth micro-cycle, or "test" week, utilizes the lowest volume of the training cycle, and the intensity decreases until the last one or two days of the week. At that time a "test set" is administered and a new 1RM is established. The advantage of doing this is that the athlete's progress can be checked regularly, and any change that needs to be made can be made in a timely fashion.

This must fall within the overall training concept: three weeks of increasing the physiological load followed by one week of decreasing the load. The unloading week is necessary for complete recovery. Obviously, if an "unloading" week is planned in the weightroom it can be largely negated unless other components in the training process and how they might affect strength performance are controlled. There must be harmony.

Once the weeks of the meso-cycle have been allotted their various levels of volume and intensity, then the days of the week are assigned their share of the weekly load. Following the principles of variable intensities of training in a three-day per week program, Monday would have the lowest intensity and the highest volume (light day). Wednesday would have a lower volume but a higher intensity (medium day), and Friday would have the highest intensity but the lowest volume (heavy day). A light day should always follow a heavy day.

PROGRESSION

Once the plan has been designed and put into practice, the next logical question to be answered is how progress is to be made. This is done by applying the principle of progressive resistance, gradually increasing the body's workload to induce it to adapt by building its capacity to tolerate that workload.

Progressive resistance may be applied by increasing the workload within each week. For example, the weights lifted on a Friday may be planned at a greater percent of 1RM than on a Monday. More total repetitions may be planned for each set at the same intensity, or more sets may be done with the same weights. Two or three of these methods may also be combined.

	Monday	Friday
Increase in % of 1RM: Back Squat	$\frac{50}{3}\frac{60}{3}\frac{70}{3}3$	$\frac{50}{3}\frac{65}{3}\frac{75}{3}3$
Increase in repetitions per set: Power Clean	$\frac{50}{3}\frac{60}{3}\frac{70}{3}3$	$\frac{50}{3}\frac{60}{4}\frac{70}{4}3$
Increase in sets per exercise: Push Press	$\frac{50}{3}\frac{60}{3}\frac{70}{3}3$	$\frac{50}{3}\frac{60}{3}\frac{70}{3}4$
Combination: Back Squats	$\frac{50}{3}\frac{60}{3}\frac{70}{3}\frac{75}{3}3$	$\frac{50}{3}\frac{60}{3}\frac{70}{3}\frac{80}{3}4$

Progressive resistance is also applied by increasing the workload from one week in a training cycle to the next. For example, in the first week of the basic strength phase, five sets of five reps might be planned like this $\frac{50}{5}\frac{60}{5}\frac{65}{5}\frac{70}{5}\frac{65}{5}$. In the second week of the meso-cycle, the workload is increased $\frac{50}{5}\frac{60}{5}\frac{70}{5}\frac{75}{5}2\frac{70}{5}$. The same principle is applied from month to month. For example, the first two weeks of the basic strength phase shown above are increased a month later in the maximum strength cycle. The first week might look like this $\frac{50}{3}\frac{60}{3}\frac{70}{3}\frac{75}{3}\frac{70}{3}$. The second week of this cycle also increases compared to its counterpart in the previous

month $\frac{60}{3}\frac{70}{3}\frac{80}{3}\frac{85}{3}2\frac{75}{3}$. It can readily be seen that the percent of 1RM of the top lifts has increased over time. A gradual increase in the % of 1RM is the best method of increasing strength.

As the training continues over the span of several years, the law of diminishing returns comes into play. As athletes approach their maximum genetic potential, big increases are no longer possible. Still, further gains may be made by increasing the volume of the training. A high school athlete, for example, may employ 1000 reps a month during the specific preparation period. A college wrestler may train for 1200 reps a month. An Olympic class athlete may train for 1400 or more. This greater volume may be achieved by increasing the number of exercises per training session or by increasing the volume of the top sets, the favored method.

NOTE: For the purposes of calculating meaningful volume only the major exercises in a program are counted, and sets with 50% of 1RM or less are ignored.

THE TRAINING SESSION

The strength training session should begin with a general warm-up first, just as any strenuous athletic activity should. The warm-up should include large muscle activities such as jogging, riding a bike, skipping rope, or variants of these to the point where the athlete is perspiring and the deep muscle temperature is raised significantly. Stretching should then follow. After this there should be a specific warm-up composed of lighter weights, usually two or three progressive sets, in each exercise. It is a mistake to charge into the weightroom, load maximal or sub-maximal weights onto the bar and begin lifting. The dangers should be obvious, especially for older athletes.

Speed exercises should be done next, for example, short sprints. These have been shown to lead to higher results when done before strength exercises. Next speed-strength exercises should be done—power snatch first, because it is the quickest of the lifts, power clean and split jerk next in order. Then it is important to do the exercises for maximum strength, beginning with the biggest muscle groups, such as squats, deadlifts, or presses. Following these should come exercises for small muscle groups such as curls or flyes, after which exercises for strength-endurance are performed, such as abdominal work. Last of all, work for cardiovascular endurance should be done, for example, running or cycling.

This order is very important and must be strictly adhered to. The best results will not be seen if exercises are interjected into the program at the wrong place. Putting squats in front of power cleans, for example, will cause a decrease in performance in the clean. Placing a lot of running in front of squats will cause a decrease in squatting performance.

The length of the training session should be about one hour. It is critical to at least get all the big exercises done within this time. This is because the best results in strength are attained with testosterone at its highest levels. The level of testosterone increases rapidly at the onset of the training session as the body mobilizes for maximum effort and then levels off somewhat. After 50 minutes it begins a steep decline. Heavy lifting must be done before this point or disappointing results will be experienced. The small lifts can be done later.

The strength workout should be planned to coincide with one of the body's metabolic high points. The best times are around 10 AM and 3 PM. A lower peak is reached around 8 PM. These are the prime times to work-out. Early morning strength sessions should be discouraged. The early morning is a time better devoted to endurance training.

The rest interval between sets of the heavy exercises is very important. With these exercises (clean, jerk, squat, etc.) the systemic effect of the workload elevates the heart rate significantly. After a set of such activity, the heart rate should be monitored. When heart rate returns to 17 beats in a 10-second pulse count, the body can be deemed ready for the next set. This period of time should be recorded and becomes the rest interval between sets. Generally, during the early stages of training the interval can be short, as little as one minute, and as the level of intensity rises to sub-maximal and maximal later on so does the rest interval,

as much as three to five minutes. Athletes should strictly adhere to a timed rest interval, otherwise the results of their training can become inconclusive. The question will always remain, "Did the athlete lift more today because he was stronger, or because he received more rest between sets?"

It is very important to train flexibility along with strength. Stretching should be done between sets throughout the workout. Particular care should be taken to include exercises which actually improve flexibility, such as the full squat or power snatch. Flexibility should be measured regularly and steps taken immediately to correct any deficiencies.

At the end of the training session stretching and loosening exercises should be performed. The muscles have been shortening and contracting forcefully, and the spinal column has been compacted by the heavy loads. It is time to lengthen out the muscles again and reverse the pressure on the spine. In addition to stretching, the athlete should hang from a horizontal bar to reverse the pull of gravity on the spine. Another athlete or coach may gently pull the hips downward, thus increasing the space between intervertebral discs. Pulling the knees up to the chest (knee lifts) from a hanging position may also be done. These are little things, often overlooked, that can make a big difference in an athlete's training and his ability to recover and avoid injury.

SUMMARY

It is critically important that the coach watch the performance of every lift during training and be actively involved in correcting technique as well as monitoring the relative difficulty or ease with which each individual athlete handles the workload imposed by the weight being lifted. It is also essential that the coach keep accurate records of each training session, and the athlete must do so, too. Without these records no fair assessment of the results of training can be made and mistakes in training will be repeated.

Above all else, the training session must be planned by the coach, and it must be a coherent part of a larger plan. Without this results will be haphazard at best. The broader principle of planning is paramount. There must be a plan, and even a bad plan is better than no plan at all. Why? Because a bad plan, once employed, can be tested out and its weaknesses exposed. Through the evaluation process those weaknesses can then be addressed, and over a period of time a bad plan will thereby evolve into a good plan.

19
Development of Strength Endurance

QUESTIONS TO CONSIDER

- What is the dominant physical attribute in wrestling?
- What are the four exercises used by the Romanian national team?
- When do injuries occur in weight training?
- At what age should kids begin lifting?

INTRODUCTION

A few words need to be said about the development of strength-endurance and its importance in wrestling. Maximum strength is the base. Speed-strength is the explosive quality that scores. But without strength-endurance, an athlete becomes a 60-second wrestler—very dangerous for 60 seconds but very tired after that. Wrestlers must have that anaerobic capacity to go hard for 5 (international) to 10 (collegiate, with overtime) minutes in the face of mounting blood lactates. Specific training in strength-endurance allows them to do this.

Much of this is done in the wrestling room through the normal demands of practice. Much as cross-country develops endurance just by doing it, so wrestling develops strength-endurance just by doing it. More is often not necessary or even desirable. In this scenario weight training may be used to develop maximum strength and speed-strength, and wrestling practice may be used to develop strength-endurance.

However, greater strength-endurance may be created through supplementary training. In wrestling general strength-endurance, the ability of the entire organism to undergo repeated sub-maximal efforts, is the dominant physical attribute. This is in the dynamic regime. However, local strength-endurance can also be a critical factor, such as the ability of the neck muscles to support a high level of stress for a long time in the bridge. In addition, static strength-endurance can be equally important, as in the ability of the hands and forearms to keep a pinhold locked up for a long period of time. These are usually developed in a circuit training format.

In circuit training, strength-endurance may be increased by using 50-80% of 1RM and performing 10-30 repetitions (Bompa, 1983). It is important for acyclic sports such as wrestling not to go above these guidelines. As Manfred Scholich has pointed out, "If an exercise is able to be repeated more than 30 times, its effectiveness for the complex development of strength ability shows a considerable decrease" (Scholich, 1986). If, specifically, the ability to repeat speed-strength movements is desired then the repetitions per exercise may be lower, as in the "Olympic" circuit presented earlier, and the intensity higher—6–12 reps at 70-80% of 1RM.

When multi-joint exercises are used on short rest intervals, this "short program" is very exhausting work.

It is the typical practice to develop muscular-endurance for wrestling by designing a circuit of isolation exercises. The concept here is that local strength-endurance is developed separately in each muscle group which, when added together, creates general body endurance. In order to do this an exercise is selected for the biceps, then the triceps, the forearm flexors, the thighs, the calves, the leg extensors, the leg flexors, the lower back, the abdomen, the upper back, the chest, the shoulders, and the neck. Thirteen exercises in all may be set up alternating antagonists and agonists, flexors and extensors. The usual prescription is to attempt the maximal number of repetitions possible in the time limit—say 30 seconds. Then 30 seconds is allowed to change stations. Once around the circuit, another set or two may be done. Successive loading is accomplished by increasing the weight of the resistance, increasing the number of repetitions for the same resistance, increasing the length of the exercise interval (to 45 seconds, then to one minute), or decreasing the rest interval (from 30 seconds to 20 seconds, etc.).

This "long program," as Scholich calls it, has been very effective in the training of a great number of wrestlers. However, from a bio-motor standpoint, the use of isolated exercises in the training of an acyclic sport like wrestling involving huge muscle groups in constantly moving, complicated patterns of coordinated effort has to be questioned particularly during the competition period. There is a better way.

General strength-endurance is needed so multi-joint exercises may be selected which involve a large number of muscle groups. Since more muscle groups are involved in each exercise, the number of exercises can be decreased. The "Olympic" circuit is a prime example. In addition, specific wrestling movements may be added, and the transfer to wrestling preparedness is even greater. The following circuit used by the Romanian national team is typical of Eastern European thought on the subject, and produces outstanding adaptations. There are only four exercises:

A. Forward bending pull against rubber cable (as in headlock)
B. Rope skipping
C. Rope climbing
D. Throwing dummy

EXERCISES	A	B	C	D
1	2	3	4
4	1	2	3
3	4	1	2
2	3	4	1

GROUP ROTATION

There may be substitutions. For example, instead of rope skipping, there may be a technical move such as repeated fireman's carries or pummeling. Instead of the rope climb, there may be neck bridging against a partner or another technical situation. The team is divided into four groups, and each station requires maximum effort for one minute. There is not rest between stations. After all four stations have been completed, a minute's rest is allowed in which the heart rate is monitored and then the next set begins with great intensity of effort. The circuit is repeated 3 or 4 times at the end of a practice session (Romanian Wrestling Federation, 1975).

A circuit of calisthenic exercises may also be planned where more exercises are used with the work interval starting at 30 seconds in what Scholich terms an extensive-intensive endurance circuit ("long program" again): (1) squat jumps over bench, (2) jack knives, (3) hip heists, (4) squat jump with medicine ball, (5) bridge rotations, (6) squat thrusts, (7) bridge and walkover, (8) bridge roll, (9) trunk rotations with medicine ball, and (10) forward walkovers (Scholich, pp. 238–239).

A circuit of partner exercises may also be done with the main drawback being the necessity of switching partners.

WEIGHT TRAINING SAFETY AND PROTOCOL

Weight training is one of the safest activities that can be undertaken if properly supervised. However, every athletic activity carries with it some degree of risk. There are at least two reported deaths on record from bench pressing (thumbless grip!). Hands frequently get smashed in weight stacks, and athletes slip and fall while lifting. All of these are avoidable.

Injuries occur when one or both of these elements are present: (1) improper technique, or (2) exceeding the physical capacity of the athlete. To eliminate the problem of incorrect technique, every athlete should be instructed by a certified U.S. Weightlifting Federation coach or Certified Strength and Conditioning Specialist. Since there is a shortage of these specialists, every effort should be made by wrestling coaches to become certified in these areas. To eliminate the problem of excessive loading, coaches and athletes should be well versed in the theory and practical application of training plans employing the proper, supervised use of % of 1RM.

There is the mistaken notion that athletes should be "trained to failure." For the big core lifts, this is worse than a mistaken assumption; it is dangerous. An example is Naim Suleymanoglu who, when he trained in Bulgaria, attempted 4,000 maximal (100% of 1RM) lifts during a year's training time—and only missed 12! (Spassov Notes, 1989). He trained not for failure but for success, within his capacity, with every set well planned, and with strictly correct technique. At 132 pounds bodyweight, he jerked 415 pounds over head. If the strongest men in the world—men like Naim— do not "train to failure," then those who wish to gain great strength shouldn't either.

Athletes should lift weights that they know they can lift. The general rule of thumb is that on the last repetition, the athlete should feel that—if he really had to—he could squeeze out one more rep. In this manner the athlete trains for success and gains great confidence. Injuries and overtraining are avoided.

Now, when doing small exercises like curls or sit-ups, particularly in a circuit program where the emphasis is on strength-endurance, the athlete may "train to failure" because the load is very small in relationship to the body's overall capacity.

A simple set of rules should be established and enforced:

1. **Never lift alone.**
2. **Never lift without the strength coach present.**
3. **Always have spotters present.**
4. Use collars at all times.
5. Lift weights you know you can lift.
6. Use strict technique.
7. Wear proper clothing (shoes, shirt and shorts, or sweatclothes).
8. Load and unload bars in balanced fashion.
9. Load plateholders from the bottom up (45's at bottom and 2½'s at top)
10. Keep the area clean and clutter-free, and equipment well maintained.

AGE CONSIDERATIONS

Strength training may begin at an early age if it is strictly controlled. However, the emphasis should be on learning the correct techniques of lifting with light loads. Exercises should be learned with broomsticks first. Plywood "plates" can be made simply by tracing around the edge of metal plates and then cutting these out in a woodshop. These can be used as light resistance later and to give a correct feel of "weightedness" to the exercises. Children 10-12 should use broomsticks and wooden plates.

During the ages of 12-14, more formal strength training can take place. Once the strength is sufficient, a metal bar can replace the broomstick and be used with the wooden plates. Wooden plates should be retained in the weightroom hereafter for use when new exercises are learned. Later still, metal plates can be used.

It is very important to keep the training intensity for children low. Coaches should be mindful of the fact that children will demonstrate increases in strength with much smaller percents of maximum than older athletes, 50-60% of 1RM. Gaining strength is no problem. They *will* get stronger.

It should also be kept in mind that 60% of their training should consist of physical preparation. A wide variety of other exercises and activities—gymnastics, calisthenics, apparatus, and related sports/skills activity—should be included in the training program. The emphasis must be on a gradual increase in the volume of training. Volume comes first in the formative years. Intensity should be introduced later.

Between the ages of 11 and 22, the volume of training can gradually be increased every year to represent a dramatic adaptation. This parallels the increase in testosterone, which peaks at age 22 (Spassov Notes, 1989). After the age of 22, the volume of training cannot be increased. A breakdown in the adaptive abilities of older athletes will occur when this happens. Eventually some reduction in the volume of training will have to take place as the athlete ages.

SUMMARY

Coaching is half science and half art. In developing the strength of wrestlers, the coach must have a thorough understanding of the way the body adapts to external stimuli, formulate a training plan based on that knowledge, and then proceed on faith. No scientific experiment can be devised which can demonstrate a correlation between a wrestler's 1RM power clean and an Olympic gold medal. But that doesn't mean that a relationship does not exist. The sports scientist would be hard pressed to find a relationship between any of the commonly accepted forms of training—running, calisthenics, bridging to name a few—because there are so many variables involved: technical, tactical, and psychological. Yet common sense says that they are all important. The coach knows that Olympians are strong men. Therefore, he devises a plan to incorporate strength exercises in the training of his athletes and he proceeds on faith. Constant evaluation, reassessment, and fine tuning strengthens his conviction as the plan improves over time. In the end, his athletes are the beneficiaries of his wisdom as they grow into stronger . . . and better wrestlers.

20
Making and Maintaining Weight

QUESTIONS TO CONSIDER

- What are the components of fat-free weight?
- How can a proper wrestling weight be determined?
- What is the best recommended way to lose weight?
- What is the recommended percent ratio of protein, carbohydrates, and fat in competitive wrestlers' diets?

INTRODUCTION

Wrestling is a sport defined by the existence of 13 body weight classes. Although the intent of the weight classes is to equalize competition by limiting body weight differences among competitors, health problems associated with attempts by wrestlers to rapidly lose weight have attracted the attention of professional organizations. Exercise science research has repeatedly demonstrated that rapid weight loss can also adversely affect athletic performance.

To wrestlers, there are few topics more important than "making" weight. Unfortunately, wrestlers turn to other wrestlers for advice about losing weight. Parents and coaches are involved providing advice about weight loss only about 30% of the time. For example, Winterstein reported that the coaches in Oregon generally select the weight class for the younger and inexperienced wrestlers but allow the older and more experienced competitors to determine their own weight classes. It has been our experience that wrestlers with marginal abilities and average performance records almost always choose a lower weight class because of the traditional perception that dropping to a lower weight class will improve their chances of success.

Approximately 25 years ago, it was reported that the average weight loss for 747 interscholastic wrestlers represented 5% of their preseason weight, an average loss of 6-9 pounds. Interestingly, their weight loss usually occurred in less than 10 days. Subsequent research conducted by Oppliger et al. indicated that most of the weight loss typically occurs no sooner than 2-3 days before dual meets. Consistent with these findings, Winterstein reported that 44 of 51 high school wrestlers in Oregon indicated that most of their weight loss occurred no more than one week prior to competition. In a study of 139 high school wrestlers, Steen and Brownell reported that 13% lost 0-2 pounds, 51% lost 3-5 pounds, 20% lost 6-10 pounds, and 7% lost 11-20 pounds on a weekly basis. This cyclic weight loss was accomplished by food restriction, fasting, and dehydration. Fifteen percent of this wrestling population restricted their fluid intake on a daily basis.

165

In a study of 49 Massachusetts interscholastic wrestlers, 8% used vomiting as a means to "make weight," and 17% limited themselves to a daily fluid intake of less than 500 mL (two cups). Of the Iowa wrestlers who lost 9% of their initial body weight, 32% regularly used rubber sweat suits, even though such use had been strongly condemned by athletic, medical, and scientific authorities. Finally, it is no surprise that the diets of many wrestlers do not meet minimum Recommended Daily Allowances (RDA) for energy and nutrients. The conclusion from these findings is that the selection of a weight class and the procedures used to lose weight are often unscientific, unhealthy, and undesirable.

EFFECTS OF WRESTLING ASSOCIATION REGULATIONS

The undesirable weight-loss practices utilized by interscholastic wrestlers are compounded by regulations of state wrestling associations. Most states have rules that require wrestlers to compete at a given weight class for a certain percentage of their dual meets in order for the wrestler to qualify to wrestle in that weight class during the state championships. Such regulations, although well-intended, serve to increase the number of weight loss/weight gain cycles during a season. The number of dual meets scheduled by high schools varies according to regions. In Iowa, some schools hold 20 matches before championship competition, whereas in Arizona the average is 12. Steen and Brownell reported that the wrestlers they studied lost weight an average of about 7 times during the season.

Because interscholastic wrestlers are still in their growing years, keeping body weight constant throughout the competitive season may be impossible for some wrestlers. Previously, wrestlers were provided an allowance of one pound each month; unfortunately, this provision has recently been eliminated by the National High School Wrestling Federation. One solution to the growth issue might be to couple the weight allowance to a change in height. When Hall et al. evaluated changes in body weight and height for several thousand, physically fit, male 4-H Club members in Illinois, they ob-

served that an inch change in height was associated by a four-pound change in weight. This evidence suggests that wrestling authorities should re-examine their provision of a no-growth allowance and institute a provision that incorporates a change in height as its reference point. In brief, numerous changes are needed to reduce the health hazards associated with the making of weight by wrestlers.

SELECTING THE PROPER WEIGHT CLASS

Body weight has fat and fat-free components. Skeletal muscle comprises approximately 48% of the mass of the fat-free component (Table 20-1).

Table 20-1. Composition of fat-free body weight

Component	Percentage
Muscle Tissue	47.6
Skeleton	15.9
Skin	13.5
Blood	8.6
Gastrointestinal Tract	3.6
Liver	2.7
Brain and Spinal Cord	2.3
Lungs	1.5
Heart	0.6
Kidney	0.5
Spleen	0.2
Pancreas	0.1
Miscellaneous	2.9
Total	100.0

Because most interscholastic wrestlers are experiencing growth, the selection of a weight class should be determined with the assistance of body composition analyses. Several years ago, it was found that of approximately 9,000 high school wrestlers in Iowa, 40% were certified in the 119-138 pound weight categories. Because of the intense competition in these weight categories, many high school wrestlers attempt to lose enough weight to qualify for lower weight categories. Since the process is predominantely accomplished by dehydration methods, this practice is a potential health hazard.

Although methods for assessing body composition have been available for years, their use has not been widely accepted or employed. This situation is slowly changing. The state of Wisconsin has initiated a minimal body weight program for wrestlers that is mandatory for all Wisconsin high school wrestlers. Before the wrestling season, all high school wrestlers in Wisconsin will have their body fat content determined by anthropometric measures, and their minimal wrestling weights will be computed. This procedure will likely have the added educational benefit of helping most wrestlers realize that they are not fat. Research indicates that the majority of wrestlers are between 9 and 12% fat a month before competition begins. At the present time, Lohman's skinfold equation appears to be most desirable and practical for use in mass testing because its total error of measurement is the lowest of the anthropometric equations evaluated for use with Caucasian interscholastic wrestlers. Regardless of the method of equation used, it is essential that wrestlers have their body fat percentages determined before the season begins and before they initiate any program to make or maintain body weight. It is recommended that wrestlers under 16 years of age maintain at least 7% body fat, while older wrestlers may drop to 5%.

MAKING WEIGHT

Weight-loss practices today are similar to those used more than 20 years ago. Because fat-free mass has a high percentage of water—approximately 70%, weight-loss by dehydration or water deprivation occurs at the expense of intracellular and extracellular fluid. While there is debate as to whether dehydration has any effect on muscular strength, there is good evidence that muscle endurance is reduced when a loss in body weight is due to water loss. As a general rule, a 150-pound individual can lose two or three pounds of weight (1.5% - 2.0% of body weight) before fluid loss affects performance. To minimize weight loss by dehydration, body weight changes during practice should be monitored, fluids should be replaced during and after practices, and weight reduction programs should be designed to promote the loss of fat rather than the loss of fluids. Athletic performance is also impaired when caloric intake is reduced to very low levels (e.g., 500 to 600 kcal/d). While most wrestlers and their coaches would scoff at the standard medical recommendation of losing no more than two pounds per week, this is a prudent and reasonable goal if the loss is to come predominantly from body fat. The oxidation of one pound of fat requires an "extra" 3,500 kcal of energy expenditure—the equivalent of 267 minutes of wrestling or 2,116 minutes of studying. Because wrestlers want to lose weight in a brief amount of time, dehydration becomes the method of choice.

THE WRESTLER'S DIET

Wrestlers who cut weight often deny themselves the very nutrients they need to perform well. Many wrestlers either don't care about proper nutrition or they simply do not know any better. Wrestlers often think of food and water only in terms of gaining weight. They forget that food provides nutrients to fuel their bodies. However, the scientific facts are simple: poor nutrition will hamper performance. The body cannot function at its best when it lacks vital nutrients. Consider these points.

- Concentrating on wrestling rather than on cutting weight will make you a better wrestler.
- To grow naturally and increase strength, wrestlers need the same nutrients as other teenagers, but need *more* calories to meet the demands of daily training.
- Fasting causes the body to use muscle proteins for energy even if fat is available. This limits muscle growth and strength development.
- A proper diet will help wrestlers lose fat weight without sacrificing muscle tissue or becoming dehydrated.
- Dehydration is a major cause of losses in strength and endurance.
- Losing weight *rapidly* results in a loss of both muscle tissue and water.
- Losing weight *gradually* (2-3 lbs/week) is the best way to lose fat and keep muscle.
- Proper training includes practicing proper nutrition *every day*.
- Practicing good nutrition and proper weight control methods is vital to achieving peak physical performance.

Determining Your Wrestling Weight

There are several factors to consider when deciding your "best" wrestling weight, but the most important is: How much weight can you safely lose and still perform well? The weight class you choose should not be so low that you have to sacrifice good nutrition for the sake of making weight. In addition to the adverse physical effects of trying to cut too much weight, unhealthy weight loss practices affect you psychologically; the more you worry about your weight, the less you concentrate on your wrestling. Here is how to determine your "minimum" safe weight for competition.

Percent Body Fat

Body fat percentage can be determined by measuring the thickness of certain skinfolds on the body. Many health care professionals will be able to perform these measurements for you. The results of the skinfold measurements will give you a good estimate of what percent of your body is fat. For example, if the results indicate a body fat reading of 14%, that simply means that 14% of your body is fat. Such measurements are only estimates, and the error is about ±2%. In this example, you could be 12% to 16% fat (14% ±2%).

The goal of safe weight loss is to *lose excess fat weight.* Not all fat on your body can be considered "excess" fat. A certain amount of fat is essential for use as energy, to act as a shock absorber for your internal organs, to insulate your body from the cold, and to store certain nutrients.

Minimum Body Fat

Seven percent body fat is considered the *lowest* healthy level of fat content for teenage males. Body fat measurements can help you determine how much fat you can lose in order to drop to 7% (See Supplement C). If you drop below 7%, you will likely lose muscle tissue, strength, and endurance. Keep in mind that 7% is *not* a magic number. It is just a guideline for you to follow. Most wrestlers perform very well at a higher percentage of body fat. So, if you are now 10% body fat, there is no reason to believe that you'll wrestle better at 7% body fat.

Many health care professionals will be able to help you determine your minimal wrestling weight.

Cutting and Maintaining Weight

Once you've determined your weight class, you should next develop a plan for making and maintaining the weight. Plan your diet to lose not more than 2-3 pounds each week. For example, if you determine you want to lose 10 pounds, allow at least 5 weeks (2 lbs./week) to accomplish your goal. If you plan ahead, the gradual reduction in weight can be easily accomplished. Also to achieve your goal, you must understand the principles of good nutrition.

Principles of Good Nutrition

Four Food Groups

Wrestlers can achieve a balanced diet by eating foods from the four basic food groups. The training table guidelines listed below indicate the *minimum* number of servings from each food group for each day. The menus in Supplement A are consistent with these recommendations.

Meat Group: This group includes high protein foods: meats, poultry, fish, eggs, legumes (such as dry beans and lentils), and nuts. Choose lean meats, fish, and poultry (without skin) to help keep your fat intake low. Remember to keep portion sizes moderate.

Dairy Group: This group is rich in protein, calcium, and other nutrients needed for healthy bones and muscles. Choose products labeled "low-fat" or "non-fat" to get the full nutritional value without the extra fat calories found in whole milk products.

Fruit/Vegetable Group: This group includes all fresh, frozen, canned, and dried fruits and vegetables and juices. This food group is loaded with vitamins and minerals and fiber. Foods in this group are mostly composed of carbohydrates.

Grain Group: This group is the main source of complex carbohydrates and fiber. It includes grains such as oats, rice, and wheat, and the

Table 20-2. Training Table Guidelines

Group	Minimum Servings/Day	Serving Sizes
Meat	2	2-4 oz. cooked meat (total 5-7 oz./day)
Milk	4	1 cup
Fruit/Vegetable	4	½ cup cooked 1 cup raw 1 med. size piece fruit ½ cup juice
Grain	4-6	1 slice bread 1 cup cereal ½ cup pasta

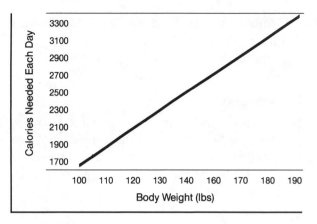

Figure 20-1. Determine the *minimum* number of calories for your goal weight.

breads, cereals, noodles, and pasta made from them.

Calories

A "calorie" is a unit used to describe the energy content of foods. Your body requires energy, and the food you eat supplies that energy. When you take in more food calories than you use, those extra calories are stored as fat, and you gain weight. Weight loss occurs when you consume fewer calories than you use. This causes your body to utilize its stored fat for energy, and you lose weight as a result. Losing weight gradually helps assure that mostly fat will be lost. Losing weight too quickly will cause you to lose muscle and water in addition to fat, sapping your strength and endurance in the process. Gradual weight loss is best accomplished by combining your training with a *slight reduction* in food intake. Remember, your body requires a certain amount of energy and nutrients just to keep you alive and healthy.

For this reason, *your caloric intake should not fall below 1,700-2,000 calories per day.*

In planning your diet, it will be helpful to estimate how many calories you need each day. Caloric needs differ from wrestler to wrestler depending upon body size and activity level. You can estimate the minimum number of calories you need each day by using the graph in Figure 20-1. Supplement A contains examples of 2,000 calorie menus to help you plan your diet. Supplement B can help you plan to eat wisely at fast-food restaurants.

Nutrients

Your body depends upon a constant supply of nutrients to keep it functioning. There are six essential groups of nutrients your body needs every day: water, carbohydrates, protein, fats, vitamins, and minerals. These nutrients work together to build and fuel your body.

Water

The most important nutrient for any athlete is water. Your body is 60-70% water. Water is absolutely essential for optimal health and peak performance. You may be surprised to know that dehydration is a major cause of decreased performance. Some wrestlers are more sensitive to dehydration than others. A fluid loss of 2-3% of your weight can quickly occur during intense training. Even modest levels of dehydration should be avoided because dehydration harms performance.

It is important to drink plenty of fluid during practice and between matches. Not only will you feel better, but you may also find you have more endurance. During physical activity, thirst is not an adequate signal of the need for fluid. Follow the fluid guidelines listed below:

- Weigh-in before and after training to monitor fluid loss. Drink two cups of fluid for every pound of body weight lost.
- Drink 2½ cups of fluid 2 hours before training or competition.
- Drink 1½ cups of fluid 15 minutes before the competition.

- Drink 1 cup for fluid every 15-20 minutes during training and competition.
- Avoid beverages containing alcohol and caffeine, as they promote dehydration.

Carbohydrates

Carbohydrates are the main food source for your body and should make up 55-65% of the total calories you consume. Excellent sources of carbohydrates include breads, pasta, cerals, fruits, and vegetables.

Fat

Everyone needs a little fat in their diets, and wrestlers are no exception. Fat should make up about 20-30% of the calories you consume. Most of the fat we consume is naturally found in foods (meats, nuts, and dairy products) or added during the preparation of food (e.g. fried foods). Sources of additional fat include margarine, peanut butter, and salad dressings.

Protein

Protein is used for growth and repair of all the cells in your body. Good sources of protein are meat, fish, and poultry. Many plant foods, like beans and nuts, are good protein sources too. However, nuts are also high in fat and so should be eaten only in small quantities. Your diet should provide 12-15% of its calories as protein. The typical American diet provides more than enough protein, so you don't need to worry too much about your protein intake.

Vitamins and Minerals

If you eat a balanced diet from the four basic food groups, you will consume all the vitamins and minerals your body needs. Including ample portions of fresh fruits and vegetables in your diet will help ensure an adequate intake of vitamins and minerals. Vitamin and mineral supplements are usually unnecessary, but if you like to have the added "insurance" of taking a supplement, choose a vitamin and mineral supplement that does not exceed 100% of the Recommended Daily Allowance (RDA) for each nutrient.

Eating Before Training or Competition

When you eat can often be as important as *what* you eat before competition and between matches in a tournament. When you eat a regular meal, it takes about three hours for the food to be completely digested and absorbed. As a result, meals are best eaten three to four hours before competition. For athletes too nervous to consume solid foods before competition, special sports nutrition supplements may be an option. Carbodydrate supplements and liquid-nutrition supplements can be taken up to one hour before training or competition, but you should experiment with such products to make certain that you do not experience discomfort. A properly-formulated sports drink can be consumed before, during, and following training or competition to help minimize dehydration and provide a source of energy to working muscles.

Methods of Weight Control That Should Be Avoided

Dehydration

Weight loss in wrestlers usually occurs in a short period of time and consists primarily of water loss. If you lose weight faster than 2-3 pounds per week, you are likely losing water (and perhaps muscle tissue). Unfortunately, when you rehydrate after weigh-in, your body absorbs water at a relatively slow rate: only about 2 pints per hour, and it takes up to 48 hours for the water balance in your tissues to be restored. The ill effects of dehydration include a decrease in muscular strength and endurance, a decrease in blood flow to muscle tissues, and an impaired ability to properly regulate your body temperature. Therefore it is recommended that:

- Wrestlers should limit weight loss by dehydration to a bare minimum.
- Use of diuretic drugs ("water pills") to help lose water weight should be avoided. These drugs can cause disorders in the way your heart and kidneys function.
- Wrestlers should not rely upon sitting in a steam room or sauna to cut weight. Exercise in a plastic suit should also be avoided. These practices are strongly discouraged because they can cause rapid dehydration and heat stroke, which may be fatal.

Fasting

When you do not eat at all (fasting), your body uses its stored nutrients, and weight loss will certainly result. However, fasting quickly reduces your blood sugar, which in turn robs your brain and muscles of their most important energy source. Fasting can cause your muscles to use muscle proteins for energy, even if fat is available. Eat at least *the minimum* calories your body requires each day so you can maintain your energy and strength while losing weight.

Yo-Yo Dieting

The greater the peaks and valleys in your body weight, the more difficult it is for your body to function correctly. Studies have shown that alternating between feast and famine may cause your body to use food more efficiently (hanging on more tightly to each calorie). Yo-yo dieting just makes cutting weight more difficult.

Diet Pills

Using diuretics (water pills) and laxatives to lose weight will dehydrate your body and rob your body of important nutrients. Diet pills can cause many adverse physical as well as psychological effects. Avoid using any of these types of products to lose or maintain weight.

SUMMARY

Research has shown that practicing proper methods of weight control are essential to maximizing your athletic performance. Peak physical performance can only occur when the body is supplied with an adequate amount of essential nutrients. Using improper methods of weight control will decrease your level of performance. The Wrestler's Diet provides the necessary information to help you achieve the highest level of performance possible. The psychological advantages of maintaining good nutritional practices are great: you'll wrestle better if you feel good physically and mentally. You will also wrestle better knowing that you have done *everything* possible to be at your best.

SUPPLEMENT A: Sample Menus and Snacks (2,000 Calories)

Breakfast

Blender Drink
Banana, 1 100
Milk, 1 cup 2% 120
Peanut Butter, 1t 95
Toast, 1 slice 70
Jam, 1t 15

Calories 400

Lunch

Hamburger on Bun
Bun 120
Grnd Beef, 2 oz 120
Catsup, 1T 20
French Fries 220
Milk, 1 cup 2% 120
Oatmeal Raisin Cookies (2)
(2½" diameter) 120

Calories 760

Dinner

Roast Pork, 3 oz. 220
Baked Potato 100
Broccoli, 1 stalk 20
Margarine, 2t 70
Bread, 1 slice 70
Sliced peaches, 1 cup 130
Milk, 1 cup 2% 120

Calories 730

Snack

Lo-cal Pudding, 1 cup 130

Total Calories 2020

Breakfast

Grapefruit juice, 6 oz. 75
Unsweetened Cereal, 1 cup 110
Banana, 1 medium 100
Milk, 1 cup 2% 120
Toast, 1 slice 70
Margarine, 1t 35
Jam, 1t 15

Calories 525

Lunch

Chicken Salad Sandwich
Bread, 2 slices 140
Chicken Breast, 2 oz. 120
Lo Cal Dressing, 1T 30
Milk, 1 cup 2% 120
Apple, 1 medium 80

Calories 490

Dinner

Chili, 2 cups 600
Saltine Crackers, 12 160
Milk, 1 cup 2% 120
Carrot & Celery Sticks 10

Calories 890

Snack

Frozen Yogurt, 4 oz. 120

Total Calories 2025

Breakfast

Apple Juice, 6 oz. 90
Oatmeal, 1 cup 145
Raisins, 1T 30
Milk, 1 cup 2% 120
Toast, 1 slice 70
Margarine 35

Calories 490

Lunch

"Sloppy Joe"
Hamburger Filling, 2 oz. 200
Bun 140
Carrot & Celery Sticks 10
Milk, 1 cup 2% 120
Chocolate Chip Cookie,
1 small 50

Calories 520

Dinner

Turkey Tacos
Taco Shells, 3 210
Picante Sauce, 2 oz. 30
American Cheese,
4 oz. shredded 220
Ground Turkey, 4 oz. 310
Lettuce, Onion, Tomato, etc. 10
Milk, 1 cup 2% 120

Calories 900

Snack

Orange, 1 medium 80

Total Calories 1990

Breakfast

Orange Juice, 6 oz.	80
English Muffin	140
Peanut Butter, 1T	90
Banana, 1 medium	100
Milk, 1cup 2%	120
Calories	**530**

Lunch

Cheese Pizza, 2 slices	400
Milk, 1 cup 2%	120
Apple, 1 medium	80
Calories	**600**

Dinner

Chicken & Noodles, 1 cup	300
Cooked Carrots, ½ cup	25
Lettuce Salad	10
Dressing, 1T	60
Milk, 1 cup 2%	120
Calories	**515**

Snack

Milk, 1 cup 2%	120
Fig Bars, 5	250
Calories	**370**

Total Calories **2015**

Breakfast

French Toast, 2 slices	300
Syrup, 2 oz.	200
Strawberries, 4 oz., unsweetened	25
Milk, 1 cut 2%	120
Calories	**645**

Lunch

Turkey Sandwich	
Bread, 2 slices	140
Turkey Breast, 3 oz.	105
Lettuce, Tomato Slices	5
Lo-cal Mayonnaise, 1T	30
Milk, 1 cup 2%	120
Calories	**400**

Dinner

Beef Stew, 2 cups	400
Dinner Roll, 1	70
Margarine, 1t	35
Applesauce, 4 oz.	55
Milk, 1 cup 2%	120
Lo-cal Pudding, 1 cup	130
Vanilla Wafers, 6	100
Calories	**910**

Snack

Popcorn, 2 cups, no butter	60
Diet Soda, 12 oz.	0
Calories	**60**

Total Calories **2015**

Breakfast

Cantaloupe, ¼	60
Egg, poached	75
Toast, 2 slices	140
Margarine, 1t	35
Jam, 2t	30
Milk, 1 cup 2%	120
Calories	**460**

Lunch

Tuna Pocket	
Pita Bread, 1	120
Tuna, 3 oz.	100
Lo-cal Mayonnaise, 2T	60
Lettuce, tomato slices	5
Pretzels, 1 oz.	110
Milk, 1 cup 2%	120
Calories	**515**

Dinner

Broiled Turkey Breast, 3 oz.	130
Wild Rice Pilaf, 1 cup	270
Spinach Salad	15
Dressing, 1T	60
Angel Food Cake, 1 slice	125
Chocolate Syrup, 2T	75
Milk, 1 cup 2%	120
Calories	**795**

Snack

Pineapple, 1 cup	150
Graham Crackers, 3 squares	80
Calories	**230**

Total Calories **2000**

You can maintain your training diet when eating at a restaurant if you are careful about what you order. Pay attention to how foods are prepared. Choose food that is baked, broiled, boiled, or poached. Avoid food that is breaded, fried, or served in gravy. Limit your use of butter, margarine, mayonnaise, sour cream, cream cheese, and regular salad dressings. Instead, use barbeque sauce, ketchup, mustard, relish, and vegetables for toppings. Do not be afraid to ask for food served "your way"; ask for extra vegetables in sandwiches or on pizza, skip the extra cheese or extra meat, request skim or 2% milk, and specify the toppings you want.

When you know you will be eating out, care-fully choose low-fat foods for your other meals that day. Also, take along your own fresh fruit to munch on after the meal instead of ordering desserts.

When eating a meal at a fast food restaurant, don't make it a dietary disaster. A typical fast food meal is high in fat and low in calcium, vitamin C, and vitamin A. It is difficult to choose a high-carbohydrate meal at a fast food restaurant. Beware or you can eat half of your caloric allotment in one meal. Satisfy your hunger and nutritional needs by using the menus listed as guidelines. For a higher carbohydrate diet, order additional servings of the food items in bold.

	Calories	Protein	Carbo-hydrate	Fat
Breakfasts				
McDonald's				
Plain English muffin (2)	747	17%	56%	25%
Strawberry jam (1 packet)				
Scrambled egg (1)				
Orange juice (6 ounces)				
2% milk (1 carton)				
or Hot Cakes with butter* and ½ syrup packet	650	11%	66%	25%
Orange juice (6 ounces)				
2% milk (1 carton)				
*If still hungry, recommend ordering plain english muffin.				
Family Style Restaurant (Perkins, Village Inn)				
Buttermilk pancakes 5" (3)	761	12%	67%	20%
Butter (1 pat)				
Egg (1)				
Syrup (3 tablespoons)				
Orange juice (6 ounces)				
Usually comes with two eggs. Order one instead. Poached, soft- or hard-boiled is recommended.				
or *Cold Cereal* with 2% milk (4 ounces)	668	15%	58%	26%
Egg (1)				
English muffin				
Butter (1 pat)				
Jelly (1 packet)				
Orange juice (4 ounces)				
Lunch/Dinner				
McDonald's				
Chicken sandwich with BBQ sauce	677	23%	51%	25%
Side salad				
½ packet low-calorie vinegar and oil dressing				
Orange juice (6 ounces)				
2% milk (1 carton)				

	Calories	Protein	Carbo-hydrate	Fat
Lunch/Dinner				
Wendy's				
Chicken breast sandwich on multigrain bread (no mayonnaise)	719	22%	53%	25%
Baked potato				
Sour cream (1 packet)				
2% milk				
or Chili (8 ounces)	1,016	16%	57%	25%
Baked potato, plain				
Frosty (small)				
Side salad: ¼ cup lettuce, ¼ cup fresh veggies, ¼ cup cottage cheese				
Arby's				
Jr. Roast Beef on multigrain bread with lettuce and tomato (no mayonnaise or horseradish)	695	22%	51%	27%
Side salad*				
2% milk				
or Arby's Regular Roast Beef or ham and cheese sandwich	970	20%	52%	30%
Side salad*				
Vanilla shake				
*½ cup lettuce, 1 cup fresh veggies, ½ cup garbanzo beans, ¼ cup cottage cheese, 2 tablespoons low-calorie dressing				
Taco Bell				
2 tostadas*	1,040	18%	56%	27%
1 bean burrito				
2 plain tortillas				
2% milk				
or 1 tostada*	1,105	18%	55%	28%
2 bean burritos				
1 plain tortilla				
2% milk				
or 3 tostadas*	785	19%	53%	28%
1 plain tortilla				
2% milk				
*If possible, ask that tostada shell be plain, not fried.				
Pizza Hut*				
Large Spaghetti with meat sauce	1,023	19%	61%	20%
Breadsticks				
2% milk				
or ½ medium onion, green pepper and cheese pizza (thin crust)	1,126	20%	55%	25%
2 breadsticks				
2% milk				
*Pizza Hut does have a salad bar.				
Family Style Restaurant (Perkins, Village Inn)				
Baked fish	1,100	25%	51%	23%
Baked potato with sour cream (1 tablespoon)				
1 muffin				
Salad bar (1 cup lettuce)				
2% milk (8 ounces)				
Sherbet (½ cup)				

Acknowledgements: Idaho Dairy Council and Marcia Rinker

1. To Calculate Your Fat Weight:
   Multiply your weight in pounds by your percent fat (as a decimal). For example, if you weigh 140 lbs. and are 12% fat:
   $140 \times 0.12 = 16.8$ lbs. of fat

2. To Calculate Your Lean Body Mass:
   Subtract your fat weight from your body weight:
   $140 - 16.8 = 123.2$ lbs. of lean body mass (LBM)

3. To Calculate Your Minimum Wrestling Weight:
   Divide LBM by .93:
   $123.2 \div .93 = 132.5$ lbs. of body weight at 7% fat

4. To Calculate Your Maximum Fat-Weight Loss:
   Subtract your calculated body weight from your present weight:
   $140 - 132.5 = 7.5$ lbs. of fat weight to lose

Section VI
Sports Medicine

21
Prevention of Common Sports Injuries

QUESTIONS TO CONSIDER

- What effect can warm-ups, cool downs, and conditioning have on preventing injuries?
- How can facilities be made safer for wrestling?
- What role does teaching wrestlers safety, appropriate sport techniques, and proper drills have in injury prevention?
- What injury prevention techniques can be implemented over the course of a season?

A thorough warm-up prior to wrestling practice will help to decrease possible injuries.

INTRODUCTION

Most sport involves the application of large muscular forces and physical contact at all levels of competition. All of the muscular force and physical contact cannot be eliminated from sport. However, if you follow several steps aimed at preventing injuries, you can make athletics safer.

As a coach, you are responsible for doing everything reasonable to allow participants to compete in an environment that is healthy and safe.

AVOIDING NEEDLESS INJURIES

It is our responsibility to have the usual safety mechanisms in place:

1. emergency numbers in the aid kit and near the phone,
2. physical exams scheduled,
3. review of emergency first aid procedures,
4. updating CPR certifications,
5. writing down our season plan and so on.

These are some of the areas of concern that usually come to our attention as we approach the season.

From another point of view there are a number of items which we often overlook until it becomes painfully obvious we have forgotten. These can cause "needless" time lost from practice—not due to serious injury, but due to the nagging problems that "show their ugly head." Many of these deal with the practice area and its control.

Proper Warm-ups

First, let us consider practice control. It is important to have an established, well planned, well organized warm-up procedure. This should include a jogging session with a large amount of basic motor fitness like skipping, hopping, galloping (single leg forward jogging), side shuffling, and backward jogging utilizing these and other basic movement patterns. During this time you can also evaluate your talent pool. The more related the footwork is to the sport, the better.

Flexibility must be included in every practice session. Again develop and monitor a program which increases the passive and active range of motion on both the front and the back of the body. All too often we stretch the back of the body (hamstrings and back muscles) without paying an equal amount of attention to the front of the body (quads and abdominal muscles). These anterior muscles must have a large range of motion so as to allow the successful completion of the back arch. The muscles of rotation of the trunk and hip area are also often overlooked. Standing rotary motion of the upper trunk countered by lower leg or foot sweeping motion in the opposite direction will assist in this rotary flexibility while also teaching the "foot sweep" motion. Remember you are helping your athletes gain better balance in some of these flexibility drills.

Stunts, tumbling, and mimetics are another aid in improving the wrestler's ability to avoid injury. Each practice in the early part of the season should include such items as:

1. forward rolls, forward rolls-split legs, forward rolls-pike legs
2. backward rolls, backward rolls-split legs, backward rolls-pike legs
3. diving forward rolls
4. back extensions
5. shoulder rolls-right and left side
6. cart wheels
7. round offs
8. round offs w/half twist
9. and other high order tumbling.

Figure 21-1. Incorporating basic skill drills into your warm-up enhances your wrestlers technique and diminishes injuries.

Mimetics are an old form of fun but valuable conditioning and motor ability activities, such as bear crawl, seal walk, snake crawl, crab walk, reverse crab walk, and many others that you may be able to get from the school physical education instructors.

These activities serve a number of purposes, but here we are concerned about helping the wrestler learn how to move his body and its parts in new and challenging patterns of motion. Again, it provides us as coaches an opportunity to assess the motor ability of the athletes and help them learn to move, fall, and recover on the mat.

Moving through the above sequence will take about 30 minutes of practice, and it will get shorter as the athletes get used to the procedure. Perhaps this is the most important aspect—they get used to following a prescribed order for the beginning of practice. This can eliminate a lot of the "horse play" which often leads to "needless injury." In addition, it aids conditioning, motor development, motor fitness, balance, and self esteem (when one learns to do something they previously could not perform).

Facilities

Next let us consider the rooms—wrestling area (cafeteria, stage, pool balcony), the gym-

Figure 21-2. A proper warm-down consisting of thorough stretching and massage will facilitate a strong and injury free body.

nasium (for sprints and endurance runs), the shower and locker room. All these areas must be considered or we will lose athletes for short periods of time from "needless injuries." It goes without saying that the areas should be safe, but what does that actually mean? What kinds of concerns need to be considered?

The Wrestling Room

Use plenty of mats. Every kind of mat that is available. Wondering what to do with the old mats or the competition mat? Before you spend $4,000 on a mat storage device, consider putting one mat under the other. They stay flat and the shock absorbency can aid in the reduction of contusion and compression injuries. Use "crash pads" to protect against bleachers, walls, doors, bars, and cages when wall padding is not available. Protect the underside of matting with corn starch and talcum powder when placing mats against mats and mats over floor tile. This must be done to protect the mat surface. Rubber floor mats or even plywood (especially supported by 2 x 4's) will offer some additional shock absorbency.

Cleaning the mat area is one of the most important aspects of preventing contagious diseases from spreading. How often you clean the mats is a function of use, heat and humidity of the room, number of participants and so forth. Cleaning the mats prior to a workout with a disinfectant solution is recommended. The best solution would contain antibacterial, antifungal, and antiviral disinfectant agents. In addition, BUT NOT ADDED TO THE SOLUTION, mats can be cleaned with a mild bleach solution.

A very good friend of wrestling, Dr. Ken Seton, has indicated that the spread of diseases in wrestling are a function of self-inoculation—we infect ourselves. We do this by picking up the virus, bacteria or fungus from others or from the mat, usually on our hands and specifically under the finger nails. We scratch, bite, dig, pick both ourselves and others, and the next thing you know an infection begins and usually means lost practice or competitive time. Herpes, staph, and other general infections get started, are difficult to control and disqualify our athletes from competing or practicing (see Chapter 25). Dr. Seton and others have noted that the anaerobic nature of the wrestling workouts coupled with dietary restriction could lead to a reduction in our ability to fight off diseases. This means an even greater concern for the cleanliness of the wrestling room and the other room we need to consider at this point.

The Shower Room

In the many discussions with Dr. Seton, Dr. Karl Wirth, Dr. Jack Harvey, and Jack Spain A.T.C., it is obvious that the least amount of attention to health and human disease in our sport is the shower and mat area. We need to be aware that a major defense against the contraction of disease is personal hygiene. Make sure the wrestlers shower immediately after practice and that they use soap which has the ability to attack the source of the problem. They must wash their hands, especially under the fingernail area, and all the other cracks and crevices on their body with soap and lots of hot water. Check out the shower room—do you have soap available? Is it the type they use to get under their fingernails? Is it the kind that is strong enough to attack the typical infectious agents that collect around the mat and on our bodies?

If you have had an experience with these kinds of problems, you know how difficult and disappointing they can be to an athlete and to those of us that coach. A little time and planning to insure that these safeguards are built into our program can pay big dividends later.

INJURY PREVENTION TECHNIQUES

Pre-Participation Exam

The cornerstone for prevention of injuries, the pre-participation athletic exam is used to determine if any defects or conditions exist that might place the athlete at an *increased* risk for injury in a particular sport. It especially is useful for identifying old, inadequately rehabilitated injuries (which easily may be reinjured).

Equipment and Apparel

A properly equipped and attired athlete is less likely to be injured. Therefore, it is important that you develop a list of essential equipment for your specific sport and distribute this information to your athletes and their parents.

Parents should be informed during a pre-season parents' orientation meeting about appropriate equipment and apparel for their children. At the start of the first practice, restate to your athletes what you told the parents about appropriate equipment and apparel.

Determine if:

- all athletes have the essential protective equipment,
- all athletes are properly attired,
- equipment is in good repair, and
- equipment properly fits.

This type of inspection should be carried out regularly. Extra essential equipment should be included in the team's equipment bag for athletes who forget their equipment. Note that wearing jewelry is inappropriate during practices and contests. Also, if eyeglasses are essential, they should be safety glasses and worn with safety straps.

Management of Practices and Contests

Every physical activity that occurs during practices and contests has some potential to result in an injury. Fortunately, most activities relating to practices and contests have only a rare chance in resulting in an injury. Injuries that do occur are the result of interactions between the situation in which the activity occurs and the physical status of the athlete. In addition to having an influence over the equipment, apparel, and facilities in reducing the risk of injuries, you have a major influence over the physical activities of your athletes during practices and contests. You can take several steps to properly manage the physical activities that occur at practices and contests to reduce the rate and severity of the injuries. These steps include the following:

Teaching Safety to Players

Whenever appropriate, inform your athletes about the potential risks of injury associated with performing certain sports activities and the methods for avoiding injury. By informing your athletes of these dangers and possibly establishing team rules that regulate their performance of high-risk activities, you will reduce the risk of injury to your wrestlers.

The key to teaching safety to your athletes is to prudently interject safety tips in your instruction whenever appropriate.

Warming Up

A warm-up at the beginning of your team's practices and before competition provides several important benefits. Specific warm-up suggestions have already been mentioned. When warm-ups and stretching are completed, the skill-oriented drills on your practice plan or the formal drills before the match may begin. A warm-up period:

- increases the breathing rate, heart rate, and muscle temperature to exercise levels;
- reduces the risks of muscle pulls and strains;
- increases the shock-absorbing capabilities of the joints; and
- prepares athletes mentally for practices and competition.

Teaching Appropriate Techniques

The instructions you provide during practices on how to perform specific sport skills have an influence on the risks of injuries to your athletes and their opponents. Teach your athletes the proper ways to perform specific techniques, and *never* teach athletes how to intentionally foul opponents. An improper technique often results in a greater chance of injury to the performer than does the correct technique. Acceptable techniques in sports usually evolve with safety as a concern.

Coaches who promote an atmosphere in which intentional violent fouls are acceptable must be eliminated from athletic programs. You should promote fair and safe participation in practices and contests with strict enforcement of the rules to encourage skill as the primary factor in determining the outcome.

Selecting Proper Drills

Drills that you select or design for your practices and the ways in which they are carried out have an influence on the risks of injuries to your athletes. Drills should be selected and designed with safety as a primary feature. Before implementing a new drill into your practice, several safety questions should be considered.

- Is the drill appropriate for the level of maturation of the athletes?
- Are the athletes sufficiently skilled to comply with the requirements of the drill?
- Are the athletes sufficiently conditioned to handle the stress of participation in the drill?
- Are other, less risky drills available to achieve the same practice results?
- Can the drill be modified to make it less risky and yet achieve the desired training result?

Conditioning

High-intensity work is part of sport. How well your athletes can handle fatigue will often determine how well they perform. Is there, however, any relationship between fatigue and injury? The sequence of events in Figure 21-3 draws an association, linking fatigue with an increased potential for injury.

In addition to improving performance, every conditioning program should be designed to minimize fatigue and the potential for injury. Being "in shape" can postpone fatigue and its detrimental effects. By progressively intensifying your practices throughout the season, you can produce a conditioning effect that can be an important deterrent to injury. Coaches must

Figure 21-3. How fatigue is linked to an increased potential for injuries.

22
Possible Serious Injuries

QUESTIONS TO CONSIDER

- What is the primary serious injury in wrestling?
- What areas of knowledge should a coach understand to reduce possible serious injuries?
- What are the guidelines for teaching progression of skills?

Although wrestling is a physical sport, major injuries occur on an infrequent basis.

INTRODUCTION

As a sport, wrestling takes precautions that make severe or serious injuries a rare occurrence. Wrestlers compete and usually train with individuals of approximately the same size. Age groups are set to limit the age discrepancies of competitors. Officials are placed on the mat to not only score the match but also to stop situations that they deem potentially dangerous. Practice and competition is done on a mat to cushion the landing. Still, because wrestling is a combative sport there is potential for serious injuries to occur.

Because of the contact nature of the sport of wrestling, there are potential situations for catastrophic injuries. The purpose of this chapter is to help the reader realize these situations, be aware of their causes, and understand the instructional responsibility of the coach.

A possible serious injury in wrestling is the fracture of the neck or back. Usually these types of injuries can be a rare occurance by educating each wrestler on the rules of the sport. It is important that the coach has knowledge of the skill levels and physiological ages of the athletes being coached. Ask the question: "What can this group do safely?"

It is also important that the mat area and workout area are well padded and kept in repair. A coach should understand and use correct conditioning and weight training methods. Coaches should teach rules, know the human body, understand strength and conditioning techniques, and be aware of growth and development stages of young athletes.

A second area of potential danger is caused by lack of proper knowledge of weight control. Coaches should understand the human body and what happens if there is a change in water content, food intake, basal metabolism, or any drastic change to the system. Coaches must monitor each athlete to be alert to changes in weight. A coach should also be cognizant of changes in personality, school attendance, excessive nose bleeds, drop in grades, or lack of energy and strength.

A third area is in teaching technique. A coach must know the level of skill of each athlete so that skills are not taught beyond the knowledge or physical ability of the athlete. For example, it would be poor practice to teach upper body throws to a physically immature boy. Further, the coach should understand the potential dangers involved with each technique as well as what makes a move legal or illegal (e.g., a throw versus a forceful throw).

PROGRESSION OF SKILLS

Some guidelines for teaching progression include:

1. **Assess the level of the athletes**
   A. Physically—strength and maturity
   B. Skill—knowledge and ability to perform at the level being taught.

2. **Perform a task analysis of each skill to be taught**

   For example, in order to most effectively teach a pinning combination, this is the order of knowledge: A. position, B. motion, C. breakdowns, D. rides, and E. pins.

3. **Monitoring**

   It is imperative in skill development that learning is monitored A new or advanced skill should not be introduced until the previous skill has been learned and mastered.

4. **Adjusting**

   As skills are introduced, a coach usually discovers that certain athletes have a difficult time learning certain skills. It might be caused by lack of mastery of an earlier skill, or it might be caused by a physical fact (e.g., body type, lack of balance). Therefore, a coach will have to adjust skills taught based upon individuals, not upon expectations. This doesn't mean individualizing the workout to a one-on-one. More than likely, groups of athletes can learn certain skills and other groups can learn another set of skills.

5. **Basic philosophy**

   Skills should be taught only if they fit into an overall coaching philosophy. The philosophy should fit into all situations that occur and should be easily understood by the athletes. It is impossible to teach a skill to cover every situation that occurs in wrestling. Therefore, a basic philosophy in coaching allows wrestlers an opportunity to adjust actions to a few basic rules. For example, at a major junior college men's wrestling team, philosophy involves two skills, basic position and basic motion. At any time in any situation, if a wrestler is in poor position or if his motion stops before it should, he knows the action was incorrect and that he will have to adjust. This allows great flexibility in group teaching and it also allows the athlete to know instantly what needs to be changed in any situation.

CONDITIONING OF PARTICIPANTS

1. Training programs

Training programs will vary according to the personal philosophy of the coaches. There are, today, successful programs that mostly drill, those that mostly exercise, and those that mostly scrimmage. All are effective. However, all follow similar guidelines in practice sessions. These guidelines consider:

A. Skill level of the athlete
B. Physical level of the athlete

C. BEFORE EACH PRACTICE answer the 3H's
   1. how much?
   2. how long?
   3. how often?
D. Adjusting as the season progresses

2. Strength programs

Today, more than ever before, strength has become an integral part of wrestling. It is a safe statement that a stronger athlete is a better athlete, in any sport. If some wrestlers are weak in comparison to others, a program must be utilized to help this aspect of their development. There are many strength programs available, but it is important to select one that fits the philosophy and the program.

3. Flexibility

Most coaches have limited knowledge concerning flexibility. Find a good exercise physiologist, biomechanist, gymnastic coach, or dance instructor (jazzersize or aerobics). Any of these people may help. Keep in mind that THIS IS A MUST and ask their assistance in developing a proper program if you do not have knowledge in this area.

Figure 22-1. Though this looks harmful, proper conditioning and technique will alleviate many possible catastrophic injuries.

Figure 22-2. The skill of throwing your opponent properly looks much more dangerous than it actually is. Very few injuries occur when done correctly.

WHAT TO BE AWARE OF AND POSSIBLE ACTIONS TO LESSEN RISK

1. Double leg takedown with lift (Opponent is lifted off the mat)

Possible injury

A. Injury to the neck region (breaks, sprains, strain)

B. Injury to shoulder area or rib cage area (break, strain)

C. Injury to offensive wrestler's back (strain, sprain)

Possible Causes

A. Spiking opponent

B. Slamming opponent

C. Incorrect lifting technique by offensive wrestler

Possible Actions to Lessen Risk

A. Proper instruction as to rules, i.e., the requirement in wrestling to return opponent safely to mat.

B. Proper instruction in taking opponent back to the mat (e.g., lowering your altitude as you lower your opponent).

C. Proper instruction in using leg muscles and hip-girdle area to lift, rather than the lower back and upper body.

2. Breakdown from behind opponent when standing

Possible injury

A. Injury to shoulder and neck (fracture, strain, bruise)

B. Injury to knee (ligament, cartilage)

C. Injury to abdomen (fractured ribs, internal injuries)

Possible Causes

A. "Tying" up opponent's near arm and tripping him toward tied-up arm.

B. Locking near leg and tripping opponent to near side.

C. Pulling opponent backward onto self.

Possible Actions to Lessen Risk

A. Teaching techniques that allow opponent always to protect self. (If near arm is tied up, opponent cannot protect shoulder area to tied up side.)

B. Teaching wrestlers to trip in the direction leg flexes, not to outside where joint does not allow flexion.

C. Proper teaching technique that emphasizes the danger of bringing opponent back on self (e.g., stay higher than opponent during takedown to the mat).

3. Belly-to-belly in folkstyle and other high amplitude throws allowed in freestyle/Greco Roman

Possible injury

A. Fractures to shoulders, neck area, or possible muscle tears or bruises

Possible Actions to Lessen Risk

A. Correct teaching technique that emphasizes correct procedure for the safety of both offensive and defensive wrestlers.

4. Front or reverse stack

Possible injury

A. Fracture or strain to neck area, shoulder area, or lower back.

Possible Causes

A. Lifting opponent at hip-girdle area and driving him forward onto neck and shoulders.

B. Lifting opponent at thigh area and driving him forward, putting pressure on lower back.

Possible Actions to Lessen Risk

A. Correct instruction on where not to apply pressure (e.g., neck area, lower back area).

5. Weight control

Possible injury

A. Ulcerated stomach lining, dehydration, poor electrolite balance, emotional stress, urinary tract infection, irregular bowel movements, poor endurance level causing fatigue (probably the most debilitating aspect of wrestling for all participants).

Possible Causes

A. Inadequate instruction in weight control by coach to athletes, inadequate understanding by coach of the human body and how it functions. Too much emphsis on winning at any cost rather than learning. Inadequate record keeping of weight and weight fluctuating of athletes by coach.

Possible Actions to Lessen Risk
A. Training of coaches in correct method of weight control and nutrition. Emphasize to coaches and parents the need to keep up-to-date records on athletes.
B. Emphasize to coaches the safety concerns with using rubber sweatsuits, saunas, steam baths.

C. Emphasize the disadvantages in use of diuretics, artificial means of weight control.

6. **Maintenance of mats**
Possible injury
A. Concussion
B. Neck injury
C. Staphylococus infection

Possible Actions to Lessen Risk
A. Proper care and cleaning of mats
B. Repair of mats
C. Taping mats where needed

23
Care, First Aid, and Handling of Injuries

QUESTIONS TO CONSIDER

- Can you identify and provide first aid for the different medical conditions commonly associated with your sport?
- What items belong in a well-stocked first-aid kit?
- What procedures should you follow when an injury occurs?
- What information should you have about your athletes in case they become injured?

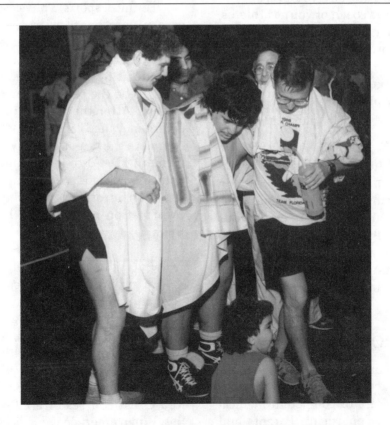

As a coach, it is important to recognize injuries and properly assist in its care.

INTRODUCTION

Paul is leading the defending state champion Ben by 1 point with 20 seconds remaining in the match. While Ben is trying to take Paul down with a double leg to win the match, he drives Paul out of bounds and violently collides with the score clock. As Paul's head struck the metal object, he slumped to the mat and lay motionless. The official, sensing the likelihood of injury, immediately signals Paul's coach to the corner to tend to the downed wrestler.

You must not rely on the likelihood that a serious injury will not occur to your athletes as an excuse for inadequate emergency preparation!

Watching from the corner, the first, and normal, reaction of a coach is to be frightened by the possible outcome of this violent collision. The sinking feeling in the stomach and the "Oh, no" message sent out by the brain when Paul went down have been felt by most coaches at some point.

If this, or some similar situation confronted you, what would you do? Are you prepared to act appropriately? As a coach of young athletes, it is your obligation to be able to deal with such an emergency. Before your first practice, you should: obtain medical information on your athletes, establish emergency procedures, and prepare to provide first aid.

MEDICAL INFORMATION

The completed Athlete's Medical Information (Supplement A) and Parental Instruction (Supplement B) forms should be in your possession whenever your athletes are under your supervision. Hopefully, the need to use this information will never arise. But, if an injury occurs, the information on these forms will help you and qualified medical personnel respond quickly.

EMERGENCY PROCEDURES

As the coach of an injured athlete, you are responsible for the actions taken until the athlete is placed in the care of competent medical personnel, parents, or guardians. Parents and players expect you to know how to proceed. An Emergency Plan Form (Supplement C) has been developed to assist you in properly responding to an emergency.

The Emergency Plan Form provides directions for a number of people to carry out responsibilities in an emergency. One completed form is needed for each of the five individuals listed below. The form also contains space for inserting site-specific information about emergency care.

Before the first practice, a number of responsible individuals must be assigned roles to carry out in an emergency. These roles are:

A. taking charge of the situation (the coach)
B. attending to an injured athlete
C. attending to the uninjured athletes
D. calling for emergency medical assistance
E. flagging down the emergency vehicle.

Note that when a medical emergency occurs, all responsibilities must be addressed simultaneously.

Part A.

For most sports, a physician or athletic trainer is not present to assist the coach in handling the medical aspects of an emergency. Thus, after taking charge of the situation and directing individuals to their assigned tasks, the coach is likely to be the person to attend to the injured athlete. After the injured player is released to emergency medical personnel, the coach should complete the On-site Injury Report form (Supplement D). Also, if the injured athlete's parents or guardians are unaware of the emergency situation, information on the Athlete's Medical Information form should be used to contact them.

Part B.

Providing emergency care includes knowledge and skill in cardiopulmonary resuscitation (CPR), controlling bleeding, attending to heat stroke, attending to shock, and knowing how to use an allergic reaction kit. This knowledge and skill are beyond the scope of USAW Bronze Certification and should be obtained through Red Cross courses offered in most communities. When emergency medical personnel arrive, responsibility for the injured athlete should be transferred to these professionals. The Athlete's Medical Information and Parental Instruction (Release) forms should be presented to the emergency medical personnel. The person designated on the Parental Instruction (Release) form (usually the coach) must accompany the injured athlete to the medical center.

Part C.

If the coach is attending the injured athlete, the uninjured athletes should be directed to a safe area within voice and vision of the coach. These responsibilities are assigned to the person in charge of the uninjured athletes. An accepted procedure for dismissing the uninjured athletes should also be developed.

Part D.

The responsibilities of the individual assigned to call for emergency medical assistance are covered here. This section also includes space for entering site-specific information for the location of the nearest telephone, emergency telephone number, directions to the injured athlete, and the location of the "flag" person. If known, the person calling for assistance should report the nature of the injury to the receptionist. After completing the call for assistance, this individual should privately report the status of emergency medical assistance to the person attending the injured athlete.

Part E.

Whether or not someone is needed to flag down and direct the emergency vehicle will depend on the site of the team's activities. If a flag person is needed, the procedures to follow are described here. In rare situations, where there is no telephone near the site of the injury, the flag person will be responsible for seeking emergency medical assistance.

Rehearsing emergency care procedures can be invaluable.

Immediate treatment of life-threatening injuries is extremely important. Being trained in basic first-aid and emergency procedures is invaluable and will give you more confidence when dealing with any type of injury.

PROVIDE FIRST AID

If the athlete is seriously injured, have your assistant coach, a parent, or a responsible athlete take the coins and the list of emergency telephone numbers from the first aid kit and call an ambulance. You or your trainer should stay with the injured athlete until help arrives.

Aids for Proper Care

If the injury is less serious and does not require assistance from trained medical personnel, you may be able to move the athlete from the sport setting to an area where care can begin. Two important aids to properly care for an injured athlete include a first aid kit and ice.

First Aid Kit

A well-stocked first aid kit does not have to be large, but it should contain the basic items that may be needed for appropriate care. The checklist in Figure 23-1 provides a guide for including commonly used supplies. Your trainer or you may wish to add and subtract from the kit on the basis of your experience and/or local policies or guidelines.

A good rule of thumb for coaches is, "If you can't treat the problems by using the supplies in a well-stocked first aid kit, then it is too big a problem for you to handle." You should be able to handle bruises, small cuts, strains, and sprains. When fractures, dislocations, back, or neck injuries occur, call for professional medical assistance.

Ice

Having access to ice is unique to every local setting. Thus, every coach or trainer may have to arrange for its provision in a different way. Ice, however, is very important to proper immediate care of many minor injuries and should, therefore, be readily available.

Care of Minor Injuries

R.I.C.E.

Unless you are also a physician, you should not attempt to care for anything except minor injuries (e.g., bruises, bumps, sprains). Many minor injuries can be cared for by using the R.I.C.E. formula (Figure 23-2).

_____ white athletic tape	_____ plastic bags for ice
_____ sterile gauze pads	_____ coins for pay telephone
_____ Telfa no-stick pads	_____ emergency care phone numbers
_____ ace bandages	_____ list of emergency phone numbers
_____ Band-aids, assorted sizes	_____ cotton swabs
_____ foam rubber/moleskin	_____ scissors/knife
_____ tweezers	_____ safety pins
_____ disinfectant	_____ soap
_____ first aid cream	_____ sling

Figure 23-1. First aid kit checklist.

The **R.I.C.E.** formula for care of minor injuries involves the following steps.

R = Rest. Keep the player out of action.

I = Ice. Apply ice to the injured area.

C = Compression. Wrap an elastic bangage around the injured area and the ice bag to hold the bag in place. The bandage should not be so tight as to cut off blood flow to the injured area.

E = Elevation. Let gravity drain the excess fluid.

Figure 23-2. The R.I.C.E. Formula.

Most minor injuries can benefit from using the R.I.C.E. formula for care.

When following the R.I.C.E. formula, ice should be kept on the injured area for 20 minutes and taken off for 20 minutes. Repeat this procedure three to four times. Icing should continue three times per day for the first 72 hours following the injury. After three days, extended care is necessary if the injury has not healed. At this time, options for care include: stretching and strengthening exercises, contrast treatments, and visiting a doctor for further diagnosis.

Contrast Treatments

If the injured area is much less swollen after 72 hours, but the pain is subsiding, contrast treatments will help. Use the following procedure:

1. Place the injured area in an ice bath or cover with an ice bag for one minute.
2. After using the ice, place the injured area in warm water (100-110°F) for three minutes.
3. Continue this rotation for five to seven bouts of ice and four to six bouts of heat.
4. Always end with the ice treatment.

Contrast treatments should be followed for the next three to five days. If swelling or pain still persists after several days of contrast treatments, the athlete should be sent to a physician for further tests. Chapter 24 of this manual deals with the rehabilitation of injuries. Read it carefully, because proper care is actually a form of rehabilitation.

COMMON MEDICAL PROBLEMS IN SPORT

Information about 23 common medical conditions that may occur in sport is presented in this section. The information about each condition includes: 1) a definition, 2) common symptoms, 3) immediate treatment, and 4) guidelines for returning the athlete to action.

ABRASION

Definition: Superficial skin wound caused by scraping.

Symptoms:
- minor bleeding
- redness
- burning sensation

Care:
- Cleanse the area with soap and water.
- Control the bleeding.
- Cover the area with sterile dressing.
- Monitor over several days for signs of infection.

Return to Action: After providing immediate care.

BACK or NECK INJURY

Definition: Any injury to the back or neck area that causes the athlete to become immobile or unconscious.

Symptoms:
- pain and tenderness over the spine
- numbness
- weakness or heaviness in limbs
- tingling feeling in extremities

Care:
- **Do not move the athlete.**
- Make sure athlete is breathing.
- Call for medical assistance.
- Do not move neck or back

Return to Action: With physician's permission.

BLISTERS

Definition: Localized collection of fluid in the outer portion of the skin (Figure 23-3).

Symptoms:
- redness
- inflammation
- oozing of fluid
- discomfort

Care:
- Clean the site with disinfectant.

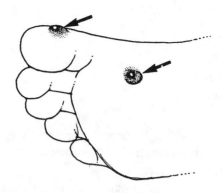

Figure 23-3. Blisters.

- Put disinfectant on the area.
- Cut a hole in a stack of several gauze or mole skin pads to be used as a doughnut surrounding the blister.
- Cover the area with a Band-aid.
- Alter the cause of the problem when possible (e.g., proper size and/or shape of the shoes).

Return to Action: Immediately, unless pain is severe.

CONTUSION

Definition: A bruise; an injury in which the skin is not broken (Figure 23-4).

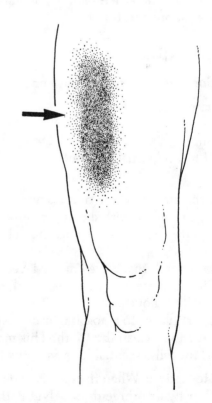

Figure 23-4. Contusion on thigh.

Symptoms:
- tenderness around the injury
- swelling
- localized pain
- discoloration

Care:
- Apply the R.I.C.E. formula for first three days.
- Use contrast treatments for days four to eight.
- Restrict activity.
- Provide padding when returning the athlete to activity.

Return to Action: When there is complete absence of pain and full range of motion and strength is restored.

CRAMPS

Definition: Involuntary and forceful contraction of a muscle; muscle spasm.

Symptoms:
- localized pain in contracting muscle

Care:
- Slowly stretch the muscle.
- Massage the muscle.

Return to Action: When pain is gone and full range of motion is restored.

DENTAL INJURY

Definition: Any injury to mouth or teeth.

Symptoms:
- pain
- bleeding
- loss of tooth (partial or total)

Care:
- Clear the airway where necessary.
- Stop the bleeding with direct pressure.
- Make sure excess blood does not clog the airway.
- Save any teeth that were knocked free; store them in a cup specially designed for this or in the athlete's mouth.
- Transport player to a hospital or dentist.
- Do not rub or clean the tooth. This may kill important cells essential for saving the tooth.

Return to Action: When the pain is gone (usually within two to three days) AND with permission of a dentist or physician.

DISLOCATION

Definition: Loss of normal anatomical alignment of a joint (Figure 23-5).

Symptoms:
- complaints of joint slipping in and out (subluxation)
- deformity
- pain at the joint

Care:
- Immobilize before moving.
- Must be treated by a physician.
- Obtain medical care. Do not attempt to put joint back into place.
- R.I.C.E.

Return to Action: With permission of physician.

EYE INJURY—CONTUSION

Definition: Direct blow to the eye and region surrounding the eye by a blunt object.

Symptoms:
- pain
- redness of eye
- watery eye

Care:
- Have the athlete lie down with his/her eyes closed.

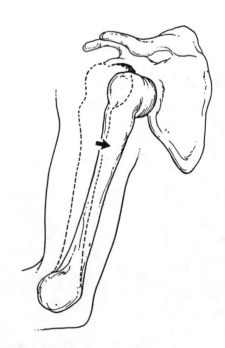

Figure 23-5. Shoulder dislocation, when upper arm (humerus) moves totally out of its normal position.

- Place a folded cloth, soaked in cold water, gently on the eye.
- Seek medical attention if injury is assessed as severe.

Return to Action: For minor injury, athlete may return to action after symptoms clear; for severe injury, with permission of physician.

EYE INJURY—FOREIGN OBJECT

Definition: Object between eyelid and eyeball.

Symptoms:
- pain
- redness of eye
- watery eye
- inability to keep eye open

Care:
- Do not rub the eye.
- Allow tears to form in eye.
- Carefully try to remove loose object with sterile cotton swab.
- If object is embedded in the eye, have the athlete close both eyes, loosely cover both eyes with sterile dressing, and bring the athlete to an emergency room or ophthalmologist.

Return to Action: With permission of physician.

FAINTING

Definition: Dizziness and loss of consciousness that may be caused by an injury, exhaustion, heat illness, emotional stress, or lack of oxygen.

Symptoms:
- dizziness
- cold, clammy skin
- pale
- seeing "spots" before one's eyes
- weak, rapid pulse

Care:
- Have the athlete lie down and elevate feet or have the athlete sit with head between knees.

Return to Action: With permission of physician.

FRACTURE

Definition: A crack or complete break in a bone. A simple fracture is a broken bone, but with unbroken skin. An open fracture is a broken bone that also breaks the skin (Figure 23-6).

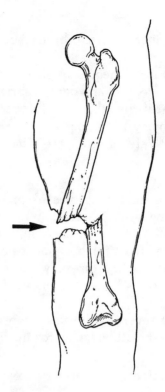

Figure 23-6. Open fracture in thigh.

Symptoms:
- pain at fracture site
- tenderness, swelling
- deformity or unnatural position
- loss of function in injured area
- open wound, bleeding (open fracture)
- [Note that a simple fracture may not be evident immediately. If localized pain persists, obtain medical assistance.]

Care:
- Stabilize injured bone by using splints, slings, or bandages.
- Do not attempt to straighten an injured part when immobilizing it.
- If skin is broken (open fracture), keep the open wound clean by covering it with the cleanest available cloth. Check for shock and treat if necessary.

Return to Action: With permission of physician.

HEAD INJURY—CONSCIOUS

Definition: Any injury that causes the athlete to be unable to respond in a coherent fashion to known facts (name, date, etc.).

Symptoms:
- Mild: dizziness, nausea, headache, and confusion
- Severe: pupils unequal in size and/or non-responsive to light and dark; disorientation
- [Note that if the athlete is unconscious, expect an injury to the back or neck and care for the athlete as if it were a back or neck injury.]

Care:
- Mild: If the mild symptoms are present, athlete may be moved carefully when dizziness disappears. Athletes with head injuries should be removed from further practice or competition that day and carefully observed for a minimum of 24 hours. Obtain medical assistance.
- Severe: If severe symptoms are present, do not move the athlete. Call for medical assistance.

Return to Action: With permission of physician.

HEAD INJURY—UNCONSCIOUS

Definition: Any injury in which the athlete is unable to respond to external stimuli by verbal or visual means.

Symptoms:
- athlete is unconscious
- cuts or bruises around the head may be evident

Care:
- ANY TIME AN ATHLETE IS UNCONSCIOUS, ASSUME AN INJURY TO THE SPINAL CORD OR BRAIN.
- If necessary, clear the airway keeping the player's neck straight. Do not move the athlete.
- Call for medical assistance.

Return to Action: With permission of physician.

HEAT EXHAUSTION

Definition: Heat disorder that may lead to heat stroke.

Symptoms:
- fatigue
- profuse sweating
- chills
- throbbing pressure in the head

- nausea
- normal body temperature
- pale and clammy skin

Care:
- Remove the athlete from heat and sun.
- Provide plenty of water.
- Rest the athlete in a supine position with feet elevated about 12 inches.
- Loosen or remove the athlete's clothing.

Return to Action: Next day if symptoms are no longer present.

HEAT STROKE

Definition: Life-threatening heat disorder.

Symptoms:
- extremely high body temperature
- hot, red, and dry skin
- rapid and strong pulse
- disorientation
- unconscious

Care:
- Immediately call for medical assistance.
- Immediately cool body by cold sponging, immersion in cool water, and cold packs.
- Remove clothing.

Return to Action: With permission of physician.

LACERATIONS

Definition: A tearing or cutting of the skin.

Symptoms:
- bleeding
- swelling

Care:
- Direct pressure to the wound for four or five minutes usually will stop bleeding.
- Clean the wound with disinfectant.
- If stitches are required, send to a doctor within five hours.

Return to Action: As soon as pain is gone, if the wound can be protected from further injury.

LOSS OF WIND

Definition: A forceful blow to mid-abdomen area that causes inability to breathe.

Symptoms:
- rapid, shallow breathing
- gasping for breath

Care:
- Check athlete for other injuries.
- Place athlete in a supine position.
- Calm the athlete in order to foster slower breathing.
- Loosen belt and clothing.

Return to Action: After five minutes of rest to regain composure and breathing has returned to normal rate.

NOSE BLEED

Definition: Bleeding from the nose.

Symptoms:
- bleeding
- swelling
- pain
- deformity of nose

Care:
- Calm the athlete.
- Get the athlete into a sitting position.
- Pinch the nostrils together with fingers while the athlete breathes through the mouth.
- Apply ice.
- If bleeding cannot be controlled, call for medical assistance.
- If the nose is deformed, refer athlete to a physician.

Return to Action: Minor nosebleed—when bleeding has stopped for several minutes. Serious nosebleed—no more competition that day; doctor's permission if a fracture has occurred.

PLANTAR FASCIITIS

Definition: Inflammation of the connective tissue (fascia) that runs from the heel to the toes.

Symptoms:
- arch and heel pain
- sharp pain ("stone bruise") near heel
- gradual onset of pain, which may be tolerated for weeks
- morning pain may be more severe
- pain may be noted after sitting
- pain may decrease throughout day

Care:
- Rest the foot.
- Stretch the Achilles' tendon before exercise.
- Use shoes with firm heel counter, good heel cushion, and arch support.

- Use of a heel lift may reduce shock to the foot and decrease the pain.
- Use adhesive strapping to support the arch.

Return to Action: When pain is gone.

PUNCTURE WOUND

Definition: Any hole made by the piercing of a pointed instrument.

Symptoms:
- breakage of the skin
- minor bleeding, possibly none
- tender around wound

Care:
- Cleanse the area with soap and water.
- Control the bleeding.
- Cover the area with sterile dressing.
- Consult physician about the need for a tetanus shot.
- Monitor over several days for signs of infection.

Return to Action: With permission of physician.

SHOCK

Definition: Adverse reaction of the body to physical or psychological trauma.

Symptoms:
- pale
- cold, clammy skin
- dizziness
- nausea
- faint feeling

Care
- Have the athlete lie down.
- Calm the athlete.
- Elevate the feet, unless it is a head injury.
- Send for emergency help.
- Control the player's temperature.
- Loosen tight-fitting clothing.
- Control the pain or bleeding if necessary.

Return to Action: With permission of physician.

SPRAIN

Definition: A stretching or a partial or complete tear of the ligaments surrounding a joint (Figure 23-7).

Symptoms:
- pain at the joint

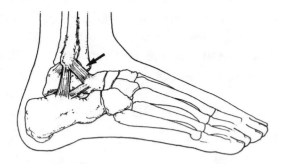

Figure 23-7. Frequently torn ligament in the ankle—the anterior talofibular ligament.

- pain aggravated by motion at the joint
- tenderness and swelling
- looseness at the joint

Care:
- Immobilize at time of injury if pain is severe; may use corner flag post as a splint.
- Use the R.I.C.E. formula.
- Send the player to a physician.

Return to Action: When pain and swelling are gone, full range of motion is reestablished, and strength and stability are within 95 percent of the non-injured limb throughout range of motion.

Also when light formal activity is possible with no favoring of the injury, or moderate to full intensity formal activity can be resumed with no favoring of the injury.

STRAIN

Definition: Stretching or tearing of the muscle or tendons that attach the muscle to the bone (commonly referred to as a "muscle pull") (Figure 23-8).

Symptoms:
- localized pain brought on by stretching or contracting the muscle in question
- unequal strength between limbs
- swelling
- discolorization after 24 hours if strain is severe

Care:
- Use the R.I.C.E. formula.
- Use contrast treatments for days four through eight.

Return to Action: When the athlete can stretch the injured segment as far as the non-injured

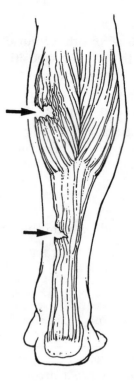

Figure 23-8. Muscle strain in belly of muscle (upper) and in muscle tendon unit (lower).

segment, when strength is equal to opposite segment, and when the athlete can perform basic skills of the sport without favoring the injury. Depending on the severity of the strain, it may take from one day to more than two weeks to return to action.

MAINTAINING APPROPRIATE RECORDS

The immediate care you provide to an injured athlete is important to limit the extent of the injury and to set the stage for appropriate rehabilitation. However, immediate care is not the end of prudent action when an injury occurs. Two additional brief but valuable tasks should be completed. First, complete an on-site injury report form (Supplement D), and second, log the injury on the summary of season injuries form (Supplement E).

On-Site Injury Report Form

It is important for you or an athletic trainer to maintain a record of the injuries that occur to your athletes. This information may be helpful to guide delayed care or medical treatment and may be very important if any legal problems develop in connection with the injury. Supplement D includes a standard form that will help guide the recording of pertinent information relative to each injury. These records should be kept for several years following an injury. You should check on legal requirements in your state to determine how long these records should be kept.

Summary of Season Injuries Form

Supplement E, the summary of season injuries form, lists each of the common medical conditions that occur in sport and also provides a space for you or your trainer to record when each type of injury occurred. At the end of the season, you should total the incidence of each injury type to see if there is any trend to the kind of injuries your team has suffered. If a trend exists, evaluate your training methods in all areas of practices and competition. Try to alter drills or circumstances that may be causing injuries. Review Chapter 21, Prevention of Common Sports Injuries, for techniques that may help you prevent injuries. Perhaps your practice routine ignores or overemphasizes some area of stretching or conditioning. Decide on a course of action that may be implemented for next season and write your thoughts in the space provided or note the appropriate changes you wish to make on your season or practice plans.

SUMMARY

This chapter attempts to acquaint you with various injuries associated with sport and how you and/or your athletic trainer should be prepared to deal with these injuries. If you have prepared your first aid kit, brought along the medical records, and familiarized yourself with the different types of injuries, you should be able to handle whatever situation arises. Follow the steps that are outlined for you, and remember—you are not a doctor. If you are in doubt about how to proceed, use the coins in your first aid kit and call for professional medical help. Do not make decisions about treatments if you are not qualified to make them.

Remember, react quickly and with confidence. Most injuries will be minor and the injured athlete will need only a little reassurance before they can be moved to the bench area. Injuries will always occur in sport. Therefore, you must prepare yourself to deal with whatever happens in a calm, responsible manner.

Athlete's Medical Information

(to be completed by parents/guardians and athlete)

Athlete's Name: _____ Athlete's Birthdate: _____

Parents' Names: _____ Date: _____

Address: _____

Phone No's.: (____)_____ (____)_____ (____)_____
                        (Home)   (Work)   (Other)

Who to contact in case of emergency (if parents cannot be immediately contacted):

Name: _____ Relationship: _____

Home Phone No.: (____)_____ Work Phone No.: (____)_____

Name: _____ Relationship: _____

Home Phone No.: (____)_____ Work Phone No.: (____)_____

Hospital preference: _____ Emergency Phone No.: (____)_____

Doctor preference: _____ Office Phone No.: (____)_____

MEDICAL HISTORY

Part I. Complete the following:

	Date	Doctor	Doctor's Phone No.
1. Last tetanus shot?	_____		
2. Last dental examination?	_____	_____	_____
3. Last eye examination?	_____	_____	_____

Part II. Has your child or did your child have any of the following?

General Conditions:	Circle one		Circle one or both		Injuries:	Circle one		Circle one or both	
1. Fainting spells/dizziness	Yes	No	Past	Present	1. Toes	Yes	No	Past	Present
2. Headaches	Yes	No	Past	Present	2. Feet	Yes	No	Past	Present
3. Convulsions/epilepsy	Yes	No	Past	Present	3. Ankles	Yes	No	Past	Present
4. Asthma	Yes	No	Past	Present	4. Lower legs	Yes	No	Past	Present
5. High blood pressure	Yes	No	Past	Present	5. Knees	Yes	No	Past	Present
6. Kidney problems	Yes	No	Past	Present	6. Thighs	Yes	No	Past	Present
7. Intestinal disorder	Yes	No	Past	Present	7. Hips	Yes	No	Past	Present
8. Hernia	Yes	No	Past	Present	8. Lower back	Yes	No	Past	Present
9. Diabetes	Yes	No	Past	Present	9. Upper back	Yes	No	Past	Present
10. Heart disease/disorder	Yes	No	Past	Present	10. Ribs	Yes	No	Past	Present
11. Dental plate	Yes	No	Past	Present	11. Abdomen	Yes	No	Past	Present
12. Poor vision	Yes	No	Past	Present	12. Chest	Yes	No	Past	Present
13. Poor hearing	Yes	No	Past	Present	13. Neck	Yes	No	Past	Present
14. Skin disorder	Yes	No	Past	Present	14. Fingers	Yes	No	Past	Present
15. Allergies	Yes	No			15. Hands	Yes	No	Past	Present
Specify:_____			Past	Present	16. Wrists	Yes	No	Past	Present
_____			Past	Present	17. Forearms	Yes	No	Past	Present
16. Joint dislocation or					18. Elbows	Yes	No	Past	Present
separations	Yes	No			19. Upper arms	Yes	No	Past	Present
Specify:_____			Past	Present	20. Shoulders	Yes	No	Past	Present
_____			Past	Present	21. Head	Yes	No	Past	Present
17. Serious or significant ill-					22. Serious or significant in-				
nesses not included above	Yes	No			juries not included above	Yes	No		
Specify:_____			Past	Present	Specify: _____			Past	Present
			Past	Present	_____			Past	Present
18. Others:_____			Past	Present	23. Others: _____			Past	Present
_____			Past	Present	_____			Past	Present

SUPPLEMENT A:

Part III. Circle appropriate response to each question. For each "Yes" response, provide additional information.

	Circle one		Additional information

1. Is you child currently taking any medication? If yes, describe medication, amount, and reason for taking. — Yes   No   _____

2. Does your child have any allergic reactions to medication, bee stings, food, etc.? If yes, describe agents that cause adverse reactions and describe these reactions. — Yes   No   _____

3. Does your child wear any appliances (e.g., glasses, contact lenses, hearing aid, false teeth, braces, etc.)? If yes, describe appliances. — Yes   No   _____

4. Has your child had any surgical operations? If yes, indicate site, explain the reason for the surgery, and describe the level of success. — Yes   No   _____

5. Has a physician placed any restrictions on your child's present activities? If yes, describe restrictions. — Yes   No   _____

6. Does your child have any existing and/or past medical or emotional conditions that require special concern and attention by a sports coach? If yes, explain. — Yes   No   _____

7. Does your child have any deformities (e.g., abnormal curvature of the spine, heart problems, one kidney, blindness in one eye, one testicle, etc.)? If yes, describe. — Yes   No   _____

8. Is there a history of serious family illnesses (e.g., diabetes, bleeding disorders, heart attack before age 50, etc.)? If yes, describe illnesses. — Yes   No   _____

9. Has your child lost consciousness or sustained a concussion ? — Yes   No   _____

10. Has your child experienced fainting spells or dizziness while exercising? — Yes   No   _____

Part IV. Has your child or did your child have any of the following personal habits?

Personal Habit	Circle one		Circle one or both		Indicate extent or amount
1. Smoking	Yes	No	Past	Present	_____
2. Smokeless tobacco	Yes	No	Past	Present	_____
3. Alcohol	Yes	No	Past	Present	_____
4. Recreational drugs (e.g., marijuana, cocain, etc.)	Yes	No	Past	Present	_____
5. Steroids	Yes	No	Past	Present	_____
6. Others Specify: _____	Yes	No	Past	Present	_____
_____	Yes	No	Past	Present	_____
_____	Yes	No	Past	Present	_____

Part V. Please explain, below, any "Yes" responses in Parts II, III, and IV or any other concerns that have present implications for my coaching your child. Also, describe special first aid requirements, if appropriate. An additional sheet may be attached if necessary.

_____

_____

_____

_____

_____

_____

_____

_____

Parental Instruction Concerning Medical Treatment

Card No. _____

Wrestler's Name _____ Date of Birth _____

Parent/Guardian Name _____

Address _____

Telephone Numbers: Home: _____

                          Work: _____

Please indicate another person to contact in the event of an accident and we are unable to reach you:

Name _____ Telephone _____

Insurance Company _____

Policy Number _____

Is this athlete presently on medication? _____

If yes, please list medication(s) _____

_____

Drug Sensitivities _____

Other Allergies _____

Please read the alternative statements below and sign under the one that you choose.
DO NOT SIGN MORE THAN ONE!

1. If my child needs medical attention, it is my wish that I be contacted before any medical procedures are done on my child, unless immediate treatment is necessary to save my child's life or to prevent permanent injury.

    Signature of Parent/Guardian _____

    Date _____

2. If my child needs medical treatment while participating, it is my wish that the treatment be begun while efforts are being made to contact me. So that treatment is not delayed, I consent to any medical procedures that the physician believes needed, on the understanding that efforts will continue to be made to contact me. I accept responsibility for all cost related to such treatment.

    Signature of Parent/Guardian _____

    Date _____

Coach's Name _____

Club Name _____

SUPPLEMENT C:

EMERGENCY PLAN FORM*

Essential Items:

1. Well-stocked first aid kit
2. Medical forms for each athlete (Athlete's Medical Information, Athlete's Medical Information Summary, and Medical Release)
3. On-Site Injury Report form

PROCEDURES

A. COACH
1. Take charge of situation
2. Alert previously assigned people to their tasks

B. _____ / _____

(Name and alternate person in charge of injured athlete; likely the coach or assistant coach.)
1. Calm and assure athlete.
2. If possible, determine nature and extent of injury.
3. If possible, privately report nature and extent of injury to person calling for emergency medical assistance.
4. If athlete is unconscious or a spinal injury is suspected, do not move the athlete.
5. Provide appropriate emergency care if warranted.
   a. ABC's (open Airways, restore Breathing, and restore Circulation)
   b. Control bleeding by direct pressure.
   c. For heat stroke, immediately cool body by cold sponging, immersion in cold water, and cold packs.
   d. For shock, have athlete lie down, calm athlete, elevate feet unless head injury, control athlete's temperature, loosen tight fitting clothing, and control pain or bleeding if necessary.
   e. For allergic reaction, use ana-kit if available.
6. Transfer care to emergency medical personnel. (Note that the Medical Release Form and one individual whose name appears on the form must accompany athletes to medical center unless parents or guardians are available.)
7. Provide Athlete's Medical Information Summary to emergency medical personnel.

C. _____ / _____

(Name and alternate person in charge of uninjured athletes.)
1. Direct uninjured athletes to safe area within voice and vision of coach.
2. Have a plan in place to divert the attention of uninjured athletes from the emergency situation.
3. Use accepted procedure to dismiss athletes from practice/competition.

D. _____ / _____

(Name and alternate person responsible for phoning for emergency medical assistance.)
1. Get coins from first aid kit if needed for phone call.
2. Location of nearest phone by site of activity:
   Site   Location
   _____   _____
   _____   _____
   _____   _____
3. Emergency phone number by site of activity:
   Site   Phone No.
   _____   _____
   _____   _____
   _____   _____
4. Report the nature of the injury and calmly respond to questions.
5. Directions to sites:
   Site   Directions
   _____   _____
   _____   _____
   _____   _____
   _____   _____
6. Location of flag person by site:
   Site   Location
   _____   _____
   _____   _____
   _____   _____
7. Remain on the phone until the other person hangs up.
8. Return to person attending to injured athlete and privately report status of emergency medical assistance.

E. _____ / _____

(Name and alternate person responsible for flagging down emergency vehicle.)
1. Go to designated location to flag down emergency vehicle.
   Site   Location
   _____   _____
   _____   _____
   _____   _____

Note that the site and location information corresponds to D.6. If no phone is within reasonable distance from the activity site, flag person should go to location where a vehicle can be flagged down.
2. Direct emergency medical personnel to injured athlete.

A. COACH, cont.
3. Use the information on the Roster Summary of Contacts in an Emergency to phone the injured athlete's parents (guardians) or their designees.
4. Complete the On-Site Injury Report form.

*A minimum of 4 completed copies of this form is needed; one for each of the individuals with assigned tasks. Make sure that information is included at all practice and competition sites.

On-Site Injury Report Form

Name _____ Date of injury ___/___/___
       (Injured Player)   mo day yr

Address _____
       (Street)   (City, State)   (Zip)

Telephone _____
        (Home)   (Other)

Nature and extent of injury: _____

_____

How did the injury occur? _____

_____

Describe first aid given, including name(s) of attendee(s): _____

_____

Disposition: to hospital   to home   to physician

Other _____

_____

Was protective equipment worn?   _____ Yes   _____ No

Explanation: _____

_____

Condition of the playing surface _____

_____

Names and addresses of witnesses:

Name	Street	City	State	Tel.
Name	Street	City	State	Tel.
Name	Street	City	State	Tel.

Other comments: _____

_____

_____

Signed	Date	Title-Position

Summary of Season Injuries Form

Injury Type	First 4 Weeks	Middle Weeks	Last 4 Weeks	Total
1. Abrasion				
2. Back or Neck Injury				
3. Blisters				
4. Contusion				
5. Cramps				
6. Dental Injury				
7. Dislocation				
8. Eye Injury—Contusion				
9. Eye Injury—Foreign Object				
10. Fainting				
11. Fracture				
12. Head Injury Conscious				
13. Head Injury Unconscious				
14. Heat Exhaustion				
15. Heat Stroke				
16. Lacerations				
17. Loss of Wind				
18. Nose Bleed				
19. Plantar Fascitis				
20. Puncture Wound				
21. Shin Splints				
22. Shock				
23. Sprain				
24. Strain				
25. Others:				

Do you see a trend?   YES   NO

Steps to take to reduce injuries next season:

(1) _____

(2) _____

(3) _____

SUMMARY OF SEASON INJURIES

(4) _____
(5) _____
(6) _____
(7) _____
(8) _____
(9) _____
(10) _____
(11) _____
(12) _____
(13) _____
(14) _____
(15) _____
(16) _____
(17) _____
(18) _____
(19) _____
(20) _____
(21) _____
(22) _____
(23) _____
(24) _____
(25) _____
(26) _____
(27) _____
(28) _____
(29) _____
(30) _____
(31) _____
(32) _____
(33) _____
(34) _____

24
Rehabilitation of Common Sports Injuries

QUESTIONS TO CONSIDER

- What are the important components of a rehabilitation program?
- How can a coach tell when athletes are trying to "come back" too fast?
- Is it necessary to obtain permission from parents and a physician before returning an injured athlete to competition?
- Following an injury, what determines if an activity is too stressful?

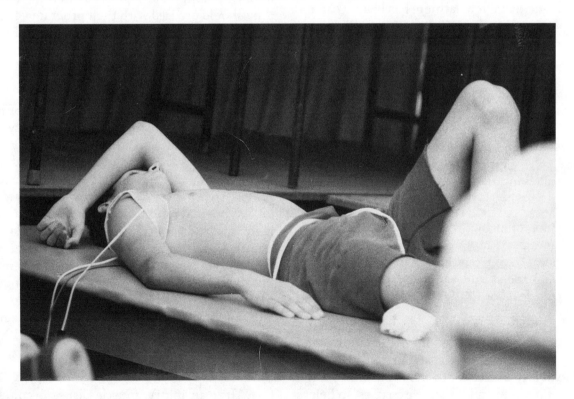

Though injuries do occur, proper care and rehabilitation will facilitate speedy recovery and return to competition.

INTRODUCTION

Decisions about the rehabilitation of injuries and re-entry into competition must be made according to a flexible set of guidelines, not hard and fast rules. Every individual on your team and each injury is unique. Therefore, rehabilitation techniques and re-entry criteria will differ for each athlete.

GENERAL PROCEDURES

Most injuries suffered by your athletes will not be treated by a physician. Therefore, you, the athlete, possibly an athletic trainer, and the athlete's parents will determine when the athlete returns to action. It is prudent to seek the parents' written permission to return a previously injured athlete to practices and games. If an athlete has been treated by a physician, written clearance from the physician should also be obtained.

Athletes, coaches, and parents realize that missing practices will reduce the athlete's ability to help the team. Pressure is often exerted on the coach to play injured athletes before they are fully recovered, especially if they are the stars of the team. If an athlete has been treated by a physician for an injury, written clearance by both the physician and the parents should be obtained before permitting the athlete to return to practice and competition. Also, clarification as to any limitations on participation should be obtained from the physician.

Chances of an injury recurring are greatly increased if an athlete returns too soon. The following five criteria should be met, in order, before allowing an injured athlete back into full physical activity:

1. absence of pain,
2. full range of motion at the injured area,
3. normal strength and size at the injured area,
4. normal speed and agility, and
5. normal level of fitness.

If a physician is not overseeing an injured player's recovery, the task of rehabilitation will probably fall upon the coach and/or athletic trainer. Flexibility exercises, to help regain normal range of motion, and resistive exercises, to help regain normal strength, form the basis of a re-habilitation program. Start with simple range of motion exercises. Presence of pain during movement is the key to determining if activity is too stressful. The onset of pain means too much is being attempted too soon. When an athlete can handle flexibility exercises, then resistive exercises may be added to the program.

ABSENCE OF PAIN

Most injuries are accompanied by pain, although the pain may not always be evident immediately when the injury occurs. Usually, the pain disappears quickly if the injury is a simple bruise, or a minor strain or sprain. For more serious injuries such as dislocations or fractures, the pain may remain for days or weeks. Once the pain is gone, the athlete can start the range of motion portion of a rehabilitation program.

The chance of an injury recurring is greatly increased if an athlete returns to action too soon.

The main goal of a rehabilitation program is to re-establish normal range of motion, strength, power, and muscular endurance at the site of the injury. As long as athletes remain free of pain, they should proceed with their programs. If pain recurs, they should eliminate pain-producing movements until they are pain-free again.

FULL RANGE OF MOTION

Injuries generally reduce the range of motion at a joint. The more severe the injury, the greater the reduction in range of motion. As soon as they are able to move an injured area without pain, athletes should be encouraged to progressively increase the range of movement until a normal range is achieved. For example, if the athlete has strained a groin muscle, the muscle should be stretched as much as possible without causing pain. Initially, the movement may be slight. With stretching, the full range of motion will eventually return. When the athlete can move the injured joint through its normal range, strengthening exercises should begin.

NORMAL STRENGTH AND SIZE

After an injury, muscle disuse occurs (by cast, splint, wrap, or simply "favoring" the area).

As a result of disuse, muscles become smaller and weaker than they were before the injury. Just because a cast is removed and the injury has "healed," does not mean that the athlete is ready to practice and compete at full speed. Loss of muscle mass means a loss of strength. Letting athletes resume normal practice schedules before their strength has returned to pre-injury levels could lead to re-injury.

Your goal is to have the athletes regain full strength through the entire range of motion before allowing them to return to competition.

Strengthening the injured area should be done conservatively. If weights are used, start with light weights and perform the exercise through the entire range of motion. If the exercise causes pain, then lighter weights should be used. To determine when full strength and size have been regained, compare the injured area to the corresponding non-injured area on the opposite side of the body. When both areas are of equal size and strength, then the athlete may progress to the next phase of recovery.

NORMAL SPEED AND AGILITY

When an athlete returns to practice, incorporate progressively greater levels of intensity of activity. You should be careful to gradually challenge the previously injured body part. In your observation of injured athletes, try to detect any favoring of an injured part or inability to smoothly perform a skill at increasing intensities. When athletes can move at pre-injury speed and agility, they are almost ready to compete.

The main goal of a rehabilitation program is to rees- tablish normal range of motion, strength, and muscular endurance to the injured area.

NORMAL LEVEL OF FITNESS

Every extended layoff reduces the level of muscular fitness. While recovering, the athlete may be able to exercise other body parts without affecting the injured area. For example, someone with a sprained ankle may not be able to run but may be able to swim. Someone with a broken wrist may be able to do a variety of lower body activities such as jogging and biking. Cautiously encourage this type of activity because it helps to maintain portions of pre-injury levels of fitness. Athletes who have missed long periods of activity due to an injury should practice for several days after meeting the previous criteria before being allowed to compete. Their cardiovascular and muscular systems need time to adjust to the demands of competition. The longer the layoff, the more conditioning work athletes will need.

SUMMARY

When the pain is gone, and the range of motion, strength, agility, and conditioning are back to normal, your athlete is ready to re-enter practice and competition. The entire process may have taken two days for a bruise to 12 or more weeks for a fracture. In either case, if you have followed the general guidelines of this chapter, you know you have acted in the best long-term interest of the athlete. Participation is important, but only if participation is achieved with a healthy body. Resist the pressure and temptation to rush athletes into competition before they are ready. Your patience will be rewarded in the contests to come.

25
Contagious Diseases

QUESTIONS TO CONSIDER

- Why are contagious diseases so common in the sport of wrestling?
- What are the two most common forms of the HIV virus transmittal?
- What is the difference between viral and bacterial skin diseases?
- What are some common conditions that mimic contagious diseases?

INTRODUCTION

The following issue pertaining to blood borne pathogens and infectious skin diseases is one that could very well bring to an end wrestling, as we know it, if not controlled within the wrestling community and public opinion.

Wrestling is the ultimate in close, one-on-one competition. The constant skin-on-skin contact makes it imperative that wrestlers avoid contagious skin diseases. If a wrestler does contract a contagious skin disease, the coach should have a rudimentary knowledge of common conditions so that the problem can be dealt with in a quick and medically correct manner. New vaccines, antibiotics, and knowledge of disease gestation and transmission has greatly aided the diagnosis and treatment of infectious diseases. No doubt this chapter will have to be rewritten in future editions of this book, to keep pace with ever changing medical science.

As wrestling coaches, it is our responsibility and duty to approach this topic with the utmost urgency and seriousness. The unethical behavior of just *one* coach who allows an infected wrestler to compete will negatively affect every

athlete who participates in the sport and threaten the continuance of wrestling forever.

BLOOD-BORNE PATHOGENS

AIDS

The Acquired Immuno Deficiency Syndrome is a disease that weakens the immune system and makes the person extremely susceptible to a variety of infections and cancerous problems. This disease is caused by the human immuno-deficiency virus (HIV). The first case was reported to the United States Centers for Disease Control in 1981. Since then, millions of people worldwide have become infected with HIV, and hundreds of thousands have died from this disease. The symptoms and signs vary depending upon which organ system in the body is a problem at the time. Anything and everything can malfunction when a person becomes weakened with the HIV virus. As far as known, the eventual outcome in all patients is death from this disease! Treatment has to be with sophisticated medications given by a medical team that is interested and knowledgeable about this epidemic disease.

The virus is usually transmitted via close sexual contact or sharing of dirty needles by drug abusers. The worry in wrestling is that an HIV positive wrestler might transfer the disease via blood during a wrestling contest. A person can have the virus in the system and not be aware of it for months or years. Since there is no protective vaccine or good antibiotic, a person must try to prevent contracting AIDS by avoiding all illicit drug usage and any unsafe sexual practices. On the wrestling mat all bleeding must be stopped before the wrestler can continue. The mat must be kept clean of blood at all times.

Because of the deadly nature of this disease, strict control of contact with blood is a necessity. It might be debated whether all wrestlers above age 16 should get an HIV test at the beginning of each wrestling season. Whether this would be economically reasonable or feasible is questioned and whether the yield would be significant is unknown. Perhaps colleges and olympic groups could set up a program with a local hospital or blood bank and get HIV tests done at a reduced rate, or simply require the wrestler to pay for the test himself, in order to be eligible to wrestle. This author feels that such a program would not be an infringement upon a person's civil rights; it would simply be a way of making this sport a safe sport for all competitors. A wrestler who is HIV positive should quit wrestling and participate only in noncontact sports.

Hepatitis B

Hepatitis is a term that means inflammation of the liver. There are many causes of liver inflammation, such as viral, chemicals, drugs, alcohol, and anatomical problems like gall bladder disease. One common cause of hepatitis is a virus called hepatitis B. The gestational period for this disease is one to three months after contact. It is commonly transmitted via exposure to blood. The most common cases involve sharing dirty, intravenous needles or unsafe sexual activity. The worry in wrestling is that exposure to blood during a contest might transmit this disease.

The signs and symptoms of hepatitis can vary dramatically from a very mild, hardly noticeable illness to one with severe weakness, loss of appetite, weight loss, headache, and abdominal pain. The urine can be dark, the skin can be yellow, and the patient can appear quite ill. In rare cases hepatitis B can cause death. Many patients clear the system of the virus and get back to a normal healthy life rather quickly. Some patients do not clear the virus for many years. Some chronic carriers seem to be fairly healthy and their body adjusts to having the virus in the system. Others can become chronically ill. Any patient with hepatitis B must be under a doctor's care. Rest and excellent nutrition is always quite helpful. Sometimes immune globulin shots are given. There is no good antibiotic for this virus.

An exciting new hepatitis B vaccine is now available. When it first came out only medical personnel got the vaccine. Then policemen, teachers, and other workers who are exposed to blood got the vaccine. Recently the American Academy of Pediatrics suggested that all newborns get the vaccine, as well as sexually active young adults. The vaccine is given as a shot in the shoulder muscle. A shot is given at one month, two months, and six months. Each shot costs about $50.00, but many patients can get the vaccine at their county or city health department for a reduced cost, or even at no charge.

The most common age group involved with hepatitis B is the 15 to 25 year old age group. It might be advisable for wrestling organizations to consider vaccinating all of their wrestlers 16 years of age and above. That would completely eliminate the possibility of any wrestler contracting this disease. If a wrestler does contract hepatitis B, he must not compete in any way until he has been cleared by his physician.

VIRAL SKIN DISEASES

Herpes Simplex

Herpes is a very common blistery, viral eruption seen on the skin or mucous membranes. The most common area for this virus is on the lips, but it can occur absolutely anywhere on the skin. Before the age of modern medicine

Precautions for Preventing the Transmission of Blood-Borne Pathogens (BBP's)

It is generally agreed among experts that the likelihood of transmission of blood-borne pathogens—such as the human immunodeficiency virus (HIV) and hepatitis B—through athletics is extremely low. In fact, to date the only case of rumored transmission of HIV in athletics—that of an Italian soccer player—has been dismissed. Even though transmission of BBP's is unlikely in athletics, coaches should exercise precautions by

- removing from play athletes who have bloody wounds and
- personally avoiding direct contact with blood and other fluids likely to contain blood.

Removing an Athlete from Competition

If an athlete sustains a wound in which blood or exudate are present, bleeding must be stopped and open skin lesions must be covered completely before permitting the athlete to return to competition.

Avoiding Direct Contact with Blood and Bodily Fluids Containing Blood

Latex gloves should be worn when tending to an injury in which blood or fluids containing blood are present. If the hands and skin become contaminated, they should be washed immediately after removing the gloves.

Disposable contaminated materials should be placed in a biohazard container. This may be a plastic trash bag that is clearly labeled as containing biohazardous materials and that can be sealed.

Contaminated structures, equipment, and instruments must be cleaned with a freshly mixed bleach solution. (This contains one part bleach and ten parts water.) Clothing that becomes contaminated must be removed, placed in an appropriately labeled container, and later washed at 160° F. (71° C.) with detergent for 30 minutes.

If mouth-to-mouth resuscitation is performed, a mouth shield should be worn.

---

if the virus would get into the eye, it would commonly cause blindness in that eye. As the cluster of blisters form, there can be throbbing, stinging, and pain. Nearby lymph nodes can also swell and cause great discomfort.

The virus enters the body through an open area in the skin or mucous membranes. It travels up the nerve to the central nervous system. The virus then never completely leaves the nerves in the backbone for the rest of the person's life. Periodically the virus can activate and leave the central nervous system. It will travel back out the nerves to the skin and manifest as blisters. When one wrestler gives it to another wrestler, this is called Herpes Gladiatorum. Nicknames for this eruption are "cold sores" and "fever blisters."

There is no vaccine to prevent a person from contracting this disease, but there is an ex-

cellent antibiotic whose brand name is Zovirax. This antibiotic does not eradicate the virus from the body, but does greatly diminish the severity of episodes. If a wrestler suffers from frequent "cold sores," Zovirax can be taken in pill form several days prior to a wrestling meet to prevent an eruption. Several other exciting new anti-herpes antibiotics are being developed and might be available in the near future. If a wrestler has an active cold sore on the lip, he should do no live wrestling unless he agrees to wear a face mask. No part of the blister fluid should be allowed to touch any other wrestler or the mat. (See Figure 25-1).

Chicken Pox (Varicella)

Chicken Pox (Varicella) is a common, highly contagious viral disease that manifests with scattered blisters. There can be only a few or hundreds of blisters. There can be fever, chills, loss of appetite, and headache. Older children or young adults are often quite sick. This eruption starts one or two weeks after contact with an infected person.

There is an exciting new vaccine for chicken pox. It is being used now in specific situations and by 1995, might be used routinely in all children to eliminate this disease. Studies are ongoing to determine the long-term safety and effectiveness of this vaccine. If a wrestler has not had the vaccine and seems to be coming down with the illness, he can be given Zovirax antibiotic pills. Sometimes a doctor will give immune globulin shots. If a wrestler has had chicken pox and is in good, overall immune health, then he need not fear catching chicken pox a second time, as he should be immune to it. A wrestler with chicken pox should not compete until the blisters are completely flat and dry and the wrestler feels well. (See Figure 25-2).

Shingles

Shingles (Zoster) is a blistery skin eruption caused by the chicken pox virus. It typically occurs in a band on either the right or left side of the body. It can be found in any area on the body, including the face. It is not caught from other people, but is simply a reactivation of the chicken pox virus that has been lying dormant in the backbone nerve tissue. The eruption can cause severe pain, burning, stinging, numbness and weakness. The wrestler can have fever, nausea, and a severe headache. Shingles can occur months or decades after a bout of chicken pox. The most common age for this to occur is after 65, but it is not uncommon in the childhood and young adult years. Shingles can be treated with Zovirax or Famvir brand antibiotic pills. An immune globulin shot can be helpful. Often pain medicines are needed. The blisters can be treated with an antibiotic ointment, gauze, and peroxide. It is not known what the incidence and severity of shingles will be if children start getting the new chicken pox vaccine at a young age. It may take a number of years before the issue of how to use the chicken pox vaccine is settled. A wrestler with shingles should not compete until all of the blisters are completely flat and dry, he feels quite well, and has no residual numbness or weakness in that area of the body. (See Figure 25-3).

Warts

Warts are scaly, rough, tan contagious bumps that occur on the skin and mucous membranes. Warts are caused by a virus. The bumps usually cause no problem but they can get quite large and irritated and split open, bleed, and hurt. If left untreated, warts can spontaneously clear, but it could take months or many years for that to happen. Some people are extremely prone to have this virus and the virus can persist for decades. After contact with the skin the virus may take weeks or months to grow.

Since there are no wart vaccines or antibiotics, these bumps are frozen, burned, lasered, or treated with acids. Because warts are considered rather harmless, a wrestler does not have to miss practice or meets. To prevent spread of this nuisance condition the wrestler should have all warts thoroughly covered with clothing or tape. It would be very unfair for a wrestler to spread warts from his fingers to his opponent's eyelid, nose, or face. Warts on these areas can be very disfiguring and difficult to treat. It might be advisable for the referee to look for hand warts at the time that he checks finger nail length prior to a match. (See Figure 25-4).

Molluscum Contagiosum

Molluscum Contagiosum is a harmless communicable viral skin disease. It manifests as small, pearly, tan bumps occurring anywhere on the skin, including the face. Usually these little bumps have no symptoms but they easily get rubbed and irritated and then they can itch, burn, or bleed, and look bad. The bumps can pop up either a few days or up to two months after direct contact with the skin rash or indirectly with clothing or articles that have touched the rash. This disease can last a few months or several years before it spontaneously clears. Since this condition is not really harmful or dangerous, it does not have to be treated in an athlete who is in a noncontact sport. Wrestlers should be treated immediately so that this virus does not spread to the whole team and to opponents. There is no vaccine or internal antibiotics for this virus. The bumps are killed with external therapies, such as acids, scrapping, burning, freezing, and blister solutions. It would be wise, but not imperative, to keep the wrestler out of live practice and unimportant matches. For important matches or meets, the wrestler can participate as long as the molluscum lesions are completely covered during the contest with clothing, tape, or gauze so that the viral bumps have no chance of touching any other wrestler, mat, mask, or head gear. (See Figure 25-5).

Hand-Foot and Mouth Disease

This is a unique viral illness with an eruption that occurs classically on the hands, soles and in the mouth. It occurs more commonly in young children and adults. This is not to be confused with the serious hoof and mouth disease of cattle. The disease manifests with small red spots on hand, foot and mouth. Most persons do not feel very ill and can continue with their daily activities. A non-contact athlete in a sport like golf or tennis could compete if he felt well. A minority of patients can get quite ill with high fever, headache, loss of appetite, and other symptoms resembling severe flu. The gestation is one or two weeks after contact. There is no medical treatment for this disorder other than rest, fluids and pain medicines. A wrestler with this disease should be kept out of the wrestling room for about 1-2 weeks on the average. (See Figure 25-6).

BACTERIAL SKIN DISEASES

Impetigo

Impetigo is a honey colored, crusty, oozing, superficial skin infection usually caused by the staph or strep bacteria. These germs are commonly found in the environment and even on normal skin. Usually, clean dry skin is a good barrier and keeps these germs out. Whenever the skin has a break, the barrier function of the skin is lost and then these bacteria can invade the skin and cause infection. Impetigo usually starts in an area that has a cut, scratch, scrap, abrasion, or burn. If these lesions are not quickly

treated, the infection can appear within a couple days. It can then spread quite easily in the local area and even on distant skin sites. This disease can be transmitted directly from skin-to-skin contact, or indirectly if the infection gets on the mat or other wrestling apparel. The rash can cause itching, burning, or pain. Early in the course of the disease this can be treated with hydrogen peroxide or an over-the-counter antibiotic ointment. This infection is a perfect example where an "ounce of prevention is worth a pound of cure." All cuts and open areas of the skin should be treated with peroxide or an antibiotic ointment. Most of these ointments can be suggested by the team physician and kept in the coach's medical box. After practice all wrestlers should shower gently and thoroughly. Any reasonable soap should be sufficient. Any wrestler with impetigo should not be engaged in active wrestling until all of the sites have completely dried up and he gets a doctor's okay to resume contact wrestling. (See Figure 25-7).

Folliculitis

Folliculitis is a common infection of the hair follicles caused by either common bacteria like staph and strep or less common germs. The pustules can pop up in a day or two after contacting another wrestler with the infection, or, these sores can pop up from one's own bacteria on the skin if the skin is irritated or excessively hot and sweaty. These bumps can itch and burn, and the pustules can be small or exceedingly large and deep. Mild cases can be treated with hydrogen peroxide, alcohol, or external antibiotic creams. Oral antibiotics or the powerful Vitamin A derivative drug Accutane can be used for severe cases. Folliculitis can be prevented by having meticulous hygiene on the mat. After practice the wrestler should shower immediately to cool off the skin and get clean. A wrestler should be very careful with shaving his beard area. Clean clothes should be worn every day at practice. The wrestler should not compete until all the pustules are dried up and flat, with no redness or pus.

Conjunctivitis

Conjunctivitis is a common, contagious infection of the eyes. It can be spread from direct contact with the pus from another wrestler's eye or from the mat or other objects that have gotten the pus on it. The infection can arise one or two days after contact. The eyes can be red and painful and sensitive to light. A common lay term for this infection is "pink eye." Antibiotic eye drops prescribed by a doctor usually clear the infection quickly. A wrestler with pink eye should not be allowed in the wrestling room until the eye infection is completely clear.

FUNGAL SKIN DISEASES

Ringworm

Ringworm is a common, itchy, red, scaly skin infection caused by one of several fungi that is common in our environment. The gestation period is a few days to a couple weeks. It is usually transmitted by direct skin-to-skin contact, but can be picked up by touching articles of clothing or mats that have the fungi on them. When the rash is large it can cause alot of itching. If the fungal infection leaves the surface of the skin and moves down into the hair follicle, it can cause quite large, oozing pustules. If this infection is on the feet, it is often called "athletes foot." In the groin the names "jock itch" or "crotch rot" are used. There are a variety of good, nonprescription antifungus creams that should be applied quickly to any rash that might be an early fungus infection. The team physician can supply the coach with a number of tubes of these ointments to be kept in the medicine bag. For more severe infections, there are a number of internal antifungus, antibiotic pills that can be prescribed by a doctor. It is almost impossible to completely prevent some members of a wrestling team from getting ringworm during the wrestling season, as this fungus loves to grow in hot, warm, moist environments like the wrestling room. To minimize the possibility of a bad ringworm infection, all wrestlers should have clean clothes daily. The bottom of the wrestling shoes should be clean. Wrestlers should take a thorough, but gentle shower after all practices, and the mat should be cleaned daily prior to practice. A wrestler with an ordinary case of ringworm should be kept out of live wrestling practices and unimportant matches or meets until he is clear. If the wrestler has an

extremely important tournament, then he can be allowed to wrestle as long as the ringworm rash is completely covered with tape and gauze so that there is no chance of an opposing wrestler touching the infected skin. (See Figure 25-8).

Yeast

Yeast infections are red, bumpy, and scaly infections of hot, sweaty areas of skin caused by a tiny round fungus. The yeast that usually cause this problem are present on everyone's skin all the time anyway, but usually do not cause any problem in normal cool, smooth skin. With heat, sweat and irritation, the yeast proliferate on the surface of the skin and cause a rash. Wrestlers will more commonly get a yeast infection from their own heat and sweat versus actually contracting it from another wrestler. There can be extreme itching and discomfort in infected areas. Many of the normal ringworm antifungus creams work well for yeast, and in bad infections there are prescription oral antibiotics. Keeping the skin as cool and dry as possible during practice and cooling down immediately after practice with a shower is quite helpful in preventing this infection. A wrestler with a severe yeast infection should probably stay out of any hot, sweaty activities for a few days and allow the infection to clear. If the wrestler has an important match, he can participate as long as the yeast infection is in a covered area, like the groin or buttocks. If the yeast infection is in the armpit, then a normal tee shirt should be adequate to cover the area.

Tinea Versicolor

Tinea Versicolor is a common, fairly harmless, superficial fungus infection of the skin. It can cause temporary discoloration of the skin, and if it gets bad, quite a bit of itching. This disease is considered very harmless and is more often caused by an overgrowth of a person's normal fungus on the skin rather than being caught from another wrestler. This fungus is a natural inhabitant of the skin and is not related to the ringworm fungus. It occurs most commonly on the trunk but can be involved in other areas. It can be treated by nonprescription antiyeast, anti-fungus creams, or in bad cases an

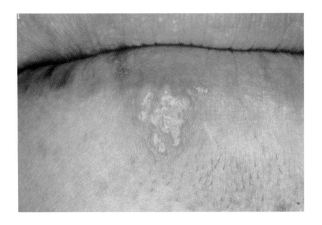

Figure 25-1. Herpes simplex on lower lip.

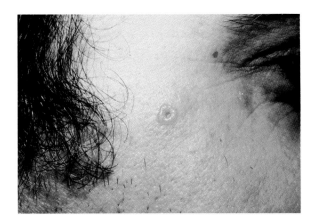

Figure 25-2. Chicken pox on face.

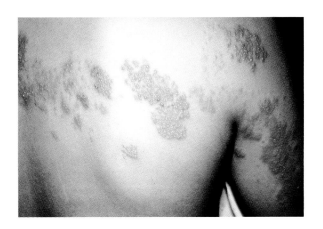

Figure 25-3. Shingles (zoster) on back and arm.

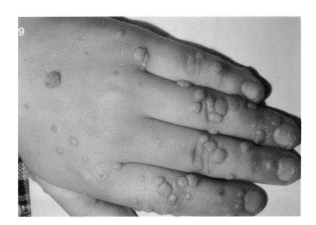

Figure 25-4. Warts on hands and fingers.

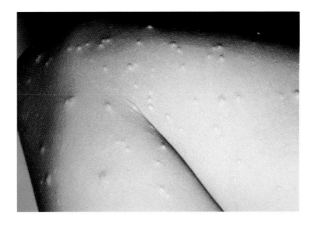

Figure 25-5. Molluscum contagiosum on leg.

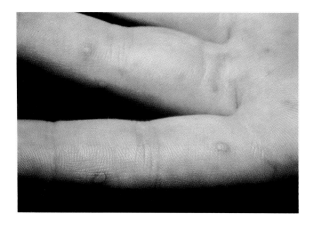

Figure 25-6. Hand-foot-mouth disease.

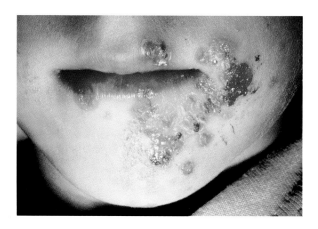

Figure 25-7. Impetigo on mouth.

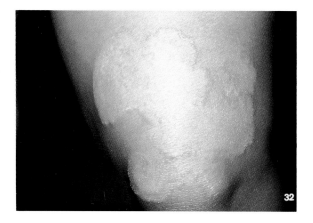

Figure 25-8. Ringworm fungus on knee.

Figure 25-9. Tinea versicolor on chest.

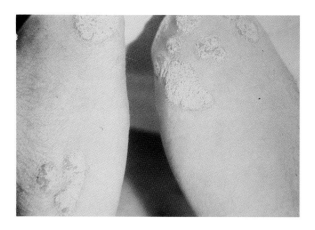

Figure 25-10. Psoriasis.

antibiotic can be prescribed by a physician. Keeping the skin cool and dry and clean will often prevent this eruption from occurring. Since the rash occurs most commonly on the trunk, a wrestler can compete in any important meets by wearing a tee shirt. (See Figure 25-9).

MISCELLANEOUS CONTAGIOUS DISEASES

Mononucleosis

Mononucleosis is a common, contagious, viral disease. The gestation period is typically a week or two, but the exact onset is difficult to pinpoint in many patients because the disease can be quite subtle. Many patients have only mild fatigue as their only complaint. Other patients can have severe fatigue, fevers, loss of appetite and huge, swollen lymph nodes in the neck area. There can be extreme liver enlargement, hepatitis, and swelling of the spleen. Severely ill patients often require hospitalization and IV fluids. There is no vaccine or antibiotic for this virus. Wrestlers with mild mononucleosis should stay out of the wrestling room, as they could pass this disease to one of their teammates who might have a much more severe episode. A wrestler may return to competition when all signs and symptoms of his Mono has cleared, he feels well and strong, and is eating and drinking normally.

Measles

Measles is a highly contagious, moderately severe viral disease with a characteristic skin rash. This is caused by a virus. The gestation period is one to two weeks after contact with another person with the disease. The patient can have fever, upper airway congestion, sweating, diarrhea, cough, and feel chills, fatigue, headache, muscle aches, and eye pain. The classical treatment is rest, fluids, and fever control. Prevention is the key in this disease. The current vaccines that are given in childhood should completely eliminate the possibility of contracting this disease. Unfortunately, many parents do not have their children vaccinated and some school systems do not force the person to get the vaccine. Until part of the population becomes

less negligent about vaccinating for measles, there will continue to be isolated breakouts. The wrestler should not compete until all of the signs and symptoms of measles have cleared, he feels completely well and strong, and is eating and drinking normally.

Scabies

Scabies is an extremely itchy, blistery, contagious, oozy skin infestation caused by a tiny mite. This mite burrows under the top layer of skin, where it lays eggs. The eggs hatch and baby mites move around the skin and burrow in other areas. The itching is very intense. Thus, the name scabies, which is derived from the Latin word scabere, which means to itch and scratch. As the infestation progresses, large blisters, hives, blotchy skin, eczema, and other allergic manifestations can occur on the skin. The patient will scratch open his itchy skin and cause deep, bloody grooves that can get infected with bacteria and fungi. The diagnosis can be proven by taking a scraping from a suspicious area and finding the tiny mite under the microscope. Once the diagnosis is proven, an appropriate insecticide lotion can be applied to the skin and the rash can come under pretty good control after only a couple treatments. Sometimes cortisone pills or lotions, and anti-itch medicines are required to help speed up the resolution of the rash.

Scabies is contracted from close skin-to-skin contact. It can easily be spread around a wrestler room. Often it takes several weeks after contracting this mite before the person actually realizes that he has a problem. The moment a wrestler is suspected of having scabies, he must be seen by a physician and treated appropriately. He must not return to competitive wrestling until he is deemed to be free of mites.

Pediculosis

Pediculosis is the medical name for a superficial infection by little bugs called lice. The three different types of Pediculosis infections are head lice, body lice, and pubic lice. The head lice by definition occur mostly on the scalp, but sometimes they can occur on the eye lashes and brows, and, on males, even on the chest hair. Symptoms can occur several days after the lice gets on the scalp. The louse lays an egg sac called a nit on the base of the hair shaft. The nit is a smooth, white blob that adheres strongly to the shaft. The lice are brown and often very difficult to find in the scalp, but the white nit is often much easier to find. As time passes this infestation can cause severe itching of the scalp. The person will scratch and cause open sores on the scalp that easily get infected. That can cause swelling of the neck lymph nodes and neck stiffness and tenderness. Treatment can be with a prescription lotion or shampoo, such as Lindane, or many of the nonprescription, over-the-counter medicines are quite adequate also. These are available at all pharmacies. A wrestler with head lice should be kept out of practices and unimportant wrestling matches until cleared by his physician. In the case of an extremely important match or tournament, the wrestler could probably compete if he fashioned a scarf under his head gear, so that his opponent could not have any contact with his scalp.

Body lice is not very common. It is seen during wars when soldiers are not able to change clothes frequently and are living in close contact with other soldiers. Soldiers call body lice "cooties." This louse can live off of the skin on clothing for long periods of time. With this disease it is important to clean or fumigate all clothing that might be infested with the louse. The skin can be treated with Lindane, or other anti-louse agents. It is not likely that a wrestling coach will ever come across this problem.

Pubic lice infections are called "crabs" because this louse is very flat and looks like a crab. The rash can cause extreme itching and if the wrestler scratches, he can cause open sores that can get infected just like head lice infections. Any of the above medicines can easily clear up this infestation. It is not likely that a wrestler will contract this disease from another wrestler, as it requires close, skin-to-skin contact and most of the time the wrestler will be adequately dressed to prevent transmission. However, in practice it is much more contagious. If a wrestler has pubic lice that is not yet treated, he can compete as long as he wears a uniform that will allow no possible contact of the infection with the opponent's skin.

CONDITIONS THAT CAN MIMIC CONTAGIOUS DISEASES

Psoriasis

Psoriasis is a rather common, harmless, red, scaly skin rash. The cause is unknown. The presentation is quite variable. Some patients have only a few, tiny, pink scaly patches of rash on their body. Others can be almost completely covered by a terribly thick, itchy, crusty rash. It is felt to be a disease of healthy people, but in rare cases it can seem to cause an associated arthritis. Psoriasis is usually a lifelong problem, but it can wax and wane through the person's life. The onset can be at any age. The therapy must be individualized to be appropriate for each person's age, health, and degree of skin involvement. There is no cure, but with an aggressive approach most psoriasis can be managed. There is no prevention as this is some sort of a genetically inbuilt tendency. Psoriasis is not contagious to other wrestlers. Most people with psoriasis do not take up wrestling as a sport because they are embarrassed by the rash, or they worry that the chronic trauma to the rash will make it worse. A wrestler with psoriasis can compete almost anytime he desires to, and feels his psoriasis is controlled enough to withstand the physical trauma of wrestling. (See Figure 25-10).

Eczema

Eczema is an itchy, scaly, harmless, non-contagious skin rash. Eczema often starts in early childhood and is commonly associated with allergies, hayfever, and asthma. The exact cause is unknown, but each patient can often pinpoint factors that worsen it. Some children outgrow eczema, but many continue to have it to one degree or another well into adulthood. Eczema is usually quite itchy and uncomfortable. It often interferes with sleeping and with concentration. If the rash itches, then the patient often scratches vigorously. This can open up the skin and cause crusting and bleeding and secondary bacterial skin infections. The long-term outcome is variable. Since there is no cure, a variety of creams, ointments, pills, and shots are used to control this disease. Eczema is not contagious but any secondary skin infection might be. Most persons with severe eczema do not wrestle because the intense heat and sweat makes the eczema far too itchy. Those patients with eczema who do desire to compete in wrestling can do so with a well thought out plan of treatment that would be designed with the help of a doctor, the coach, and parents.

Acne

Acne is a very common pustular eruption seen from puberty and extending into the adult years. The pimples are seen mostly on the face but can be seen on the neck, chest, back, and shoulders. The pimples can be quite small or huge, deep, and cause severe scarring. Often there is an excess of oiliness and blackheads. In severe cases the patient can run a fever and have swollen lymph nodes. Acne can have its onset at any age but it usually does not start until after puberty. There are a variety of treatments that can control this condition. The heat, sweat, and rubbing of wrestling might aggravate acne. Acne is not contagious. The pustules are usually sterile. Most persons with ordinary acne can compete. If the acne is cystic and the lesions can easily break open and bleed, then the wrestler must have those areas completely covered with clothing and gauze or tape, or consider not wrestling until his acne is better controlled.

Appendix
Wrestling Opportunities for Disabled

Nondisabled NGB: U.S.A. Wrestling (USAW)
Federation Internationale de Lutte Amateur (FILA)
Disabled Sports Organization: N/A
Official Sport Of: ✓ AAAD   DAAA   NHS
              NWAA   * SOI   ✓ USABA
              USCPAA   USLASA
          *=Prohibited

SPORT OVERVIEW

For many years, wrestling has enabled individuals with certain disabilities to compete on an equal basis with their nondisabled peers. Scrapbooks from across the country are filled with stories about high school and college athletes with disabilities participating and succeeding in wrestling, in integrated (nondisabled vs. disabled) and disabled only (blind and deaf) competition. Only two disabled sports organizations, the United States Association for Blind Athletes (USABA) and the American Athletic Association of the Deaf (AAAD), offer wrestling as an official sport. Many athletes from each organization wrestle in high school and college against nondisabled opponents.

Competition is usually conducted in freestyle wrestling. However, in certain cases, such as the 1987 United States Olympic Festival, competition in Greco-Roman wrestling, in which legs cannot be used for offensive maneuvers, is also offered.

Wrestling was a promising event in Special Olympics until it was prohibited by the organization in the mid 1980s due to the risk of injury to athletes.

RULE ADAPTATIONS

Rules for blind and deaf wrestling are identical to nondisabled rules with one exception: the finger touch start rule for blind competitions (Mastro, Montelione & Hall, 1986). This rule involves a finger touch start while both wrestlers are in the vertical position. If contact is broken during competition, restarts also use the finger touch (*USABA Official Sports Rules*, 1986, pp. WR 1-5).

ADDITIONAL RESOURCES

U.S.A. Wrestling (USAW)
6155 Lehman Dr.
Colorado Springs, CO 80918
(719) 597-8333

Canadian Amateur Wrestling Association
1600 James Naismith Drive, #505
Gloucester, Ontario K1B 5N4
(613) 748-5686
(613) 748-5756 (FAX)

Federation Internationale de Lutte Amateur
(FILA)
AV. Ruchonnet 3
CH-1003
Lausanne, Switzerland
Tele: (845) 45 59 58

USABA Sports Director for Wrestling
c/o USABA
311 North Institute Street
Brown Hall, Suite 015
Colorado Springs, CO 80903
(719) 630-0422

United States Deaf Wrestling Association
James Schartner
4835 Mount Zion Road
Frederick, MD 21702
(301) 473-5255

References

DISABLED

Jones, J., Todd, T., & Tetreault, P. (1987). U.S. Olympic Festival: Disabled athlete participation. *Palaestra* 4 (1):48–53,64.

Mastro, J.V., Montelione, T.L. & Hall, M.M. (1986). Wrestling: A viable sport for the visually impaired. *Journal of Physical Education, Recreation and Dance*, 57(9):61–64.

Paciorek, M., Jones, J. (1994). *Sport & Recreation for the Disabled, 2nd*, Carmel, IN: Cooper Publishing Group.

USABA Official Sports Rules. (1986). Beach Haven Park, NJ: USABA.

NUTRITION & WEIGHT CONTROL

AMA Committee on the Medical Aspects of Sports, Wrestling and Weight Control. *J. Am. Med. Assoc.* 201:541-453, 1967.

Burke, E., Berning, J. (1995). *Training Nutrition*, Carmel, IN: Cooper Publishing Group.

Lamb, D., Knuttgen, H., Murray, R. (1994). *Physiology and Nutrition for Competitive Sport*, Carmel, IN: Cooper Publishing Group.

PSYCHOLOGY

Barzdukas, A. (1995). *Goldminds: Gold Medal Mental Strategies for Everyday Life*. Carmel, IN: Cooper Publishing Group.

Gould, D. (1980). *Motivating young athletes*. East Lansing, MI: Institute for the Study of Youth Sports.

Gould, D. & Weiss, M. (1980). *Teaching sports skills to young athletes*. East Lansing, MI: Institute for the Study of Youth Sports.

Harney, D.M. & Parker, R. (1972). Effects of social reinforcement, subject sex, and experimenter sex on children's motor performance. *Research Quarterly* 43:187–196.

Martens, R. (Ed.). (1978). *Joy and sadness in children's sports*. Champaign, IL: Human Kinetics Publishers, Inc.

Rushall, B. & Pettinger, J. (1969). An evaluation of the effect of various reinforcers used as motivators in swimming. *Research Quarterly*, 40 (3).

Seefeldt, V. (Ed.) (1995). *Program for Athletic Coaches' Education*, Carmel, IN: Cooper Publishing Group.

Smith, R.E., Smoll, F.L. & Curtis, B. (1978). Coaching behaviors in Little League baseball. In F.L. Smoll & R.E. Smith (Eds.), *Psychological perspectives in youth sports* (pp. 1:73–201). Washington, D.C.: Hemisphere, 173–201.

Smoll, F.L. & Smith, R.E. (1979). *Improving relationship skills in youth sport coaches*. East Lansing, MI: Institute for the Study of Youth Sports.

State of Michigan (1978). *Joint legislative study on youth sports programs phase II*. East Lansing, MI: Institute for the Study of Youth Sports.

SPORTS MEDICINE/ INJURY PREVENTION

Agre, J.C. & Krotee, M.L. (1981). Soccer safety—Prevention and care. *Journal of Health, Physical Education, Recreation and Dance*, 52(5). 52–54.

American College of Sports Medicine, American Orthopaedic Society for Sports Medicine & Sports Medicine Committee of the United State Tennis Association (1982). *Sports injuries—an aid to prevention and treatment*. Coventry, CT: Bristol-Myers Co.

Estrand, J. & Gillquist, J. (1983). Soccer injuries and their mechanisms: A prospective study. *Medicine and Science in Sports and Exercise*, 15(3), 267–270.

Jackson, D. & Pescar, S. (1981). *The young athletes health handbook*. New York: Everest House.

Micheli, L.J. (1985). Preventing youth sports injuries. *Journal of Health, Physical Education, Recreation and Dance*, 76(6), 52–54.

Mirkin, G. & Marshall, H. (1978). *The Sportsmedicine Book*. Boston, MA: Little Brown, & Co.

Rutherford, G., Miles, R., Brown, V., & MacDonald, B. (1981). *Overview of sports related injuries to persons 5-14 years of age*. Washington, DC: U.S. Consumer Product Safety Commission.

Seefeldt, V. (Ed.) (1987). *Handbook for youth sport coaches*. Reston, VA: American Alliance for Health, Physical Education, Recreation and Dance.

WEIGHT TRAINING

Bompa, Tudor. *Theory and Methodology of Training*. Dubuque, Iowa: Kendall/Hunt Publishing Company, 1983.

Goldstein, Grigory. "Recommendations on Physical Development of Football Players," *NSCA Journal*, Volume 11, No. 9, 1989, p. 50.

Katsen, Pavel. Training Plans. Olympic Training Center, 1979.

O'Bryant, Harold and Stone, Michael. *Weight Training: A Scientific Approach*. Minneapolis, Minnesota: Bellwether Press, 1987.

Parker, Johnny. "Modern Principles of Strength Training." New York, 1991.

Petrov, Rojko. *Freestyle and Greco-Roman Wrestling*. Switzerland: International Amateur Wrestling Federation, 1987, p. 41.

Romanian Wrestling Federation. "Planning the Training of Wrestlers." Presentation in Bucharest, Romania, 1975.

Scholich, Manfred. *Circuit Training*. Dresden, GDR: Sportverlog Beslin, Grafischer Grofbtrieb Volkerfruendschaft, 1986.

Spassov, Angel. "The Bulgarian Approach to Maximal Strength and Power Development." NSCA Seminar, New Jersey, 1989.

Verkhoshansky, Yuri I. *Fundamentals of Special Strength Training in Sport*. Moscow: Fizkultura i Sport Publishers, 1977.